Lecture Notes in Computer Science 9370

Commenced Publication in 1973
Founding and Former Series Editors:
Gerhard Goos, Juris Hartmanis, and Jan van Leeuwen

More information about this series at http://www.springer.com/series/7412

Aasa Feragen · Marcello Pelillo
Marco Loog (Eds.)

Similarity-Based Pattern Recognition

Third International Workshop, SIMBAD 2015
Copenhagen, Denmark, October 12–14, 2015
Proceedings

 Springer

Editors
Aasa Feragen
University of Copenhagen
Copenhagen
Denmark

Marco Loog
Delft University of Technology
Delft, Zuid-Holland
The Netherlands

Marcello Pelillo
DAIS
Università Ca' Foscari Venezia
Venezia Mestre
Italy

ISSN 0302-9743 ISSN 1611-3349 (electronic)
Lecture Notes in Computer Science
ISBN 978-3-319-24260-6 ISBN 978-3-319-24261-3 (eBook)
DOI 10.1007/978-3-319-24261-3

Library of Congress Control Number: 2015949444

LNCS Sublibrary: SL6 – Image Processing, Computer Vision, Pattern Recognition, and Graphics

Springer International Publishing AG Switzerland is part of Springer Science+Business Media
(www.springer.com)

Preface

This volume of Springer's well-known Lecture Notes in Computer Science series presents the papers from the Third International Workshop on Similarity-Based Pattern Analysis and Recognition (SIMBAD), held in Copenhagen, Denmark, from October 12–14, 2015. The aim of this series of workshops, of which the previous two editions were held in Venice and York in 2011 and 2013, respectively, is to consolidate research efforts in the area of similarity-based and dissimilarity-based machine learning, pattern recognition, and statistical learning. The workshop provides an informal discussion forum for researchers and practitioners interested in this important yet diverse subject. The idea of running these workshops originated from the EU FP7 Project SIMBAD (http://simbadfp7.eu), which was devoted to this theme in full.

The call for papers resulted in 23 papers being accepted for this workshop. Fifteen of these contributions are full-length papers and report on original and worked-out research. The remaining eight works are extended abstracts whose length is limited to two pages only. These contributions present abstracts of previously-accepted work, preliminary results, open problems, topics for discussion, appeals for novel research directions, or any other essay that suits the aim of SIMBAD and underlines the workshop's character. The 23 papers cover a wide range of problems, techniques, applications, and perspectives: from supervised to unsupervised learning, from generative to discriminative models, and from theoretical issues to empirical validations. In addition to talks and posters based on the peer-reviewed papers, the workshop was graced by invited keynote talks by Barbara Hammer (Bielefeld University, Germany), Nina Balcan (Carnegie Mellon University, USA), and Morten Mørup (Technical University of Denmark, Denmark).

We would like to take this opportunity to express our sincere gratitude to all those who helped to make this workshop a success. First of all, thanks go to the members of the Program Committee. A special thanks goes to Eyasu Zemene Mequanint for maintaining the web site. We would like to thank the Department of Environmental Science, Informatics, and Statistics of Ca' Foscari University of Venice for providing financial support. We also offer our appreciation to the editorial staff at Springer for producing this book and supporting the event through publication in their LNCS series. Finally, we thank all the invited speakers and enthusiastic participants, and of course you as a reader of these proceedings.

July 2015

Aasa Feragen
Marcello Pelillo
Marco Loog

Program Committee

Contents

A Novel Data Representation Based on Dissimilarity Increments

Helena Aidos[✉] and Ana Fred

Instituto de Telecomunicações, Instituto Superior Técnico, Universidade de Lisboa,
Lisbon, Portugal
{haidos,afred}@lx.it.pt

Abstract. Many pattern recognition techniques have been proposed, typically relying on feature spaces. However, recent studies have shown that different data representations, such as the dissimilarity space, can help in the knowledge discovering process, by generating more informative spaces. Still, different measures can be applied, leading to different data representations. This paper proposes the application of a second-order dissimilarity measure, which uses triplets of nearest neighbors, to generate a new dissimilarity space. In comparison with the traditional Euclidean distance, this new representation is best suited for the identification of natural data sparsity. It leads to a space that better describes the data, by reducing the overlap of the classes and by increasing the discriminative power of features. As a result, the application of clustering algorithms over the proposed dissimilarity space results in reduced error rates, when compared with either the original feature space or the Euclidean dissimilarity space. These conclusions are supported on experimental validation on benchmark datasets.

Keywords: Dissimilarity representation · Euclidean space · Dissimilarity increments space · Clustering · Geometrical characterization

1 Introduction

The learning process encompasses developing computer methods to model categories/classes of objects or to assign objects to one of the different classes. In that sense, a representation of the objects is required, which can be a vector, string of symbols or even a graph. Afterwards, a decision rule may be constructed based on that representation of objects, and the objective is to discriminate between different classes achieving high accuracy values [1,3,8].

Typically, objects are represented by a set of features, which should characterize the objects and be relevant to discriminate among the classes; the Euclidean vector spaces are the most popular representation of objects [3]. A problem with the feature-based representation of objects is the difficulty to obtain a complete description of objects, forcing to an overlap of the classes, leading to an inefficient learning process. That difficulty in describing objects through a set of

© Springer International Publishing Switzerland 2015
A. Feragen et al. (Eds.): SIMBAD 2015, LNCS 9370, pp. 1–14, 2015.
DOI: 10.1007/978-3-319-24261-3_1

features is due to high-dimensional data or sometimes it is necessary to describe objects using continuous and categorical variables.

To overcome the limitations of feature-based representations, another representations of data can be used. One possibility is the dissimilarity representation, which is based on comparisons between pairs of objects [10]. This representation solves the problem of class overlap that exists in feature representations, since only identical objects have a dissimilarity of zero.

Also, a suitable dissimilarity measure can be used to compare pairs of objects, and dissimilarity vectors for each object are constructed to obtain the dissimilarity space. Measures that compare the entire objects may be considered or measures can be derived from raw measurements, strings or graphs. Defining features that can have a high discriminant power may be a difficult task for some applications (*e.g.* shape recognition) than define a dissimilarity measure.

Dissimilarities have been used in pattern recognition, either explicitly or implicitly, in many procedures, like in cluster analysis, which uses dissimilarities instead of feature spaces [14]. In the last years, based on the work of Pekalska and Duin [11], some classification methods for dissimilarity data have been proposed [2,4,13]. This type of classifiers are useful to tackle problems in computer vision, bioinformatics, information retrieval, natural language processing, among other fields [5,9].

Moreover, the dissimilarity space can be constructed using a feature representation and some appropriate dissimilarity measure [4,12]. This measure may be asymmetric and does not require to fulfill mathematical properties for metrics. Over the dissimilarity space, any classifier or clustering procedure that works in vector spaces can be applied.

The purpose of this paper is to present a novel dissimilarity representation of data, the *dissimilarity increments space*, based on a second-order dissimilarity measure, consisting on triplets of nearest neighbors [6]. This dissimilarity space is built by the increment in dissimilarity between an object and a set of representative objects, which are defined as an edge between a prototype and its nearest neighbor. To fairly compare the proposed dissimilarity space, an Euclidean space is built by relying on the Euclidean distance to measure the set of representative objects. Both dissimilarity spaces are used as feature-based dissimilarity spaces, which consist in representing each object as a vector of dissimilarities, and typical clustering algorithms are applied to those spaces.

To compare the spaces, we use two different approaches. We start by presenting an insightful characterization of the spaces by relying on a set of geometrical measures. Then we apply a set of unsupervised learning methods in order to analyze the spaces behavior under clustering problems. Experimental results with an extensive set of datasets show that the proposed second-order dissimilarity space leads to a substantial improvement in accuracy when compared to the original feature space and to the feature-based Euclidean space.

This paper is organized as follows: Sect. 2 explains how to build dissimilarity spaces, and proposes a new dissimilarity space based on a second-order dissimilarity measure – the dissimilarity increments space. Section 3 presents some measures to characterize each dissimilarity space and understand if a learning problem becomes easier in these spaces. The proposed dissimilarity increments space is evaluated in the context of unsupervised learning, in comparison with other dissimilarity spaces, in Sect. 4. Conclusions and final remarks are drawn in Sect. 5. The datasets used in the experimental evaluation of methods are described in appendix.

2   Dissimilarity Representation

A dissimilarity representation consists of a matrix with the dissimilarities between an object and a set of representative objects. Thus, the resulting dissimilarity matrix is considered as a set of row vectors, where each vector represents a direction from the dissimilarity space, whose dimension corresponds to the cardinality of the set of representative objects.

Let $X = \{\mathbf{x}_1, \ldots, \mathbf{x}_n\}$ represent a set of objects. In general, $\mathbf{x}_i$ may not be a vector, but an image or signal. However, in this paper and given the datasets used in the experimental validation (see appendix), we assume that $\mathbf{x}_i$ is a feature vector in $\mathbb{R}^p$, $\mathbf{x}_i = [x_{i1} \ldots x_{ip}]$. Also, let $R = \{\mathbf{e}_1, \ldots, \mathbf{e}_r\}$ be the set of representative or prototype objects, such that $R \subseteq X$.

In [11], a dissimilarity space is defined as a data-dependent mapping

$$D(\cdot, R) : X \to \mathbb{R}^r, \tag{1}$$

given a dissimilarity function. Therefore, each object $\mathbf{x}_i$ from the set X is described by a r-dimensional dissimilarity vector

$$D(\mathbf{x}_i, R) = [d(\mathbf{x}_i, \mathbf{e}_1) \ldots d(\mathbf{x}_i, \mathbf{e}_r)], \tag{2}$$

where $d(\cdot, \cdot)$ is a dissimilarity measure. So, $D(\mathbf{x}_i, R)$ is a row of the $n \times r$ dissimilarity matrix D, obtaining the **dissimilarity space**. Now, we define the dissimilarity space as a vector space Y by $Y = D$, where the i-th object is represented by the dissimilarity vector of the D_{ij} values.

For simplicity, we assume that R is the entire set X, meaning that all objects of X are used as representatives. Therefore, in this paper, the dissimilarity space is represented as a $n \times n$ dissimilarity matrix.

In this paper, we consider two dissimilarity spaces: the Euclidean space and the Dinc space, detailed below.

Euclidean space. This space is obtained assuming that $d(\cdot, \cdot)$ in (2) is the Euclidean distance,

$$d(\mathbf{x}_i, \mathbf{e}_j) = \left(\sum_{k=1}^{p} (x_{ik} - e_{jk})^2 \right)^{1/2}. \tag{3}$$

Thus, each element, D_{ij}, of the dissimilarity matrix D, is the Euclidean distance between i-th and j-th objects.

Dinc space. This space is obtained using a second-order dissimilarity measure between triplets of neighboring objects, and its explained in detail in Sect. 2.1.

2.1 Dissimilarity Increments Space

Firstly, we need to define the concept of dissimilarity increments. Given $\mathbf{x}_i$, $(\mathbf{x}_i, \mathbf{x}_j, \mathbf{x}_k)$ is a triplet of nearest neighbors, obtained as follows:

$$(\mathbf{x}_i, \mathbf{x}_j, \mathbf{x}_k) - \text{ nearest neighbor triplet}$$
$$\mathbf{x}_j : j = \arg\min_l \{d(\mathbf{x}_l, \mathbf{x}_i), l \neq i\}$$
$$\mathbf{x}_k : k = \arg\min_l \{d(\mathbf{x}_l, \mathbf{x}_j), l \neq i, l \neq j\}.$$

The *dissimilarity increments* [6] between neighboring objects is defined as

$$d_{\mathrm{inc}}(\mathbf{x}_i, \mathbf{x}_j, \mathbf{x}_k) = |d(\mathbf{x}_i, \mathbf{x}_j) - d(\mathbf{x}_j, \mathbf{x}_k)|, \tag{4}$$

where $d(\cdot, \cdot)$ is any dissimilarity measure between pairs of objects; in this paper, we assume that $d(\cdot, \cdot)$ is the Euclidean distance.

This measure gives information about the structure of a dataset compared to pairwise distances, *i.e.* the dissimilarity increments between neighboring objects should not occur with abrupt changes, and between well separated classes will have higher values. Moreover, this measure can identify easily objects in a sparse class, while most of the distance measures used in the literature discard objects that are far apart in a sparse class.

We propose to define the set of representative objects as edges between two specific objects, *i.e.*, a representative object $\mathbf{e}_j$ is an edge between a prototype $\mathbf{m}_j$ (a sample of the dataset) and its nearest neighbor $\mathbf{x}_{\mathbf{m}_j}$. So, $d(\mathbf{e}_j)$ is the weight of that edge, *i.e.* $d(\mathbf{e}_j) = d(\mathbf{m}_j, \mathbf{x}_{\mathbf{m}_j})$. Moreover, the distance between any object $\mathbf{x}_i$ and the representative object $\mathbf{e}_j$ is defined as

$$d(\mathbf{x}_i, \mathbf{e}_j) = \min\{d(\mathbf{x}_i, \mathbf{m}_j), d(\mathbf{x}_i, \mathbf{x}_{\mathbf{m}_j})\}. \tag{5}$$

Furthermore, we propose a new representation of data based on the dissimilarity increments measure, called *dissimilarity increments space* and we will refer to that space as **Dinc space**. Similar to the Euclidean space, each object is described by a n-dimensional dissimilarity vector (2). However, $d(\cdot, \cdot)$ is no longer the Euclidean distance, but a dissimilarity increment between each object $\mathbf{x}_i$ and a representative object $\mathbf{e}_j$ (see Fig. 1 for an example how to compute the elements in Dinc space). Thus, the (i, j)-th element of our dissimilarity space is defined as

$$D(\mathbf{x}_i, \mathbf{e}_j) = |d(\mathbf{x}_i, \mathbf{e}_j) - d(\mathbf{e}_j)|. \tag{6}$$

From (6), it is easy to see that the dissimilarity matrix D is non-negative. Moreover, D is asymmetric, and to see that consider a set of patterns distributed as shown in Fig. 1. If a is a prototype, e_a is an edge between a and its nearest neighbor b, and will be the representative object. Now, the dissimilarity increment between c and the representative object, e_a, is $D(c, e_a)$. On other hand, when c is a prototype, the representative object, e_c, is the edge between c and its nearest neighbor d, and, thus, $D(a, e_c)$ is the dissimilarity increment between a and the representative object. Therefore, $D(c, e_a) \neq D(a, e_c)$ (see Fig. 1).

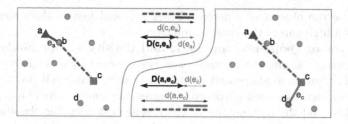

Fig. 1. Set of patterns to illustrate how to compute elements from the Dinc space D and to demonstrate its asymmetry. If a is a prototype, e_a is the representative object constructed as an edge between a and its nearest neighbor b. Then, $D(c, e_a)$ is the dissimilarity increment between c and the representative object, e_a, computed from (6). $D(c, e_a) \neq D(a, e_c)$ since different triplets of patterns are used to compute D.

3 Characterization of the Dissimilarity Spaces

So far, we constructed feature-based dissimilarity spaces to represent a set of objects. Both dissimilarity spaces, Euclidean and Dinc spaces, are constructed on top of feature spaces. In the following we will characterize these spaces based on some measures to characterize the geometrical complexity of classification problems proposed by Ho *et al.* [7]. Those measures are based on the analysis of different classifiers to understand the separability of classes or even the geometry, topology and density of manifolds. Thus, we used some of those measures to understand if a learning problem in the dissimilarity space becomes easier than in the feature space. According to [7], those measures can be divided into three categories:

1. **Measures of overlaps in feature values from different classes** focus on how good the features are in separating the classes. These type of measures examine the range and spread of values in the dataset within each class, and check for overlaps among different classes. Here, we only consider two measures: the maximum Fisher's discriminant ratio (**F1**) and the collective feature efficiency (**F4**). F1 computes the maximum discriminant power of each feature, and high values of this measure indicates that, at least, one of the features turns the problem of separating the samples of different classes easier. On the other hand, F4 computes the discriminative power of all the features.
2. **Measures of separability of classes** evaluate, based on the existence and shape of class boundary, to what extent two classes are separable. Here, we consider three measures: the training error of a linear classifier (**L2**), the ratio average intra/inter class nearest neighbor distance (**N2**) and the leave-one-out error rate of the one-nearest neighbor classifier (**N3**). L2 shows if the classes of the training data are linearly separable. N2 compares the within class distances with distances to the nearest neighbors of other classes, and higher values indicate that samples of the same class are disperse. N3 verifies

how close the objects of different classes are, and lower values means that there is a high gap in the class boundary.

3. **Measures of geometry, topology, and density of manifolds** characterize classes, assuming that each class is composed by a single or multiple manifolds, and their shape and position determines how well two classes are separated. Here, we considered two measures: the nonlinearity of a linear classifier (**L3**) and the nonlinearity of the one-nearest neighbor classifier (**N4**). L3 measures, for linearly separable problems, the alignment of the decision surface of linear classifiers with the class boundary, and N4 measures the alignment of the nearest neighbor boundary with the shape of the gap or overlap between the convex hulls of the classes.

Some of the measures are designed for two-class problems, namely L2 and L3. In this paper, we consider the average value between one versus all classes problems for datasets with more than two classes. Table 1 presents the results of the measures presented above, over the datasets described in the appendix, in the Feature space and in both dissimilarity spaces.

From Table 1 we notice that both dissimilarity spaces have high discriminant power of features in separating the classes, corresponding to higher values of F1 and F4 than the Feature space. Moreover, F4 in the Feature space has a minimum of zero and that value increased in both dissimilarity spaces, which means that the collective feature efficiency increased. Thus, the datasets are better described in the dissimilarity spaces, even with the increase of dimensionality on those spaces, compared to the Feature space.

In both dissimilarity spaces, there is a decrease in L2 and N2 values, indicating that there exists less overlap between the classes, which may facilitate the learner to separate the samples of different classes. However, in both dissimilarity spaces, the measure for geometry and topology of the manifold N4 has higher values, indicating that, even if the classes are more separable they are nonlinearly separable by the one-nearest neighbor classifier.

4   Unsupervised Learning in Dissimilarity Spaces

Typically, dissimilarity measures have been used in cluster analysis or in classification, as a tool to decide which objects are closer to each other. They also can be used to describe objects, and, consequently, build dissimilarity spaces. In this paper we proposed a new dissimilarity space based on a second-order dissimilarity measure. We further investigate if clustering results can be improved by transforming a feature space into a dissimilarity space, namely the Euclidean space and the Dinc space.

We applied, to the datasets described in appendix, four hierarchical clustering algorithms: single-link (SL), average-link (AL), centroid-link (CeL) and median-link (MeL). Moreover, we set the number of clusters in each clustering algorithm as being equal to the true number of classes (see Table 4). The results presented in this section are error rates, *i.e.* the percentage of misclassified samples, and

Table 1. Measures to characterize the geometrical complexity of classification problems in the original feature space, and in both dissimilarity spaces considered in this paper, Euclidean space and Dinc space. High values for F1 and F4 is better (thus the ↑ sign), while lower values for the remaining measures is better (↓ sign). The values presented correspond to median (Med), minimum (Min), maximum (Max), first and third quartiles (Q1 and Q3, respectively), over all datasets. The best space (on median) according to each geometrical measure are boldfaced.

FEATURE SPACE							
	F1↑	F4↑	L2↓	N2↓	N3↓	N4↓	L3↓
Med	1.88	0.91	0.20	0.64	**0.13**	**0.08**	0.50
Min	0.06	0.00	0.00	0.18	0.02	0.00	0.00
Max	22.06	18.73	0.42	0.91	0.38	0.46	0.50
Q1	0.60	0.48	0.10	0.52	0.05	0.03	0.37
Q3	5.20	1.08	0.33	0.75	0.24	0.19	0.50

EUCLIDEAN SPACE							
	F1↑	F4↑	L2↓	N2↓	N3↓	N4↓	L3↓
Med	**2.86**	**1.00**	**0.14**	**0.54**	0.14	0.14	0.45
Min	0.04	0.96	0.03	0.11	0.03	0.00	0.00
Max	23.04	20.25	0.42	0.95	0.43	0.62	0.50
Q1	0.44	1.00	0.07	0.43	0.05	0.03	0.15
Q3	4.18	1.00	0.25	0.70	0.26	0.24	0.50

DINC SPACE							
	F1↑	F4↑	L2↓	N2↓	N3↓	N4↓	L3↓
Med	2.76	**1.00**	**0.14**	0.56	0.15	0.14	**0.40**
Min	0.03	0.96	0.03	0.11	0.02	0.00	0.01
Max	27.84	19.31	0.42	0.96	0.45	0.63	0.50
Q1	0.45	1.00	0.07	0.43	0.06	0.03	0.11
Q3	4.35	1.00	0.23	0.71	0.26	0.23	0.50

number of datasets with better error rates (see Table 2). Also, a statistical significance difference between each space, in each clustering algorithm considered, is achieved by applying the Wilcoxon signed rank test over all datasets [15]. A statistical significance difference is achieved for p-value < 0.05.

Figure 2 shows the error rates, for each clustering algorithm, comparing the Feature space with the Euclidean space. Notice that if the points (which represents a dataset) in the plots are lying on the line $y = x$, this means that the error rate are equal in both spaces. This situation happens for SL: almost all points (datasets) have equal error in both spaces. Furthermore, all the remaining clustering algorithms are better in the Euclidean space compared to the Feature space, being the CeL the one with better error rates for the Euclidean space.

Table 2. Number of datasets with better error rate, for single-link (SL), average-link (AL), centroid-link (CeL), and median-link (MeL), when comparing pairs of spaces. "=" means equal error rate in both spaces. Mean difference indicates that, when one space wins, it is better on average x% than the other space. Last column presents the p-value for the Wilcoxon signed rank test between two spaces, in each clustering algorithm. A statistical significance difference is achieved when p-value < 0.05.

FEATURE SPACE VS EUCLIDEAN SPACE						
Clustering	Count			Mean difference		p-value
Method	Feat	=	Eucl	Feat	Eucl	
SL	8	17	11	1.3 %	**5.5 %**	0.355
AL	10	4	22	3.3 %	**12.5 %**	**0.002**
CeL	11	3	22	2.9 %	**16.1 %**	**0.001**
MeL	9	2	25	2.6 %	**11.8 %**	**0.001**

FEATURE SPACE VS DINC SPACE						
Clustering	Count			Mean difference		p-value
Method	Feat	=	Dinc	Feat	Dinc	
SL	9	15	12	1.3 %	**4.3 %**	0.408
AL	10	3	23	3.1 %	**11.6 %**	**0.002**
CeL	9	3	24	2.7 %	**15.9 %**	**<0.001**
MeL	6	2	28	2.2 %	**13.6 %**	**<0.001**

EUCLIDEAN SPACE VS DINC SPACE						
Clustering	Count			Mean difference		p-value
Method	Eucl	=	Dinc	Eucl	Dinc	
SL	3	29	4	**4.3 %**	0.7 %	0.859
AL	12	14	10	**2.6 %**	2.4 %	0.523
CeL	7	12	17	1.7 %	**2.8 %**	**0.029**
MeL	8	10	18	4.0 %	**7.1 %**	**0.030**

Table 2 presents the number of datasets that have lower error rates for each clustering algorithm. We notice that the Euclidean space is always better than the Feature space, and that difference is statistically significant (p-value < 0.01), except when we apply SL (p-value = 0.355). For all the remaining clustering algorithms, the Euclidean space is better in more than 20 datasets compared to the Feature space. The most significant difference on average error rates occurs for CeL, because when the Feature space is better than the Euclidean space, its improvement is on average 2.9 %, and it is better on average 16.1 %, when the Euclidean space is better than the Feature space.

Figure 3 shows the error rates of the comparison between the Feature space and the Dinc space. Again, SL seems to have similar performance in both spaces, except for three datasets. However, all the remaining clustering algorithms perform better in the Dinc space, with the highest improvement for the CeL. From

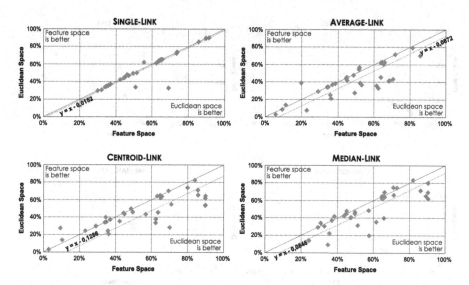

Fig. 2. Error rates with different clustering algorithms when comparing the Feature space with the Euclidean space. Dots represent datasets and the solid line, $y = x$, indicate equal error rate between the two spaces. The dash line represents a linear regression line forced to be parallel to $y = x$, to indicate which space is better (on average) and how much is the improvement.

Table 2, the Dinc space wins the Feature space in more than 20 datasets out of 36 when we apply any clustering algorithm, except SL, which it wins, by 12 out of 36 datasets against 9 datasets. When the Dinc space wins, it is better over 11 % on average than the Feature space for any clustering algorithm, and around 3 % when the Feature space wins, except for SL. The differences between Dinc and Feature spaces are statistically significant for all clustering algorithms, except for SL, since p-value < 0.01.

So far we compared both dissimilarity spaces with the Feature space. Now, we present in Fig. 4 the comparison between both dissimilarity spaces. All clustering algorithms have similar error rates in both dissimilarity spaces. However, MeL has a tendency to have lower error rates in the Dinc space. MeL wins in 18 out of 36 datasets, for the Dinc space, against 8 out of 36 datasets for the Euclidean space, corresponding to an improvement of 7.1 % on average, when the Dinc space is better and 4.0 % on average when the Euclidean space is better (see Table 2). There are statistically significant differences between Euclidean and Dinc spaces (p-value < 0.05) for CeL and MeL. For AL and SL, the differences are not statistically significant, as can be seen from the higher number of datasets with equal error rate between the two spaces.

Table 3 presents the correlations between the measures of geometrical complexity mentioned in Sect. 3 and the error rates of each clustering algorithm. We notice that there exists a negative correlation between F1 and the error rate of each clustering algorithm, and that correlation is higher in the dissimilarity

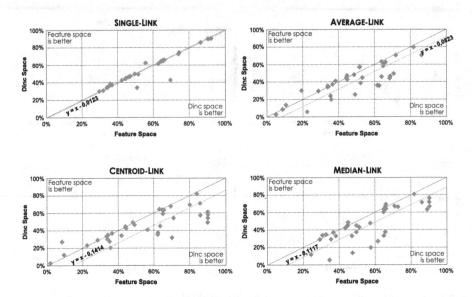

Fig. 3. Error rates with different clustering algorithms when comparing the Feature space with the Dinc space. Dots represent datasets and the solid line, $y = x$, indicate equal error rate between the two spaces. The dash line represents a linear regression line forced to be parallel to $y = x$, to indicate which space is better (on average) and how much is the improvement.

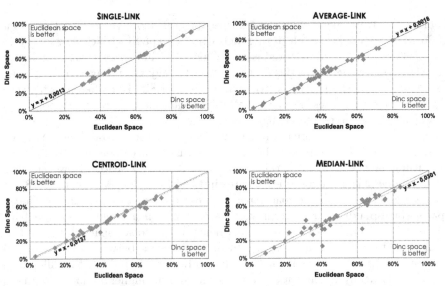

Fig. 4. Error rates with different clustering algorithms when comparing the Euclidean space with the Dinc space. Dots represent datasets and the solid line, $y = x$, indicate equal error rate between the two spaces. The dash line represents a linear regression line forced to be parallel to $y = x$, to indicate which space is better (on average) and how much is the improvement.

Table 3. Correlations between measures of geometrical complexity and error rates of each clustering algorithm (single-link (SL), average-link (AL), centroid-link (CeL), and median-link (MeL) for each space).

FEATURE SPACE							
	F1	F4	L2	N2	N3	N4	L3
SL	−0.01	0.35	−0.46	0.16	−0.08	−0.06	0.14
AL	−0.23	0.27	0.03	0.28	0.21	0.28	0.36
CeL	−0.13	0.34	−0.26	0.29	0.01	0.02	0.25
MeL	−0.01	0.40	−0.47	0.16	−0.06	−0.08	0.04
EUCLIDEAN SPACE							
	F1	F4	L2	N2	N3	N4	L3
SL	−0.28	0.16	−0.15	0.23	0.03	0.07	0.45
AL	−0.46	0.30	0.13	0.50	0.48	0.50	0.37
CeL	−0.37	0.25	0.00	0.42	0.33	0.35	0.43
MeL	−0.35	0.22	−0.10	0.36	0.22	0.24	0.41
DINC SPACE							
	F1	F4	L2	N2	N3	N4	L3
SL	−0.24	0.19	−0.11	0.23	0.00	0.08	0.50
AL	−0.47	0.28	0.20	0.52	0.46	0.50	0.44
CeL	−0.39	0.27	0.08	0.44	0.33	0.40	0.43
MeL	−0.37	0.27	−0.03	0.45	0.31	0.39	0.45

spaces, indicating that whenever F1 increases, the error rate decreases. In fact, from Table 1, F1 is higher in both dissimilarity spaces than in the Feature space, and looking at the plots of the error rates between the Feature space and one of the dissimilarity spaces (Figs. 2 and 3), the dissimilarity spaces have lower error rates, except for SL.

Figures 3 and 4 shows that, for CeL and MeL, the Dinc space is better than the Feature space and the Euclidean space. The correlations between L3 and the error rates may explain these results. The Feature and Euclidean spaces have lower correlations, than the Dinc space and those correlations are positive correlations. This means that if L3 decreases, then the error rate decreases, and L3 has a lower value in the Dinc space compared to the other two spaces (see Table 1). Moreover, N2 have higher and positive correlation in both dissimilarity spaces compared to the Feature space, indicating that whenever N2 decreases, the error rate also decreases. Analysing Figs. 2 and 3, we notice that AL, CeL and MeL have better performances than the Feature space. Accordingly, CeL and MeL have a better performance in both dissimilarity spaces, however the Dinc space shows a slightly improvement compared to the Euclidean space.

Overall, if we do not consider SL, F1, N2, N3, N4 and L3 have a higher correlation in the dissimilarity spaces than in the Feature space, and the Dinc space

Table 4. Datasets used in the analysis of dissimilarity spaces. N is the number of samples, p the dimension of the feature space and Nc the number of classes.

Dataset	N	p	Nc	Dataset	N	p	Nc	Dataset	N	p	Nc
crabs	200	5	2	house-votes	232	16	2	ionosphere	351	33	2
iris	150	4	3	log-yeast	384	17	5	pima	768	8	2
std-yeast	384	17	5	wine	178	13	3	80x	45	8	3
biomed	194	5	2	breast	683	9	2	chromo	1143	8	24
ecoli	272	7	3	glass	214	9	4	imox	192	8	4
kimia	216	4096	18	liver	345	6	2	mfeat-fac	2000	216	10
mfeat-fou	2000	76	10	mfeat-kar	2000	64	10	mfeat-pix	2000	240	10
mfeat-zer	2000	47	10	nist16	2000	256	10	sonar	208	60	2
soybean1	266	35	15	soybean2	136	35	4	diff300	300	20	3
same300	297	20	3	sim300	291	10	3	austra	690	15	2
derm	366	11	6	german	1000	24	2	heart	270	9	2
uci-image	2310	18	7	vehicle	846	16	4	wdbc	569	14	2

has higher correlation values than the Euclidean space. This suggests that, the dissimilarity spaces, especially the Dinc space, have better discriminant features and the classes are easier to separate using clustering techniques. Although we increased the dimensionality of the dissimilarity spaces, the assigning of samples to each class by a clustering algorithm seems much effective.

5   Conclusions

In this paper we proposed a novel dissimilarity representation for data based on a second-order dissimilarity measure. That measure is computed over triplets of nearest neighbors and has some advantages over pairwise dissimilarities, namely it can identify sparse classes. Each element of the Dinc space is a dissimilarity increment between an object and a set of representative objects, which are defined as an edge between an object and its nearest neighbor.

In this paper we considered that the set of representative objects corresponds to the entire dataset, which increased the dimensionality of the each dissimilarity space. Although, the dimensionality of the Dinc space was higher than the Feature space, we have shown that features in the Dinc space are more discriminative and the overlap of the classes has decreased, which facilitate the learning task to separate the objects from different classes. In future work, we will study different techniques for prototype selection, in order to obtain a smaller set of representative objects, leading to lower dimensionality of dissimilarity spaces.

Unsupervised learning techniques were also applied, namely hierarchical clustering algorithms, to the Dinc space, the original Feature space and to a dissimilarity space, built using the Euclidean distance. Overall, the Dinc space had lower error rates compared to the other two spaces, especially for centroid-link and median-link.

Acknowledgments. This work was supported by the Portuguese Foundation for Science and Technology, scholarship number SFRH/BPD/103127/2014, and grant PTDC/EEI-SII/2312/2012.

Appendix: Datasets

A total of 36 benchmark datasets from two repositories are used for the experimental evaluation of methods. The majority of the datasets are from the UCI Machine Learning Repository[1], and only a few datasets are from the 20-Newsgroups database[2]. A summary of the datasets in terms of number of samples, dimension of the feature space and number of classes is presented in Table 4.

References

1. Bishop, C.M.: Pattern Recognition and Machine Learning, Information Science and Statistics. Information Science and Statistics, vol. 1, 1st edn. Springer, New York (2006)
2. Chen, Y., Garcia, E.K., Gupta, M.R., Rahimi, A., Cazzanti, L.: Similarity-based classification: concepts and algorithms. J. Mach. Learn. Res. **10**, 747–776 (2009)
3. Duda, R.O., Hart, P.E., Stork, D.G.: Pattern Classification, 2nd edn. John Wiley & Sons Inc., New York (2001)
4. Duin, R.P.W., Loog, M., Pękalska, E., Tax, D.M.J.: Feature-based dissimilarity space classification. In: Ünay, D., Çataltepe, Z., Aksoy, S. (eds.) ICPR 2010. LNCS, vol. 6388, pp. 46–55. Springer, Heidelberg (2010)
5. Eskander, G.S., Sabourin, R., Granger, E.: Dissimilarity representation for handwritten signature verification. In: Malik, M.I., Liwicki, M., Alewijnse, L., Blumenstein, M., Berger, C., Stoel, R., Found, B. (eds.) Proceedings of the 2nd International Workshop on Automated Forensic Handwriting Analysis: A Satellite Workshop of International Conference on Document Analysis and Recognition (AFHA 2013). CEUR Workshop Proceedings, vol. 1022, pp. 26–30. CEUR-WS, Washington DC, USA August 2013
6. Fred, A., Leitão, J.: A new cluster isolation criterion based on dissimilarity increments. IEEE Trans. Pattern Anal. Mach. Intell. **25**(8), 944–958 (2003)
7. Ho, T.K., Basu, M., Law, M.H.C.: Measures of geometrical complexity in classification problems. In: Ho, T.K., Basu, M. (eds.) Data Complexity in Pattern Recognition. Advanced Information and Knowledge Processing, vol. 16, 1st edn, pp. 3–23. Springer, London (2006)
8. Jain, A.K., Duin, R.P.W., Mao, J.: Statistical pattern recognition: a review. IEEE Trans. Pattern Anal. Mach. Intell. **22**(1), 4–37 (2000)
9. Liao, L., Noble, W.S.: Combining pairwise sequence similarity and support vector machines for detecting remote protein evolutionary and structural relationships. J. Comput. Biol. **10**(6), 857–868 (2003)
10. Pekalska, E., Duin, R.P.W.: Dissimilarity representations allow for building good classifiers. Pattern Recogn. Lett. **23**, 943–956 (2002)

---

[1] http://archive.ics.uci.edu/ml.

[2] http://www.ai.mit.edu/people/jrennie/20Newsgroups/.

11. Pekalska, E., Duin, R.P.W.: The Dissimilarity Representation for Pattern Recognition: Foundations and Applications. World Scientific Pub Co Inc, River Edge, NY (2005)
12. Pekalska, E., Duin, R.P.W.: Dissimilarity-based classification for vectorial representations. In: 18th International Conference on Pattern Recognition (ICPR 2006). vol. 3, pp. 137–140. IEEE Computer Society, Hong Kong, China August 2006
13. Johl, T., Nimtz, M., Jänsch, L., Klawonn, F.: Detecting glycosylations in complex samples. In: Iliadis, L., Maglogiannis, I., Papadopoulos, H. (eds.) Artificial Intelligence Applications and Innovations. IFIP AICT, vol. 381, pp. 234–243. Springer, Heidelberg (2012)
14. Theodoridis, S., Koutroumbas, K.: Pattern Recognition, 4th edn. Elsevier Academic Press, San Diego (2009)
15. Wilcoxon, F.: Individual comparisons by ranking methods. Biometrics Bull. 1(6), 80–83 (1945)

Characterizing Multiple Instance Datasets

Veronika Cheplygina[1,2](✉) and David M.J. Tax[2]

[1] Biomedical Imaging Group Rotterdam, Erasmus Medical Center,
Rotterdam, The Netherlands
`v.cheplygina@tudelft.nl`
[2] Pattern Recognition Laboratory, Delft University of Technology,
Delft, The Netherlands

Abstract. In many pattern recognition problems, a single feature
vector is not sufficient to describe an object. In multiple instance learning (MIL), objects are represented by sets (*bags*) of feature vectors
(*instances*). This requires an adaptation of standard supervised classifiers
in order to train and evaluate on these bags of instances. Like for supervised classification, several benchmark datasets and numerous classifiers
are available for MIL. When performing a comparison of different MIL
classifiers, it is important to understand the differences of the datasets,
used in the comparison. Seemingly different (based on factors such as
dimensionality) datasets may elicit very similar behaviour in classifiers,
and vice versa. This has implications for what kind of conclusions may
be drawn from the comparison results. We aim to give an overview of the
variability of available benchmark datasets and some popular MIL classifiers. We use a dataset dissimilarity measure, based on the differences
between the ROC-curves obtained by different classifiers, and embed this
dataset dissimilarity matrix into a low-dimensional space. Our results
show that conceptually similar datasets can behave very differently. We
therefore recommend examining such dataset characteristics when making comparisons between existing and new MIL classifiers. Data and
other resources are available at http://www.miproblems.org.

1 Introduction

Images portraying several objects, text documents covering a range of topics or
molecules with conformations with different chemical properties are all examples
of data, where a single example (image, document, molecule) cannot always be
faithfully represented by a single feature vector. Representing each part (object
in an image, paragraph in a text document, molecule conformation) of an example by a single feature vector preserves more information about the example, but
requires a finer level of annotation, which is not always available. To deal with
such problems, supervised learning has been extended to multiple instance learning (MIL): a learning scenario where examples are sets (*bags*) of feature vectors
(*instances*), but where labels are available only for bags. Originally, the goal in
MIL was to classify previously unseen bags, however MIL classifiers which are
able to classify instances have also received a lot of attention because of their
ability to be trained with only coarse annotations.

© Springer International Publishing Switzerland 2015
A. Feragen et al. (Eds.): SIMBAD 2015, LNCS 9370, pp. 15–27, 2015.
DOI: 10.1007/978-3-319-24261-3_2

Since the introduction [8] of MIL in 1997, many classifiers have been proposed in the literature. A typical strategy in comparisons is to evaluate on the early benchmark problems (Musk [8], Fox, Tiger and Elephant [2]) as well as a number of larger sources, such as MIL adaptations of Corel [5] image datasets, or Newsgroups [27] text classification problems, which consist of 20 datasets each. Usually one of the following strategies is used when choosing datasets for a comparison: (i) targeting a particular application, such as image classification, and choosing few sources with many datasets per source (ii) choosing diverse datasets, for example by choosing many sources, with a few datasets per source, and/or choosing datasets with different characteristics, such as dimensionality.

A potential pitfall in choosing datasets this way is that, while they may seem diverse to a human observer, this may not be the case for a classifier, and vice versa. For example, in a related study on characterizing standard datasets [9], Duin et al. show that when changing dataset size and dimensionality for three different problems, some modified datasets remain similar (in dataset space) to their original versions. This is very important for the types of conclusions that can be drawn from an empirical comparison on a "observer-diverse" or "observer-similar" set of problems. For example, a classifier which performs well on a "observer-diverse" set of problems, may in fact only be suitable for problems in a small area of the dataset space. On the other hand, a classifier that is very good in one area of the dataset space, but not performing well on "observer-similar" problems might delay (or even prevent) the paper from being published.

In this paper we review a large number of problems that have been used as benchmarks in the MIL literature. We propose to quantify the dataset similarity based on the behavior of classifiers, namely by comparing the ROC curves, or the area under the ROC curves, that different classifiers obtain on these datasets. Our results show that conceptually similar datasets can behave quite differently. When comparing MIL classifiers, we therefore recommend not choosing datasets based on the application (images, text, and so forth) or on the dataset properties (bag size, dimensionality), but on how differently existing classifiers perform on these datasets.

2   Multiple Instance Learning

In multiple instance learning [8], a sample is a set or *bag* B_i of feature vectors $\{\mathbf{x}_i^1, \ldots, \mathbf{x}_i^{n_i}\}$. Each bag is associated with a label $y_i \in \{0, 1\}$, while the instances are unlabeled. Often assumptions are made about the existence of instance labels $\{z_i^k\}$, and their relationships to y_i. The standard assumption is "a bag is positive if and only if it has a positive instance", but over the years, more relaxed assumptions have been explored [10]. The positive instances are often called concept instances, and an area in the feature space with positive instances is often referred as "the concept".

Originally, the goal in MIL is to train a classifier f_B, which can label previously unseen bags. Globally, this can be achieved either by (1) training an instance classifier f_I, which relies on the assumptions about the instance and bag labels, and defining f_B by combining outputs of f_I, or (2) training f_B directly, by defining a supervised representation of the bags, or by distance- and kernel-based methods. We call these approaches instance-level and bag-level approaches, respectively. These approaches, which are also summarized in Fig. 1, are as follows:

Supervised Classifier By assuming that all the instances in a bag share the bag's label, a supervised classifier can be trained. A test bag is classified by combining the outputs of its instances. We call this approach simpleMIL.

MIL Classifier By using the standard MIL assumption of a concept (or a generalization thereof), an instance classifier can be trained, which is consistent with the training bag labels. Examples used in this paper are Diverse Density [16], EM-DD [25], MILBoost [24] and miSVM [3]. In Diverse Density the concept is explicitly modeled as an ellipsoidal region around one location. This location, and the dimensions of the ellipsoid, are optimized by maximizing the data likelihood. The concept should have high "diverse density": high density of positive instances but low density of instances from negative bags. EM-DD is an expectation-maximization algorithm which searches for the concept. The expectation step selects the most positive instance from each bag according to the current estimate for the concept, and the maximization step updates the concept by maximizing the diverse density. The miSVM classifier extends the regular SVM by searching not only for the optimal decision boundary, but also for the instance labels, which, given the decision boundary, are consistent with training bag labels.

Bag Vector, Kernel or Dissimilarity This approach converts the bag into an alternative representation before training a supervised, bag-level classifier. Examples used in this paper are Citation-kNN [23], bag statistics [11], bag-of-words, MILES [5] and MInD [6,22]. Citation-kNN defines a bag distance based on the number of "referencing" nearest neighbors, and the number of "citing" neighbors, and applies a nearest neighbor classifier. The other approaches represent each bag by a single feature vector, and apply a supervised classifier. The representation is absolute (instance statistics per bag) or relative, in terms of similarities to instance clusters (bag of words), instances in the training set (MILES), and bags in the training set (MInD).

A complete overview of MIL classifiers can be found in [1].

3   Datasets

In this section we describe the datasets we use in the experiments. These include 6 artificial datasets and 34 real-life datasets from 13 groups. For the artificial datasets, we use three datasets where only a number of concept instances are informative, and three datasets where all instances are informative. For the real-life datasets, different groups represent different sources of data. In some cases, different datasets from the same source are obtained by splitting up a multi-class problem into different one-against-all problems. For such groups, we use a small

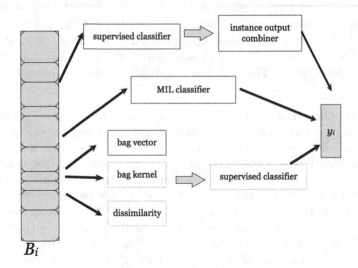

Fig. 1. A dataset with bags B_i of varying number of instances, and three general approaches how to arrive at bag labels y_i

number of datasets per group to make sure that the influence of each group is not too large. The complete list of datasets is shown in Table 1.

3.1   Artificial Datasets

Gaussian For the positive bags, instances are drawn from the positive concept Gaussian centered around (7,1), and a random set of instances is drawn from a background Gaussian distribution around (0,0). For the negative bags, the instances are drawn from the background distribution.

Maron Instances are randomly drawn from a uniform distribution in a unit square. For positive bags, one instance is also drawn from the 5 interval in the center of the square. This dataset is originally defined in [16].

Concept Instances are randomly drawn from 4 Gaussian distributions with centers [+2,−2], [−2,+2] or [−2,−2]. For positive bags, at least one instance is also drawn from [+2,+2].

Difficult Both positive and negative instances are drawn from elongated Gaussian distributions, that differ in mean in only the first feature.

Rotated The instances are drawn from an elongated Gaussian distributions. Instances from positive bags are drawn from a slightly rotated version of the negative instance distribution.

Widened The instances are drawn from two Gaussian distributions. For positive bags, this Gaussian is slightly wider than for negative bags.

3.2   Real-Life Datasets

Biology

Musk are molecule activity prediction problems. Each bag is a molecule, each instance is one of that molecule's conformations. The molecule is active if at least one of its conformations is active.

Mutagenesis is a molecule activity prediction problem [20]. Each bag is a molecule and each instance is a pair of atoms in that molecule, described by their chemical properties.

Protein is a problem of predicting whether a protein belongs to a family of TrX proteins [21]. A bag is protein, and an instance is part of that protein's sequence, represented by its molecular and chemical properties.

Images

Corel are scene classification problems [5]. Each bag is an image, each instance is a patch of that image. The images depict scenes of a beach, historical buildings, and so forth. Using the original 20 classes, 20 datasets are generated using the one-against-all approach.

SIVAL are image classification problems [18]. The images show a particular object (such as an apple) from different perspectives and in front of different backgrounds. Datasets are generated by the one-against-all approach.

Fox, Tiger, Elephant are image classification problems [2]. The positive images show the respective animal, the negative images are selected randomly from other (more than just these three) classes.

Breast is an image classification problem [14]. A bag is a tissue microarray image and an instance is a patch. The task is to predict whether the image is malignant (positive) or benign (negative).

Messidor is an image classification problem [13]. A bag is an eye fundus image and an instance is a patch. The task is to predict whether the image is of a subject with diabetes (positive) or a healthy subject (negative).

Text

Web are text classification problems [26]. A bag is a webpage, and an instance is a webpage that the original page links to. The goal is to predict whether to recommend a particular webpage to a user based on the content of the linked pages. The data in each of the datasets are the same, but the labels are different for each user.

Newsgroups are text classification problems [27]. A bag is a collection of newsgroup posts, each described by frequencies of different words. A positive bag for a category contains 3 % of posts about that category, whereas negative bags contain only posts about other topics.

Table 1. List of MIL datasets and their properties: number of positive and negative bags, number of features, number of instances and minimum/maximum number of instances per bag.

	+ bags	− bags	Features	Total inst	Min	Max
Musk 1	47	45	166	476	2	40
Musk 2	39	63	166	6598	1	1044
Gaussian-MI	50	50	2	692	5	9
Maron-MI	50	50	2	1000	10	10
MI-concept	10	10	2	126	5	8
Difficult-MI	10	40	2	352	5	9
Rotated-MI	30	30	2	1359	15	29
Widened-MI	30	30	2	1259	15	29
Corel African	100	1900	9	7947	2	13
Corel Beach	100	1900	9	7947	2	13
Corel Historical	100	1900	9	7947	2	13
Corel Buses	100	1900	9	7947	2	13
Corel Dinosaurs	100	1900	9	7947	2	13
Corel Elephants	100	1900	9	7947	2	13
Corel Food	100	1900	9	7947	2	13
Sival AjaxOrange	60	1440	30	47414	31	32
Sival Apple	60	1440	30	47414	31	32
Sival Banana	60	1440	30	47414	31	32
Sival BlueScrunge	60	1440	30	47414	31	32
Web recomm. 1	17	58	5863	2212	4	131
Web recomm. 2	18	57	6519	2219	5	200
Web recomm. 3	14	61	6306	2514	5	200
Web recomm. 4	55	20	6059	2291	4	200
Text(Zhou) alt.atheism	50	50	200	5443	22	76
Text(Zhou) comp.graphics	49	51	200	3094	12	58
Text(Zhou) comp.os.ms-windows.misc	50	50	200	5175	25	82
Fox (Andrews)	100	100	230	1320	2	13
Tiger (Andrews)	100	100	230	1220	1	13
Elephant (Andrews)	100	100	230	1391	2	13
Harddrive (positive=non-failed)	178	191	61	68411	2	299
Protein	25	168	8	26611	35	189
Mutagenesis easy	125	63	7	10486	28	88
Mutagenesis hard	13	29	7	2132	26	86
Birds, target class Brown Creeper	197	351	38	10232	2	43
Birds, target class Winter Wren	109	439	38	10232	2	43
Birds, target class Pacific-slope Flycatcher	165	383	38	10232	2	43
Birds, target class Red-breasted Nuthatch	82	466	38	10232	2	43
Biocreative component	359	359	200	13129	1	53
UCSB Breast cancer	26	32	708	2002	21	40
Messidor retinopathy	654	546	687	12352	8	12

Biocreative is a text classification problem [19]. A bag is a biomedical text and an instance is paragraph in the document. The task is to predict whether the text should be annotated as relevant for a particular protein.

Other

Harddrive is a problem of predicting harddrive failures [17]. Each bag are time series (instance = time point) of different measurements of hard drives, and each bag is labeled with whether a failure has occured or not.

Birds are concerned with classifying whether a particular bird is present in a sound recording [4]. A bag is a recording's spectrogram, an instance is a segment of that spectrogram. Datasets are generated by the one-against-all approach.

4 Proposed Approach

To summarize and embed the results of all classifiers on all datasets, we define a distance or similarity between datasets and results. The most simple representation uses basic metadata about a dataset. These features can be, for instance, the dimensionality, the number of bags, the number of instances, and so forth. When this metadata representation of a dataset i is $M^{(i)}$, the distance between two datasets is easily defined as:

$$D_{meta}(X_i, X_j) = \|M^{(i)} - M^{(j)}\|. \tag{1}$$

These metadata features are typically not very informative for how classifiers perform on these datasets. For this, the outputs of the classifiers are needed. A standard approach is to compare the predicted labels and count how often two classifiers disagree in their prediction [9]. Unfortunately, for MIL problems this approach is not very suitable, because MIL classification problems can have a very large class imbalance (as is visible in the Corel and SIVAL datasets). The alternative is to use the receiver-operating characteristic (ROC) curves instead. An ROC curve shows the true positive rate as a function of the false positive rate. Because the performances on the positive and negative class is decoupled onto two independent axes, class imbalance does not influence the curve.

A drawback of the ROC curve is that it is not straightforward to compare two different curves. We choose two different approaches to do this. The first approach is to summarize each ROC curve by its area under the curve (AUC), and compare the different AUCs. This may be suboptimal, because two ROC curves can have an identical AUCs, while their shapes may still be very different. This is illustrated in Fig. 2, where two curves with equal AUCs are shown, $\mathbf{ROC}_1$ and $\mathbf{ROC}_2$ (solid line and dashed line, respectively). In order to differentiate between these two curves, a second approach is used. Here the area of the difference between the two ROC curves is used as the distance between the curves. This is indicated by the gray area in Fig. 2.

Let the ROC curve of classifier k on dataset i be $\mathbf{ROC}_k^{(i)}$, and the AUC performance of classifier k on dataset i be $\mathbf{AUC}_k^{(i)} = \mathcal{A}(\mathbf{ROC}_k^{(i)})$. In the first approach, the distance between datasets X_i and X_j is defined as:

$$D_{auc}(X_i, X_j) = \|\mathbf{AUC}^{(i)} - \mathbf{AUC}^{(j)}\| \tag{2}$$

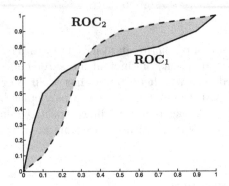

Fig. 2. Two ROC curves $\mathbf{ROC}_1$ and $\mathbf{ROC}_2$ with an equal area under the ROC curve ($\mathcal{A}(\mathbf{ROC})$), but where the two curves differ. The area of the gray region is the area $\mathcal{A}(\mathbf{ROC} - \mathbf{ROC})$.

where $\mathbf{AUC}^{(i)}$ is the vector of AUC performances, i.e. all performances of all classifiers on dataset X_i:

$$\mathbf{AUC}^{(i)} = \begin{bmatrix} \mathcal{A}(\mathbf{ROC}_1^{(i)}), \\ \vdots \\ \mathcal{A}(\mathbf{ROC}_L^{(i)}) \end{bmatrix} \tag{3}$$

In the second approach the area under the difference between two ROC curves is used:

$$D_{roc}(X_i, X_j) = \sqrt{\sum_k \mathcal{A}(\mathbf{ROC}_k^{(i)} - \mathbf{ROC}_k^{(j)})^2} \tag{4}$$

In the above, we have chosen the Euclidean norm to ensure that differences in the embeddings are caused by the choice of representation of the data, rather than by differences in the (non-)Euclideanness of the distances.

Embedding and Out-of-Sample Extension. Given the distances (1), (2) or (4), we embed the datasets using multi-dimensional scaling (MDS) [7]. MDS places a 2D vector for each dataset, such that the (Euclidean) distances in the 2D embedding match the given distances as good as possible. To compare a previously unseen dataset Z to the datasets in the embedding, the procedure is as follows. First all classifiers are trained on Z and the resulting ROC curves of the test sets are determined. Then the distances D_{auc} or D_{roc} are computed, and finally the 2D location of the Z is optimized to reproduce the original distances as well as possible.

Other algorithms could be considered for embedding as well. We have briefly experimented with t-SNE [15], which had a tendency to position the samples on a uniform grid, failing to reveal structure inside the data. In our experience, this happens when only a few samples need to be embedded. Furthermore, the out-of-sample extension is not as straightforward as for classical scaling approaches [12].

5   Experiments

In the experiments, we aim to demonstrate the embeddings for distances D_{meta}, D_{auc} and D_{roc} for the datasets described in Sect. 3. For D_{meta}, we use 6 features which are displayed in Table 1 and normalize these to zero mean and unit variance. For D_{auc} and D_{roc}, we use a set of 22 classifiers: simpleMIL, diverse density, EM-DD, MILBoost, Citation k-NN × 2, miSVM × 2, MILES × 2, MIL kernel × 3, bag statistics × 3, bag of words × 3, bag dissimilarity × 3. The base classifier for simpleMIL, bag statistics, bag of words and bag dissimilarity approaches is the logistic classifier. The different versions per classifier type correspond to different classifier parameters for which we have observed different behaviors in earlier work [6, 22]. These performances of these classifiers are available through http://homepage.tudelft.nl/n9d04/milweb/.

Clearly, the embeddings of D_{auc} and D_{roc} depend on the classifiers which are evaluated. Therefore, we first verify that we are using a diverse set of classifiers. We first create a 22-dimensional dataset where each feature contains all pairwise distances based a single classifier. We then compute the correlations between the features of this dataset. We also perform principal component analysis on this data, and compute the cumulative fraction of variance explained by the principal components. The results are shown in Fig. 3. The slope of the cumulative fraction of variance suggests that the classifiers are diverse, i.e., if there were two groups of highly correlated classifiers, the slope would be much steeper.

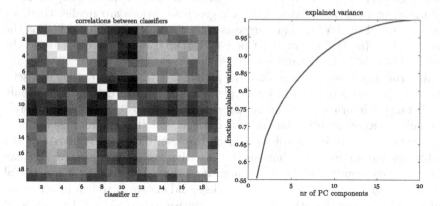

Fig. 3. Left: Correlations (white = 1, black = 0) between distances (D_{roc}) given by each of the 22 classifiers. Right: Cumulative fraction of variance explained in the D_{roc} distances between all datasets of 22 MIL classifiers.

We now compare the embeddings given by the three distances. D_{auc} and D_{roc} have very similar embeddings, so we show only D_{roc}. This means that the situation sketched in Fig. 2 does not occur very often, i.e. classifiers with similar AUCs also have similar ROC curves.

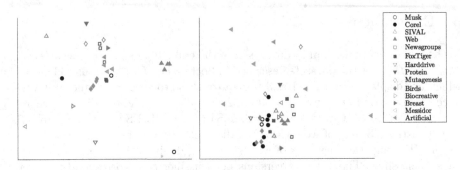

Fig. 4. Left: MDS embedding of the Euclidean distances between the meta-representations of the datasets. Right: MDS embedding of D_{roc} based on differences of ROC curves.

When comparing D_{meta} and D_{roc} the differences are very large. With D_{meta} some datasets from the same source have exactly the same representation and are on top of each other in the embedding, while the classifiers behave differently on these datasets. Another big difference is in the artificial datasets: these are relatively clustered together in D_{meta}, but display drastically different behaviors with D_{roc}.

We now zoom in more on the D_{roc} embedding. In the Web datasets, the most similar behavior within a dataset group can be observed. For most other dataset groups, we see different behavior of the datasets inside a group. In some situations, such as Birds data, the inside-group variations are smaller than, for example, Corel or SIVAL. This suggests that choosing a different class as the positive class (as is done in the Corel and SIVAL datasets) can change the character of a MIL dataset quite a lot.

A surprising observation is that the artificial datasets are outlier datasets, although they are supposed to be simpler versions of different situations (only one instance is informative, or all instances are informative) encountered in MIL. The differences of the artificial and real data suggest that the real-life datasets may contain a mixture of a concept region (or several concept regions), as well as different background distributions (i.e. negative instances in positive bags are different from negative instances in negative bags). The concept-like artificial datasets are generated such that these background instances are not informative. But in real-life cases, negative instances in positive bags could still be correlated with the bag label. For example, if foxes are photographed in forests more often than other animals, negative instances in a positive bag, i.e. patches of forest in an image of a fox, would still help in classifying the bag as positive.

Another interesting observation is that the datasets which have not been used as benchmarks very often, such as Harddrive, Breast and Biocreative are all quite different from each other. They are also quite different from the more frequently used datasets, such as Musk or Corel. Including these newer datasets in comparisons would therefore be helpful to get a more complete picture of the differences between classifiers.

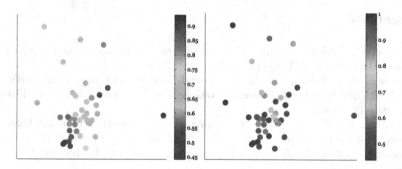

Fig. 5. Left: the average performance of a dataset, averaged over all MIL classifiers and all crossvalidation folds. Right: the performance of only a concept-based MIL classifier, the EMDD. Low performance is indicated in blue, high performance is indicated in yellow or red (Color figure online).

An attempt can be made to interpret the main variations in the MDS embedding of Fig. 4. It appears that the main direction is, not surprisingly, the average performance that the classifiers can achieve on the datasets. In Fig. 5 again the datasets are shown, embedded by MDS. In the left subplot the datasets are colored by the average performance of all classifiers. The scatter plot suggests that the "easier" datasets are in the bottom left. In the right subplot only the performance of the EM-DD classifier is shown. Here it can be observed that datasets on the left tend to have higher performances. It appears that these datasets have a concept present, that is in particular suitable for EM-DD, but also Diverse Density or MILBoost classifiers.

6   Conclusions

We proposed to characterize multiple instance learning datasets by quantifying their differences by the differences of ROC curves that different classifiers obtain on these datasets. We have shown that datasets which have similar properties such as the number of bags or instances, can have very different characteristics in terms of classifier behavior. Datasets from the same source, such as datasets derived from a multi-class problem, do not necessarily display similar characteristics. Finally, some datasets which are have not been used in comparisons of MIL classifiers often, behave quite differently from the more frequently used benchmarks. We believe that the proposed approach is useful when deciding which MIL datasets to use in a comparison of classifiers, and in interpreting results obtained by a novel MIL classifier.

A possible extension to the current work is to characterize the datasets by the ranks of the classifiers, rather than the actual performances. Perhaps in such a comparison a more apparent trend between datasets with a concept, multiple concepts, and so forth, would be seen. Another interesting direction of investigation is creating datasets – artificially, or by subsampling the real-life datasets – which will fill in the gaps in the dataset space we have investigated.

References

1. Amores, J.: Multiple instance classification: review, taxonomy and comparative study. Artif. Intell. **201**, 81–105 (2013)
2. Andrews, S., Hofmann, T., Tsochantaridis, I.: Multiple instance learning with generalized support vector machines. In: National Conference on Artificial Intelligence, pp. 943–944 (2002)
3. Andrews, S., Tsochantaridis, I., Hofmann, T.: Support vector machines for multiple-instance learning. In: Becker, S., Thrun, S., Obermayer, K. (eds.) Advances in Neural Information Processing Systems, vol. 15, pp. 561–568. MIT Press, Cambridge (2002)
4. Briggs, F., Lakshminarayanan, B., Neal, L., Fern, X.Z., Raich, R., Hadley, S.J.K., Hadley, A.S., Betts, M.G.: Acoustic classification of multiple simultaneous bird species: a multi-instance multi-label approach. J. Acoust. Soc. Am. **131**, 4640 (2012)
5. Chen, Y., Bi, J., Wang, J.: Miles: multiple-instance learning via embedded instance selection. IEEE Trans. Pattern Anal. Mach. Intell. **28**(12), 1931–1947 (2006)
6. Cheplygina, V., Tax, D.M.J., Loog, M.: Multiple instance learning with bag dissimilarities. Pattern Recogn. **48**(1), 264–275 (2015)
7. Cox, T.F., Cox, M.A.: Multidimensional Scaling. CRC Press, Boca Raton (2000)
8. Dietterich, T.G., Lathrop, R.H., Lozano-Pérez, T.: Solving the multiple instance problem with axis-parallel rectangles. Artif. Intell. **89**(1–2), 31–71 (1997)
9. Duin, R., Pekalska, E., Tax, D.: The characterization of classification problems by classifier disagreements. In: Proceedings of the 17th International Conference on Pattern Recognition 2004, ICPR 2004, vol. 1, pp. 141–143, August 2004
10. Foulds, J., Frank, E.: A review of multi-instance learning assumptions. Knowl. Eng. Rev. **25**(1), 1 (2010)
11. Gärtner, T., Flach, P.A., Kowalczyk, A., Smola, A.J.: Multi-instance kernels. In: International Conference on Machine Learning, pp. 179–186 (2002)
12. Gisbrecht, A., Lueks, W., Mokbel, B., Hammer, B.: Out-of-sample kernel extensions for nonparametric dimensionality reduction. In: Proceedings of European Symposium on Artificial Neural Networks (ESANN), pp. 531–536 (2012)
13. Kandemir, M., Hamprecht, F.A.: Computer-aided diagnosis from weak supervision: a benchmarking study. Comput. Med. Imaging Graph. **42**, 44–50 (2015, in press)
14. Kandemir, M., Zhang, C., Hamprecht, F.A.: Empowering multiple instance histopathology cancer diagnosis by cell graphs. In: Golland, P., Hata, N., Barillot, C., Hornegger, J., Howe, R. (eds.) MICCAI 2014, Part II. LNCS, vol. 8674, pp. 228–235. Springer, Heidelberg (2014)
15. Van der Maaten, L., Hinton, G.: Visualizing data using t-sne. J. Mach. Learn. Res. **9**(2579–2605), 85 (2008)
16. Maron, O., Lozano-Pérez, T.: A framework for multiple-instance learning. In: Jordan, M.I., Kearns, M.J., Solla, S.A. (eds.) Advances in Neural Information Processing Systems, vol. 10, pp. 570–576. MIT Press, Cambridge (1998)
17. Murray, J.F., Hughes, G.F., Kreutz-Delgado, K.: Machine learning methods for predicting failures in hard drives: a multiple-instance application. J. Mach. Learn. Res. **6**(1), 783 (2006)
18. Rahmani, R., Goldman, S.A., Zhang, H., Krettek, J., Fritts, J.E.: Localized content based image retrieval. In: International Workshop on Multimedia Information Retrieval, pp. 227–236, ACM (2005)

19. Ray, S., Craven, M.: Learning statistical models for annotating proteins with function information using biomedical text. BMC Bioinform. **6**(Suppl 1), S18 (2005)
20. Srinivasan, A., Muggleton, S., King, R.D.: Comparing the use of background knowledge by inductive logic programming systems. In: International Workshop on Inductive Logic Programming, pp. 199–230 (1995)
21. Tao, Q., Scott, S.D., Vinodchandran, N.V., Osugi, T.T.: Svm-based generalized multiple-instance learning via approximate box counting. In: International Conference on Machine Learning, p. 101 (2004)
22. Tax, D.M.J., Loog, M., Duin, R.P.W., Cheplygina, V., Lee, W.-J.: Bag dissimilarities for multiple instance learning. In: Pelillo, M., Hancock, E.R. (eds.) SIMBAD 2011. LNCS, vol. 7005, pp. 222–234. Springer, Heidelberg (2011)
23. Wang, J.: Solving the multiple-instance problem: a lazy learning approach. In: International Conference on Machine Learning, pp. 1119–1125 (2000)
24. Zhang, C., Platt, J.C., Viola, P.A.: Multiple instance boosting for object detection. In: Weiss, Y., Schölkopf, B., Platt, J.C. (eds.) Advances in Neural Information Processing Systems, vol. 18, pp. 1417–1424. MIT Press, Cambridge (2005)
25. Zhang, Q., Goldman, S.A., et al.: EM-DD: an improved multiple-instance learning technique. In: Dietterich, T.G., Becker, S., Ghahramani, Z. (eds.) Advances in Neural Information Processing Systems, vol. 14, pp. 1073–1080. MIT Press, Cambridge (2001)
26. Zhou, Z.H., Jiang, K., Li, M.: Multi-instance learning based web mining. Appl. Intell. **22**(2), 135–147 (2005)
27. Zhou, Z.H., Sun, Y.Y., Li, Y.F.: Multi-instance learning by treating instances as non-iid samples. In: International Conference on Machine Learning, pp. 1249–1256 (2009)

Supervised Learning of Diffusion Distance to Improve Histogram Matching

Tewodros M. Dagnew and Umberto Castellani[✉]

Università degli Studi di Verona, via Strada le Grazie 15, 30172 Verona, Italy
{tewodros.dagnew,umberto.castellani}@univr.it

Abstract. In this paper we propose a learning method properly designed for histogram comparison. We based our approach on the so called *diffusion distance* which has been introduced to improve the robustness against the quantization effect and the limitations of the standard *bin-to-bin* distance computation. We revised the diffusion distance definition in order to cast the histogram matching as a distance metric learning problem. In particular, we exploit the Large Margin Nearest Neighbor (LMNN) classification procedure to introduce a supervised version of the standard nearest neighbor (NN) classification paradigm.

We evaluate our method on several application domains namely, brain classification, texture classification, and image classification. In all the experiments our approach shown promising results in comparison with other similar methods.

1 Introduction

Histogram-based representations are very important in computer vision and pattern recognition to encode complex data, like texture or shapes, in a compact and effective form. The choice of a proper distance for histogram comparison is therefore crucial for matching purposes. Typically the most used measures are L_2 distance, χ^2 distance [8], histogram intersection [19], and Jensen-Shannon distance [11]. The main disadvantage of these methods comes from the assumption that a perfect alignment between histogram bins is available. However, this hypothesis is often violated by confounding variables like light variations, shape deformations, and so on. In particular, these distances are strongly conditioned by the data quantization process. There is a trade off in the definition of histogram size (i.e., the number or bins). When the number of bins is low the distance is robust, but not discriminative. Conversely, when the number of bins is high the distance becomes very discriminative but it loses its robustness. In order to attenuate this effect, some distances based on a cross-bin comparison strategy can be exploited leading to both robust and discriminative performances. Some example of methods addressing cross-bin distance are quadratic-form distance [15], earth mover's distance (EMD) [18], and diffusion distance [12]. All these methods are based on a hand-crafted distance definition. Another popular and very effective approach to deal with generic distances is based on supervised metric learning procedure (see [3] for a recent survey). Metric learning has

© Springer International Publishing Switzerland 2015
A. Feragen et al. (Eds.): SIMBAD 2015, LNCS 9370, pp. 28–37, 2015.
DOI: 10.1007/978-3-319-24261-3_3

been successfully employed for object recognition, image classification, and data retrieval. The overall idea consists in adopting a *data-dependent* framework to automatically estimate a *metric* specialized on the specific application at hand. The training samples are organized in a set of pairwise constraints: "must-link" for pairs of similar samples, and "cannot-link" for pairs of dissimilar samples. In this fashion the metric learning algorithm is able to find the parameters of the metric that best agree with these constraints. The metric learning methods basically differ by the problem formulation and by the used optimization strategy [3].

In this paper we aim at exploiting how metric learning methods can improve histogram comparison. Early real metric learning work has been shown in [9]. Very few work has been proposed recently starting from popular histogram-based distances. For instance a supervised version of the earth mover's distance has been introduced in [6,21]. In [21] authors proposed to learn a ground distance matrix and a flow-network by estimating an optimal transportation scheme. Similarly, in [6] the supervised EMD is further improved taking into account metric constraints for the ground metric. In [10] a supervised version of the χ^2 distance is exploited. The original formulation is generalized by introducing and estimating a metric matrix that strictly preserve the histogram properties of input data on a probability simplex.

Contribution. In our work we propose a supervised version of the diffusion distance [12] for histograms comparison. We revised the diffusion distance definition to cast the histogram matching as a distance metric learning problem. The so called *Large Margin Nearest Neighbor* (LMNN) metric learning procedure is adopted to estimate the optimal metric [22]. In this fashion we obtain an effective and easy way to compute version of a nearest neighbor classification scheme for applications that use histogram-like data descriptors.

Road-Map. The rest of the paper is organized as following. Section 2 describes the proposed method. The original definition of diffusion distance and an overview of LMNN approach is given and the proposed supervised diffusion distance is defined. Preliminary results are reported in Sect. 3 on different domains. Finally conclusions are drawn in Sect. 4.

2   Proposed Method

We based our method on the integration between the diffusion distance and a metric learning procedure. In this section we report the general definition of diffusion distance for histogram comparison as described in [12]. Then a very general overview on *metric learning* is introduced highlighting in particular the case of Large Margin Nearest Neighbor (LMNN) approach [22]. Finally, we revised the diffusion distance definition in order to propose its supervised version.

2.1 Diffusion Distance for Histogram Comparison

Given two histograms $h_1(x)$ and $h_2(x)$, the diffusion distance is defined as [12]:

$$d(h_1, h_2) = \sum_{l=0}^{L} ||(h_1(x) - h_2(x)) * \phi(x, \sigma_l)||_1, \tag{1}$$

where $(\sigma_0 = 0 < \sigma_1 < \cdots < \sigma_L)$ define a set of Gaussian filters with increasing smoothing effect. The underlined idea is to emulate a *diffusion* process on the difference between histograms that attenuate the conditioning of possible bin-to-bin dis-alignment. In order to reduce the computational complexity of Eq. 1 a recursive procedure is combined with a sub sampling process leading to:

$$d(h_1, h_2) = \sum_{l=0}^{L} ||d_l(x)||_1, \tag{2}$$

where $d_0(x) = (h_1(x) - h_2(x))$, and

$$d_l(x) = [d_{l-1}(x) * \phi(x, \sigma)] \downarrow_2, l = 1, \cdots, L. \tag{3}$$

The notation $\downarrow_2$ denotes half size down sampling, and L is the number of Gaussian pyramid layers with a fixed σ.

2.2 Metric Learning

The overall aim of distance metric learning is to replace Euclidean distances by so-called *Mahalanobis* distances. A Mahalanobis distance metric computes the distance between two vectors X and Y as $D_M = \sqrt{(X - Y)^\top M(X - Y)}$, where M is a full positive semidefinite matrix. When M becomes Identity matrix, the general equation becomes standard euclidean distance equation. This matrix M can be learned using *Large margin nearest neighbor* distance metric learning [22]:

$$\min_{M} \sum_{i,j:j \to i} D_M(x_i, x_j)^2 + \mu \sum_{k:y_i \neq y_k} [1 + D_M(x_i, x_j)^2 - D_M(x_i, x_k)^2]_+ \tag{4}$$

$[f]_+$ implies a hinge-loss $[f]_+ = \max(0, f)$. The first term pull target neighbors together. In the equation above j→i implies i and j are neighbors. The second term pushes away differently labeled $(k : y_i \neq y_k)$ instances from the target instances by a large margin so that the differently labeled instances are located further with higher distance unit in the space (see Fig. 1). μ sets the trade-off between the pulling and pushing objectives. For solving the above equation convex optimization as an instance of semi-definite programming using sub-gradient method is adopted.

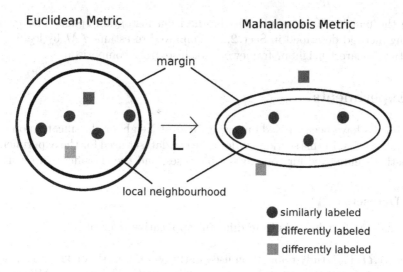

Fig. 1. Illustration of large margin nearest neighbor distance metric learning. Before training (left) and after training (right) (Color figure online).

2.3 Learning Diffusion Distance

The definition of diffusion distance described in Sect. 2.1 can be revised in order to make its learned version clearer. Exploiting the linear properties of the convolution operator Eq. 1 becomes:

$$d(h_1, h_2) = \sum_{l=0}^{L} ||(h_1(x) * \phi(x, \sigma_l)) - (h_2(x) * \phi(x, \sigma_l))||_1, \qquad (5)$$

or in a more general definition:

$$d(h_1, h_2) = ||\hat{h}_1 - \hat{h}_2||_1, \qquad (6)$$

where $\hat{h} = [h(x) * \phi(x, \sigma_l)]_{l=0}^{L}$. More precisely, the "diffusion" process is applied to the original histogram by acting as a sort of feature extractor that lead to a new histogram representation. Similarly, in the more efficient version we obtain $\hat{h} = [h^l(x) * \phi(x, \sigma)]_{l=0}^{L}$ where $h^0(x) = h(x)$ and $h^l(x)$ is a half size down sampled version of $(h^{l-1} * \phi(x, \sigma))$. In practice, the new representation is composed by the concatenation of L resized and filtered versions of the original histogram. Note that this method is coherent with the approaches that extract features from a given basic descriptor to enrich its discriminative property [4,5,16,20]. A similar approach was proposed in [17] to exploit a diffusion kernel in a Counting Grid framework. Finally, in order to integrate the new diffusion histogram representation in a metric learning framework we simply redefine Eq. 6 to:

$$d(h_1, h_2) = D_M(\hat{h}_1 - \hat{h}_2), \qquad (7)$$

where the matrix M is learned on the diffusion histogram space. The metric learning method described in Sect. 2.2 is employed to estimate M by leading to an optimal nearest neighbor framework for histogram comparison.

3   Experiments

Experiments have been carried out using Nearest Neighbor classification on several applications. In this section we describe the dataset used for the experiments, the methods employed for comparison purposes, and the classification results.

3.1   Datasets

We considered five datasets from different applicative domains.

Brain MRI The study population used in this work consists of 42 patients who were being treated for schizophrenia and 40 controls. The original MRI image size is $384 \times 512 \times 144$. A Regions of Interest (ROIs) approach was adopted in order to focus the analysis on well defined brain subparts [2]. In this work, we used left Thalamus which is found to be impaired in schizophrenic patients. DARTEL [1] tools within SPM software [7] was used to pre-process the data in order to align properly the subjects onto the canonical space and normalize the MRI intensity according to a well defined medical protocols [7]. Finally, we computed the histogram of normalized intensities of Thalamus for every subject. Number of bins in each histogram is chosen to be 40.

Outex from texture classification domain [13] containing surface textures and natural scenes. 168 images categorized into 28 distinct texture classes each having 6 example images were considered. The 6 images in each category are scale variated (i.e. 100, 120, 300, 360, 500 and 600 dpi). 12 sample categories with minimum and maximum resolution are reported in Fig. 2. Binary Gabor Pattern (BGP) texture histogram [23] is used as the image's texture descriptor/feature with dimension of 216. The process of extracting the BGP feature from an image involves gabor filtering with varying orientations, binarization and rotation invariant coding.

Webcam from object classification domain. 795 images categorized into 31 categories/classes were considered. These images are photos of several objects taken by people in unconstrained scenario as reported in Fig. 3. Local binary pattern (LBP) descriptor [14] which is commonly used for texture description is used as the image's feature with dimension of 256. Even though it may sound strange to apply descriptors commonly used for texture domain in object categorization domain, we believe, the results on 'Webcam' column as reported in Table 1 indicates texture descriptors may play important role in object detection and categorization domain too.

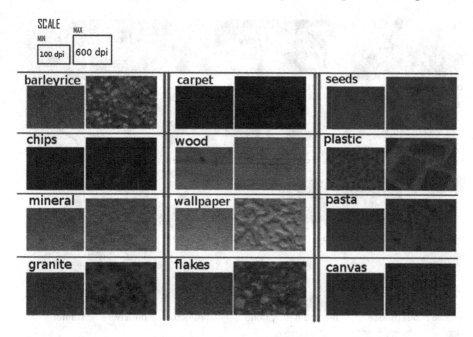

Fig. 2. Sample texture images from Outex dataset.

Amazon from image classification domain. 2817 images with 31 categories/classes were considered. These images are similar to Webcam images reported above, the difference is that, they are taken with constrained scenarios suitable for clear online displays as reported in Fig. 4 and the dataset is fused with noises. In Fig. 4 only 8 out of 31 categories are reported just to show the difference between the Webcam dataset. Surf-Bag-of-words (surf-BoW) is used as the image's descriptor with dimension of 800.

Corel Vision from image classification domain. 700 images categorized into 6 classes were considered as reported in Fig. 5. Visual bag-of-words is used as the image's descriptor with dimension of 200.

3.2 Methods Evaluated

In the Experiments 80/20 percent training/test set split is used then the error is averaged over the results of 20 random trials. K-nn classification error is used as evaluation criteria fixing $k = 3$ following the trend of the work in [10]. For comparison purposes we evaluate the following methods:

L2 :- k-nn classification is performed using L2 norm distance.

Diff :- k-nn classification is performed using diffusion distance [12] as described in Sect. 2.1.

$\mathbf{X}^2$:- k-nn classification is performed using χ^2 distance [8]. This metric is based on the χ^2 test for testing the similarity between histograms. It is defined as:

back pack   bike   helmet   book case   bottle   calculator   desk chair

headphone desk lamp tape dispenser monitor   keyboard   laptop   pen

letter tray   desktop PC mug   ring binder   note book   trash can   printer

mobile phone mouse   file cabinet phone   projector   puncher   stapler

ruler   scissor   speaker

Fig. 3. Sample images from Webcam dataset.

$$\chi(h_1, h_2) = \sum_{i=1}^{n} \frac{(h_1^i - h_2^i)^2}{h_1^i + h_2^i} \, .$$

lmnn-L2 :- k-nn classification is performed using large margin distance metric [22] reported in Sect. 2.2.

lmnn-Diff :- k-nn classification is performed using our supervised diffusion distance metric proposed in Sect. 2.3.

lmnn-X^2 :- k-nn classification is performed using supervised χ^2 distance metric [10].

3.3   Results

Results for all the experiments are reported on Table 1. As expected in the most of the cases a drastic improvement is observed when the learning procedure is introduced. Indeed, overall we can claim that the supervised distance version performs always better than the original one. This is clearly shown in the challenging scenarios of texture retrieval. We further highlight that in these experiments our

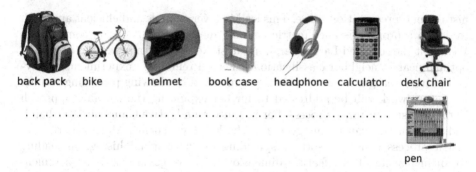

back pack   bike   helmet   book case   headphone   calculator   desk chair

pen

Fig. 4. Sample images from Amazon dataset.

wild cats   cars   elephants   clouds   buildings   rural

Fig. 5. Sample images from Corel image database.

Table 1. K-NN classification error in percentage.

	Brain MRI	Outex	Corel vision	Amazon	Webcam
L_2	53.4375	22	54.0357	65.04	54.56
Diff	38.125	22	53.5	62.46	54.18
X^2	46.875	-	62.3571	63.41	54.3
lmnn-L_2	50.9375	1	42.8571	52.40	37.09
lmnn-Diff	**29.0625**	**0**	**42.6429**	**51.33**	**36.96**
lmnn-X^2	50.625	4	53.9286	54.98	37.01

supervised diffusion distance always outperforms all other methods. In particular the benefit of our method is more relevant when quantization procedure is very critical as it has been seen in the biomedical case.

4   Conclusions

In this paper we introduce a supervised version of the diffusion distance for histogram matching. We revised the original version of diffusion distance by showing that it can be reformulated as a method for feature extraction on the histogram domain. Therefore we propose to exploit distance metric learning on this new histogram representation space. This lead to a very simple and efficient approach to design a proper distance metric learning method for histogram comparison. We adopt the so called Large Margin Nearest Neighbors framework to obtain an optimal nearest neighbor classification scheme. Preliminary experiments on several pattern recognition applications are reported by showing promising results.

Future work will be addressed to further exploiting the learning approach in the diffusion distance process. For instance an adaptive Gaussian filter bandwidth estimation can be integrated in the learning scheme. Moreover, the diffusion process caused a sort of spreading of the original histogram leading to an increasing of the feature dimensions. To overcome this issue a dimensional reduction procedure should be included in the optimal metric estimation framework.

Acknowledgements. We acknowledge financial support from the FSE project 1695/1/10/1148/2013.

References

1. Ashburner, J.: A fast diffeomorphic image registration algorithm. Neuroimage **38**(1), 95–113 (2007)
2. Baiano, M., Perlini, C., Rambaldelli, G., Cerini, R., Dusi, N., Bellani, M., Spezzapria, G., Versace, A., Balestrieri, M., Mucelli, R.P., Tansella, M., Brambilla, P.: Decreased entorhinal cortex volumes in schizophrenia. Schizophr. Res. **102**(1–3), 171–180 (2008)
3. Bellet, A., Habrard, A., Sebban, M.: A survey on metric learning for feature vectors and structured data. CoRR abs/1306.6709 (2013). http://arxiv.org/abs/1306.6709
4. Cristani, M., Perina, A., Castellani, U., Murino, V.: Geo-located image analysis using latent representations. In: IEEE Conference on Computer Vision and Pattern Recognition, CVPR, pp. 1–8, June 2008
5. Csurka, G., Perronnin, F.: Fisher vectors: beyond bag-of-visual-words image representations. In: Richard, P., Braz, J. (eds.) VISIGRAPP 2010. CCIS, vol. 229, pp. 28–42. Springer, Heidelberg (2011)
6. Cuturi, M., Avis, D.: Ground metric learning. J. Mach. Learn. Res. **15**(1), 533–564 (2014). http://dl.acm.org/citation.cfm?id=2627435.2627452
7. Friston, K., Ashburner, J., Kiebel, S., Nichols, T., Penny, W. (eds.): Statistical Parametric Mapping: The Analysis of Functional Brain Images. Academic Press, London (2007)
8. Hafner, J., Sawhney, H., Equitz, W., Flickner, M., Niblack, W.: Efficient color histogram indexing for quadratic form distance functions. IEEE Trans. Pattern Anal. Mach. Intell. **17**(7), 729–736 (1995)
9. Hastie, T., Tibshirani, R.: Discriminant adaptive nearest neighbor classification. IEEE Trans. Pattern Anal. Mach. Intell. **18**(6), 607–616 (1996). http://dx.doi.org/10.1109/34.506411
10. Kedem, D., Tyree, S., Weinberger, K., Sha, F., Lanckriet, G.: Non-linear metric learning. In: Bartlett, P., Pereira, F., Burges, C., Bottou, L., Weinberger, K. (eds.) Advances in Neural Information Processing Systems, vol. 25, pp. 2582–2590. MIT Press, Cambridge (2012)

11. Lin, J.: Divergence measures based on the shannon entropy. IEEE Trans. Inf. Theor. **37**(1), 145–151 (1991)
12. Ling, H., Okada, K.: Diffusion distance for histogram comparison. IEEE Comput. Vis. Pattern Recogn. (CVPR) **1**, 246–253 (2006)
13. Ojala, T., Mäenpää, T., Pietikäinen, M., Viertola, J., Kyllöenen, J., Huovinen, S.: Outex - new framework for empirical evaluation of texture analysis algorithms. In: Proceedings 16th International Conference on Pattern Recognition, Quebec, Canada, vol. 1, pp. 701–706 (2002)
14. Ojala, T., Pietikäinen, M., Mäenpää, T.: Multiresolution gray-scale and rotation invariant texture classification with local binary patterns. IEEE Trans. Pattern Anal. Mach. Intell. **24**(7), 971–987 (2002)
15. Pele, O., Werman, M.: The Quadratic-Chi histogram distance family. In: Daniilidis, K., Maragos, P., Paragios, N. (eds.) ECCV 2010, Part II. LNCS, vol. 6312, pp. 749–762. Springer, Heidelberg (2010)
16. Perina, A., Cristani, M., Castellani, U., Murino, V., Jojic, N.: Free energy score spaces: using generative information in discriminative classifiers. IEEE Trans. Pattern Anal. Mach. Intell. **34**(7), 1249–1262 (2012)
17. Perina, A., Peruzzo, D., Kesa, M., Jojic, N., Murino, V., Bellani, M., Brambilla, P., Castellani, U.: Mapping brains on grids of features for Schizophrenia analysis. In: Golland, P., Hata, N., Barillot, C., Hornegger, J., Howe, R. (eds.) MICCAI 2014, Part II. LNCS, vol. 8674, pp. 805–812. Springer, Heidelberg (2014)
18. Rubner, Y., Tomasi, C., Guibas, L.J.: A metric for distributions with applications to image databases. In: IEEE International Conference on Computer Vision (ICCV), pp. 59–66 (1998)
19. Swain, M.J., Ballard, D.H.: Color indexing. Int. J. Comput. Vis. **7**(1), 11–32 (1991)
20. Ulas, A., Duin, R.P.W., Castellani, U., Loog, M., Mirtuono, P., Bicego, M., Murino, V., Bellani, M., Cerruti, S., Tansella, M., Brambilla, P.: Dissimilarity-based detection of schizophrenia. Int. J. Imaging Syst. Technol. **21**(2), 179–192 (2011)
21. Wang, F., Guibas, L.J.: Supervised earth mover's distance learning and its computer vision applications. In: Fitzgibbon, A., Lazebnik, S., Perona, P., Sato, Y., Schmid, C. (eds.) ECCV 2012, Part I. LNCS, vol. 7572, pp. 442–455. Springer, Heidelberg (2012)
22. Weinberger, K., Saul, L.: Distance metric learning for large margin nearest neighbor classification. J. Mach. Learn. Res. **10**, 207–244 (2009)
23. Zhang, L., Zhou, Z., Li, H.: Binary gabor pattern: an efficient and robust descriptor for texture classification. In: 2012 19th IEEE International Conference on Image Processing (ICIP), pp. 81–84, September 2012

Similarity Analysis from Limiting Quantum Walks

Manuel Curado[1,2,3], Francisco Escolano[1,2,3]([✉]), Edwin R. Hancock[1,2,3],
Farshad Nourbakhsh[1,2,3], and Marcello Pelillo[1,2,3]

[1] Department of Computer Science and AI, University of Alicante, Alicante, Spain
[2] Department of Computer Science, University of York, York, UK
[3] DAIS - Unversità Ca' Foscari Venezia, Venezia, Italy
sco@dccia.ua.es

Abstract. Similarity compression is a critical step to improve the efficiency of edge detection. In this paper, we compare two approaches for compressing/decompressing similarity matrices, being edge detection our application domain. In this regard, state-of-the-art contour detectors rely on spectral clustering where pixel or patch similarity is encoded in a symmetric weight matrix and the eigenvectors of the normalized Laplacian derived from this matrix are clustered in order to find contours (normalized cuts and its variants). Despite significant interest in learning the similarity measure for providing well localized boundaries, the underlying spectral analysis has played a subsidiary role, and has mostly been based on classical random walks and the heat kernel. However, recent findings based on continuous-time quantum walks suggest that under the complex wave equation there are long-range interactions not present in the classical case. In the case of the edge map this opens up a means of controlling texture in the edge map by a simple thresholding. In this paper, we use the long-time averages of quantum walks for edge detection, and show that texture is a consequence of short-rangeness of these interactions. This is due to the local-to-global property of limiting quantum walks. In addition, when analyzing the role of limiting quantum walks as intermediate/indirect similarity decompression, we find that quantum walks are able of recovering the original edge structure when a factorization compressor is used, whereas this is not the case when compression relies on the Szemeéredi Regularity Lemma, despite this latter method is by far more efficient.

Keywords: Edge detection · Spectral clustering schrödinger operator · Quantum walks

1 Introduction

Since the seminal work of Canny [1], principled edge detection has been approached as a multi-stage process. First, local filters are designed so as to capture which capture the desireable details of local edges structure, and then

© Springer International Publishing Switzerland 2015
A. Feragen et al. (Eds.): SIMBAD 2015, LNCS 9370, pp. 38–53, 2015.
DOI: 10.1007/978-3-319-24261-3_4

global effects emerge from multi-resolution analysis or from more global methods usually based on supervised learning (e.g. Martin (Pb) [2] and Dollár [3]). Recent developments have addressed the problem of edge gap filling by learning from contours traced by human observers and those captured algorithmically. To this end Lim et al [4] use a dictionary of human generated contours. More recently) [5], attention has focussed on the need for learning a similarity function so that edges with properties close to those located by human eye to be located automatically by spectral clustering. In fact, the well known gPb method of Arbeláez [6] et al. has been merely used as a subsidiary tool.

In this paper we explore the potential of the underlying spectral clustering methods in more depth, and then to use them in order to understand the power of the similarity measure itself.

To understand more clearly what is attempted, we briefly provide a formal statement of the problem studied. Given a set of points $\mathcal{X} = \{x_1, \ldots, x_N\} \subset \mathbb{R}^d$ to be clustered, and a metric $d : \mathcal{X} \times \mathcal{X} \to \mathbf{R}$, the spectral approach consists of mapping the x_i to the vertices V of an undirected weighted graph $G(V, E)$ so that the edge weight $W(i, j) = e^{-d^2(x_i, x_j)/t}$ is a similarity measure between x_i and x_j. The analysis of the similarity/affinity matrix W is usually accomplished through the study of the Laplacian matrix $L = D - W$ or of its normalized counterpart. Then, despite the fact that W contains just pairwise relations, the spectrum and eigenvectors of L contain global information. However, it has been recently pointed out [7] that the limit analysis of a graph Laplacian, for instance setting $t \to 0$ as a consequence of $N \to \infty$, reveals some flaws or degenerate behaviors. For instance, ranking functions, which are usually implemented by Green's functions (the pseudo-inverse of the Laplacian), diverge when $N \to \infty$. Zhout et al. propose to solve this problem by computing Green's functions of "higher-order" Laplacians, i.e. L^m and $m \geq 0$.

One well known example of the spectral approach is provided by the normalized cuts clustering method [8]. This method has been improved by introducing topological distances which are consistent with a metric (commute-times) [9]. State-of-the-art methods for image segmentation do not only combine different eigenvectors of the Laplacian (normalized in this case) [6] but also incorporate better dissimilarity measures to make the weight matrix W more discriminative.

Further impovements of spectral clustering have exploited the random walk concept. For instance, in [10] pixels are labeled by the probability that a random walk will reach them from a given seed. Here the underpinning principle is to minimize the combinatorial Dirichlet integral associated with the weighted Laplacian of a graph. Seeds are assumed to be the boundary conditions of a Dirichlet problem and minimization seeks the values of the unknown labels so that the Dirichlet integral is the smoothest one. This means that a harmonic solution is preferred. As a result uniassigned probabilities can be estimated using semi-supervised learning, and are the averages of the probabilities of neighboring pixels). This method relies on solving a linear system, and is shown to be more robust to noise than normalized cuts.

Recently, quantum walks have been shown to offer interesting alternatives to the classical random, which offer non-classical properties such as non-stationartity, exponentially faster hitting times and as a result the possibility of long-range interactions. In particular, quantum walks suggest alternative ways of incorporating "high-order"information. For instance, in [11] a quantum version of the Jensen-Shannon divergence is used to compute a graph kernel, whereas in [12] it is exploited to detect both symmetric and anti-symmetric structures in graphs. In [13] and the references therein, it is suggested that quantum walks provide information about long-range interactions. For instance, in dendrimers (trees structured in strata or "generations") a quantum random walk starting at the root reaches (in the limit) nodes lying in the same generation with similar probability.

Our long-term aim is to address the question whether the improvement of spectral methods for clustering can be driven from quantum walks. In this paper, we will focus on uncovering the impact of quantum walks in recovering from similarity compressors in the context of edge detection.

2 Quantum Walks for Analyzing Transport

2.1 Unitary Evolution and the Schrödinger Operator

Let $\mathcal{H} = span\{|j\rangle \mid j = 1, \ldots, N\} = \mathbb{C}^N$ be a N−dimensional Hilbert space where $\langle j| = (0 \ldots 1 \ldots 0)$ with a 1 at the $j - th$ position. We use the Dirac bra-ket notation where: $|a\rangle = \boldsymbol{a}$, $\langle a| = \boldsymbol{a}^*$, $\langle a|b\rangle = \boldsymbol{a}^*\boldsymbol{b}$ is the inner product and therefore $\langle j|k\rangle = \boldsymbol{j}^*\boldsymbol{k} = \delta_{jk}$ and $\sum_{j=1}^{N} |j\rangle\langle j| = \mathbf{1}$. Then, a point in the Hilbert space is given by $|\psi\rangle = \sum_{j=1}^{N} c_j|j\rangle$ with $c_j \in \mathbb{C}$ so that $|c_1|^2 + |c_2|^2 + \ldots + |c_N|^2 = 1$ and $|c_j|^2 = \bar{c}_j c_j$.

The Schrödinger equation describes how the complex state vector $|\psi(t)\rangle \in \mathbb{C}^n$ of a continuous-time quantum walk varies with time:

$$\frac{\partial|\psi(i)\rangle}{\partial t} = -i\boldsymbol{L}|\psi_t\rangle. \tag{1}$$

Given an initial state $|\psi(0)\rangle = \sum_{j=1}^{N} c_j^0|j\rangle$ the latter equation can be solved to give $|\psi(t)\rangle = \boldsymbol{\Psi}(t)|\psi(0)\rangle$, where $\boldsymbol{\Psi}(t) = e^{-i\boldsymbol{L}t}$ is a complex $n \times n$ *unitary matrix*. In this paper we refer to $\boldsymbol{\Psi}(t)$ as the *Schrödinger operator*. In this regard, Stone's theorem [14] establishes a one-to-one correspondence between a time parameterized unitary matrix $\boldsymbol{U}(t)$ and a self-adjoint (Hermitian) operator $\boldsymbol{H} = \boldsymbol{H}^*$ such that there is a unique Hermitian operator satisfying $\boldsymbol{U}(t) = e^{it\boldsymbol{H}}$. Such an operator $\boldsymbol{H}$ is the *Hamiltonian*. In the case of graphs $\boldsymbol{H} = -\boldsymbol{L}$ and then we have that $\boldsymbol{\Psi}(t) = e^{-it\boldsymbol{L}}$ is a unitary matrix for $t \in \mathbb{R}$. Therefore, given a initial state $|\psi(0)\rangle$, the Schrödinger Operator characterizes the evolution of a Continuous-Time Quantum Walk (CTQW). The probability that the quantum walk is at node j is given by $|\langle j|\psi\rangle|^2 = |c_j|^2$. The $|c_j|^2$ are known as the amplitudes of the wave traveling through the graph.

2.2 Long-Time Averages from Magnitude

Different choices of the initial state $|\psi(0)\rangle = \sum_{j=1}^{N} c_j^0|j\rangle$ lead to different ways of probing the graph by exploiting properties of quantum superposition and quantum interference. For instance, in [11], initial amplitudes are set to $c_j^0 = \sqrt{\frac{d_j}{\sum_{k=1}^{N} d_k}}$, in order to compute de quantum version of the Jensen-Shannon divergence. However, in [12], where the focus is on identifying whether the vertices i and j are symmetrically placed in the graph, we have that either $c_j^0 = 1/\sqrt{2}$ and $c_k^0 = 1/\sqrt{2}$ (in phase) or $c_j^0 = 1/\sqrt{2}$ and $c_k^0 = -1/\sqrt{2}$ (in antiphase). Actually, the Quantum Jensen-Shannon divergence has a low value when pairs or vertices are located anti-symmetrically and a high value when they are symmetrically placed.

In this paper, we use the classical choice proposed by Farhi and Gutman for studying transport properties of quantum walks in trees [15]. In such approach, states $|j\rangle$ are associated with excitations at the nodes j. Therefore, the evolution of a CTQW commencing at node $|j\rangle$ is given by $|j(t)\rangle = e^{-itL}|j\rangle$. In this regard, the amplitude of a transition between nodes j and k at time t is given by $c_{jk}(t) = \langle k|j(t)\rangle = \langle k|e^{-itL}|j\rangle$, and the quantum-mechanical probability of such a transition is $\pi_{jk}(t) = |c_{jk}(t)|^2 = \left|\langle k|e^{-itL}|j\rangle\right|^2$.

Since the spectral decomposition of the Laplacian is $L = \Phi\Lambda\Phi^T$, where $\Phi = [\phi_1|\phi_2|\dots|\phi_n]$ is the $N \times N$ matrix of ordered eigenvectors according to the corresponding eigenvalues $0 = \lambda_1 \leq \lambda_2 \leq \dots \leq \lambda_n$, and $\Lambda = diag(\lambda_1 \; \lambda_2 \; \dots \; \lambda_n)$, we have that $e^{-itL} = \Phi e^{-it\Lambda}\Phi^T$ where $e^{-it\Lambda} = diag(e^{-it\lambda_1} \; e^{-it\lambda_2} \; \dots \; e^{-it\lambda_n})$. Then, the probability of a transition between j and k at time t is given by

$$\pi_{jk}(t) = \left|\langle k|e^{-itL}|j\rangle\right|^2 = \left|\langle k|\Phi e^{-it\Lambda}\Phi^T|j\rangle\right|^2$$
$$= \left|\langle k|\sum_{u=1}^{N} e^{-it\lambda_u}|\phi_u\rangle\langle\phi_u|j\rangle\right|^2 = \left|\sum_{u=1}^{N} e^{-it\lambda_u}\langle k|\phi_u\rangle\langle\phi_u|j\rangle\right|^2, \qquad (2)$$

where $\langle k|\phi_u\rangle = \phi_u(k)$ and $\langle\phi_u|j\rangle = \phi_u(j)$ respectively. Therefore we have

$$\pi_{jk}(t) = \sum_{u=1}^{N}\sum_{v=1}^{N} e^{-it(\lambda_u - \lambda_v)} z_u(k,j) z_v(k,j), \qquad (3)$$

where $z_u(k,j) = \phi_u(k)\phi_u(j)$ and $z_v(k,j) = \phi_v(k)\phi_v(j)$ account for the correlations between the k-th and j-th components of the eigenvectors ϕ_u and ϕ_v. Then, since $e^{-it(\lambda_u - \lambda_v)} = \cos(t(\lambda_u - \lambda_v)) - i\sin(t(\lambda_u - \lambda_v))$ we have that the long-time limit of $\pi_{jk}(t)$ does not exist, whereas the corresponding long-time limit of a classical continuous-time random walk is $1/N$. However, in the quantum mechanical case it is possible to compute the long-time average:

$$\chi_{jk} = \lim_{T\to\infty} \frac{1}{T}\int_0^T \pi_{jk}(t)dt$$
$$= \lim_{T\to\infty} \frac{1}{T}\int_0^T \sum_{u=1}^{N}\sum_{v=1}^{N} e^{-it(\lambda_u - \lambda_v)} z_u(k,j) z_v(k,j)$$

$$= \lim_{T \to \infty} \sum_{u=1}^{N} \sum_{v=1}^{N} z_u(k,j) z_v(k,j) \frac{1}{T} \int_0^T e^{-it(\lambda_u - \lambda_v)} dt$$

$$= \sum_{u=1}^{N} \sum_{v=1}^{N} \delta_{\lambda_u, \lambda_v} z_u(k,j) z_v(k,j) \,, \tag{4}$$

where $\delta_{\lambda_u, \lambda_v} = 1$ if $\lambda_u = \lambda_v$ and 0 otherwise. Therefore, the long-time averaged probabilities do not depend directly on the eigenvalues of the Laplacian but on their multiplicity. Mülken and Blumen have recently related the multiplicity to the transport efficiency of CTQWs [13]. More precisely, the averaged return probability $\bar{\pi}(t) = (1/N) \sum_{k=1}^{N} \pi_{k,k}(t)$ decays faster with time than that of a classical continuous-time random walk under conditions of low multiplicity. This means that in the long-time limit more probabilistic mass is allocated to nodes lying far away from the origin of the quantum walk, provided that there is low degeneracy (i.e. multiplicity).

3   Edges from Quantum Walks

3.1   Local-to-Global Role of Quantum Walks

The diagonal of the symmetric matrix χ contains the long-time probabilities that a CTQW returns to each node. The off-diagonal elements $\chi(j,k)$ are the probabilities that a CTQW commencing at the j−th node reaches the k−th one in the limit. Then, since $\sum_{k=1}^{T} \chi(j,k) = 1$, $\forall j$ we can associate a probability density function (pdf) to each node j. The fraction of off-diagonal probability mass $e(\boldsymbol{W}) = \sum_{j=1}^{N} \sum_{k \neq j}^{N} \chi(j,k)/N$ measures the transport efficiency of the weighted graph. Since the CTQWs have a coherent behavior, $e(\boldsymbol{W})$ increases when there is enough similarity support, provided that the eigenvectors of the Laplacian matrix $\boldsymbol{L}$ are not degenerated. For instance, if $\boldsymbol{W}$ encodes a complete graph we have $\chi = \boldsymbol{1}$, that is, $e(\boldsymbol{W}) = 0$ since the eigenvalues of the Laplacian are: 0 with multiplicity one, and N, with multiplicity $N - 1$.

Since the similarity support is not homogeneous, but piecewise smooth, we have that $\boldsymbol{W}$ is sparser than χ. We also have that off-diagonal probabilities typically correspond to long-range interactions, i.e. to transitive links, under certain regimes. More precisely, if we sort the off-diagonal entries $\chi(j,k)$ in descending order, the sequence of graphs generated by incrementally decreasing the threshold γ used for retaining an edge if $\chi(j,k) \geq \gamma$ this process leads to a structural level set $\boldsymbol{S}_1, \boldsymbol{S}_2, \ldots, \boldsymbol{S}_r, \ldots$ dominated by long-range interactions as r grows.

In an image this means that CTQWs progressively establish links between more and more dissimilar regions, however these links are very weak but not zero.

3.2   Filtering Texture

In our preliminary experiments with edge detection we have checked that CTQWs play the role of a *similarity compressor*, i.e., given the original range of similarities the result is the new range $[0, 1]$ since $\chi(j, k)$ are probabilities. However, the bulk of the probability mass is under a small threshold $\alpha > 0$ (see Fig. 1).

Since edge detection is focused on dissimilarity, we retain the probability mass corresponding $\chi(j, k) \leq \alpha$ to build a filtered version $\boldsymbol{W}_S$ of the original similarity matrix $\boldsymbol{W}$:

$$W_S(j, k) = \begin{cases} \chi(j, k) & \text{if j=k or } \chi(j, k) \leq \alpha \\ 0 & \text{otherwise} \end{cases} \tag{5}$$

The doubly stochasticity of the χ matrix suggests that $\boldsymbol{W}_S$ contains a compressed solution of the clustering problem. Actually, the structure of its associated normalised Laplacian $\tilde{\boldsymbol{L}}_S = \boldsymbol{I} - \boldsymbol{D}_S^{-1/2} \boldsymbol{W}_S \boldsymbol{D}_S^{-1/2}$ is as follows:

1. Since $diag(\chi)$ is retained to form $\boldsymbol{W}_S$, the have that $\boldsymbol{D}_S = diag(\boldsymbol{W}_S \boldsymbol{1}) \leq \boldsymbol{I}$ for $\alpha \leq 1$ and equality holds for $\alpha = 1$. In that latter case, we have $\tilde{\boldsymbol{L}}_S = \boldsymbol{I} - \boldsymbol{W}_S$ and $trace(\tilde{\boldsymbol{L}}_S) = \sum_{k=1}^{N} \tilde{\lambda}_k = N - \sum_{k=1}^{N} \chi_{kk} > 0$.
2. For $\alpha \rightarrow 0$ we have $\boldsymbol{D}_S = 1 - \boldsymbol{\epsilon}$, where $\boldsymbol{\epsilon} > 0$ is a vector of residuals. Then $\boldsymbol{D}_S^{-1/2} = (1 - \boldsymbol{\epsilon})^{-1/2}$ and $\tilde{\boldsymbol{L}}_S = \boldsymbol{I} - (1 - \boldsymbol{\epsilon})\boldsymbol{W}_S$. Then, we have $trace(\tilde{\boldsymbol{L}}_S) = \sum_{k=1}^{N} \tilde{\lambda}_k = N - \sum_{k=1}^{N} (1 - \epsilon_k)\chi_{kk}$. When $\epsilon \rightarrow 0$ (as a consequence of $\alpha \approx 0$) we have $trace(\tilde{\boldsymbol{L}}_S) = \sum_{k=1}^{N} \tilde{\lambda}_k \approx \boldsymbol{0}$.

Therefore, the smaller is α, the the closer to $\boldsymbol{0}$ becomes the spectrum of $\tilde{\boldsymbol{L}}_S$ and we capture less texture. This is due to the fact that for small values of α long-range interactions dominate over short-range ones which provide texture. This means that more global (close-to-human) contours are retained (see Fig. 2) with respect to the crisp-boundaries approach [5] for $\alpha < 1$. In addition, both methods work poorly when the object is embedded in a high-textured background. Our filtering does not merely introduces a low-pass filter (see water reflection in Taj Mahal) but localizes better the parts of objects (e.g. wheels in the car).

3.3   The Effect of Similarity Compression

Spectral clustering methods applied to image segmentation typically require the computation of a large amount of affinity pairs, even when superpixels are considered). This limits the applicability of these methods. In this paper, we explore the effect of compressing the affinity matrix before computing the Schrödinger texture filter and the subsequent edges.

We consider two different compression methods: a factorization one, based on transforming the original $\boldsymbol{W}$ into a reduced similarity matrix $\hat{\boldsymbol{W}}$ through a many-to-one mapping, and a regularization method based on the Szemeredi Regularity Lemma [16]. In this section we analyze to what extent limiting CTQWs can help recovering the edge structure from compression.

Compression Through Factorization Let $\boldsymbol{W}$ a $N \times N$ similarity matrix and $K \ll N$ a constant, being K/N the compression rate. The goal of similarity

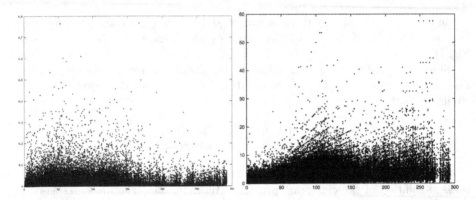

Fig. 1. CTQWs as similarity compressors: Original similarities from crisp boundaries (x-axis) vs χ probabilities (y-axis). Left: without similarity compression. Right: with similarity compression (see text).

compression is to determine both a reduced similarity matrix $\hat{\boldsymbol{W}}$ of order $K \times K$ and a many-to-one mapping $\psi(.)$ between the pixels being compared $\boldsymbol{W}$ and their corresponding pixels in $\hat{\boldsymbol{W}}$ so that $W_{ij} = \hat{W}_{\psi(i)\psi(j)}$. Following the factorisation approach introduced in [17], we express the mapping ψ in terms of a left stochastic (i.e. column stochastic) matrix $\boldsymbol{Y} \in \mathcal{S}$, where $\mathcal{S} = \{\boldsymbol{Y} \in \mathbb{R}_+^{K \times N} : \boldsymbol{Y}^T \mathbf{1}_K = \mathbf{1}_N\}$. Thus, any of the N pixels in the j−th column of $\boldsymbol{Y}$ must be mapped to the k−th pixel in the K rows of $\boldsymbol{Y}$.

In matrix form, we seek $\boldsymbol{Y}$ and $\hat{\boldsymbol{W}}$ so that

$$\boldsymbol{W} = \boldsymbol{Y}^T \hat{\boldsymbol{W}} \boldsymbol{Y}, \tag{6}$$

meaning that the essential affinity information of $\boldsymbol{W}$ must be transferred to $\hat{\boldsymbol{W}}$ through $\boldsymbol{Y}$. In order to ensure the proper affinity transfer, we must minimize $\|\boldsymbol{W} - \boldsymbol{Y}^T \hat{\boldsymbol{W}} \boldsymbol{Y}\|^2$. However it is more flexible to enforce: (i) pairwise affinities between i and j in $\boldsymbol{W}$ must be transferred to pixels k and l in $\hat{\boldsymbol{W}}$ when $\psi(i) = k$ and $\psi(l) = j$ are likely, i.e. when $Y_{ki}Y_{lj}$ is high; (ii) self-affinity transfer is enforced. These requirements are consistent with minimizing

$$f(\boldsymbol{Y}, \hat{\boldsymbol{W}}) = \sum_{i,j \in \{1,2,\dots,N\}} \sum_{k,l \in \{1,2,\dots,K\}} \delta_{(k,i) \neq (l,j)} Y_{ki} Y_{lj} (W_{ij} - \hat{W}_{kl})^2$$

$$+ \sum_{i \in \{1,2,\dots,N\}} \sum_{k \in \{1,2,\dots,K\}} (W_{ii} - \hat{W}_{kk})^2 \tag{7}$$

s.t. $\boldsymbol{Y} \in \mathcal{S}$ and $\hat{\boldsymbol{W}} \in \mathbb{R}^{K \times K}$.

The latter minimization can be addressed by a EM approach which starts by a random choice of $\hat{\boldsymbol{W}} \in \mathcal{S}$ and proceeds by alternating estimations of $\boldsymbol{Y}$ given $\hat{\boldsymbol{W}}$ and re-estimations of $\hat{\boldsymbol{W}}$ given $\boldsymbol{Y}$ until convergence. Finally, a discrete solution is obtained through *clean-up* (projection on the space of binary left stochastic matrices) [17].

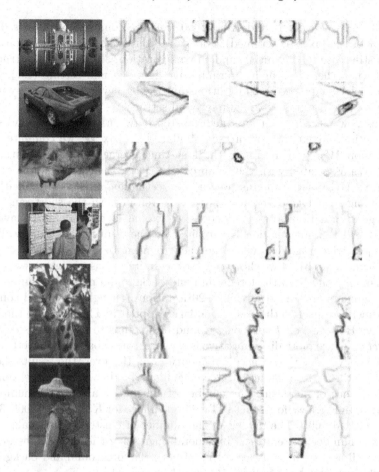

Fig. 2. Edge-detection results. First column: images from BSDS500. Second column: Crisp-boundaries from [5]. Third column: edges from quantum walks for $\alpha = 0.1$. Fourth column: edges for $\alpha = 0.05$

The above compression process does not necessarily lead to a clustering solution (in some cases it is not ensured that pixels in W mapped to the same pixel in $\hat{W}$ share a similar affinity, which in turn is different from those between pixels in W mapped to different pixels of $\hat{W}$). However, this method produces good clustering results in practice. Therefore it can be used, in principle, to simplify the spectral clustering process. If so, the *lossy decompressed matrix* $Y^T \hat{W} Y$ should induce a low-frequency edge map through spectral clustering. This is not the case of the crisp-boundaries method [5] despite the fact that incoming affinities in W are derived from mutual information. Actually, the resulting edge map obtained directly from $Y^T \hat{W} Y$ is very noisy.

For instance, in Fig. 3 we compare different levels of compression with the compression-free crisp-boundary approach (right). The size of all images is

$125 \times 83 = 10,375$ pixels and $K = 1000$ (i.e. the compression rate is 0.09 - only 10 % of the pixels is retained). For $t = 10$ iterations the compression algorithm is still close to the initial random configuration, although some structure is found when there is a high discriminative figure-ground setting (car). Low-frequency edges improve $t = 20$ iterations but the background is still very noisy, specially at low discriminative figure-ground settings.

Let us now introduce an intermediate step between compression and spectral clustering. Given the compressed similarity matrix $\hat{\boldsymbol{W}}$ we compute a filtered version $\hat{\boldsymbol{W}}_S = \hat{\chi}$ retaining the long-time average of the magnitude of the CTQWs associated with the compressed matrix, then we decompress $\hat{\boldsymbol{W}}_S$ through $\boldsymbol{Y}^T\hat{\boldsymbol{W}}_S\boldsymbol{Y}$ (we call this process *indirect decompression*). Implicitly we are assuming $\alpha = 1$ (no filtering) in order to retain both the short-range and long-range information between clusters (we exploit local-to-global behavior of CTQWs). All this information is exploited by the limiting quantum walks in order to join edge fragments while the background noise is suppressed.

For instance, in Fig. 4 we show that for $t = 10$ iterations, quantum walks find edge fragments and both the foreground and background noises are suppressed. These fragments are joined after $t = 20$ iterations, though the global contrast decreases with respect to the crisp-boundaries approach. This is due to the long-rangedness However, for $t = 20$ background noise tends to be suppressed. As in the *direct* case, the more discriminative is the foreground-background setting the faster the convergence to an acceptable edge map. However, the results showed in Fig. 4 is still far from an acceptable edge map. To that end we must analyze the convenience of increasing the number of clusters K and/or the number of iterations t. In Fig. 5 we focus on the Taj Mahal image for $K = \{1000, 2000, 3000\}$ and $t = \{10, 40, 100\}$. The impact of the number of clusters K is smaller than that of the number of iterations. In general, increasing t leads to high-contrast edges as well as a significant decreasing of both the foreground and background noise (which cannot be done with the *direct* approach).

The above *indirect* results are partially explained by the fact that CTQWs are *similarity compressors* (see Fig. 1-right). Since the above factorization also leads to similarity compression, limiting quantum walks tend to find significant correlations between the initial similarities $\boldsymbol{W}$ and those of $\boldsymbol{Y}^T\hat{\boldsymbol{W}}_S\boldsymbol{Y}$ (left).

Consequently, in addition to control texture, CTQWs are also helpful for retaining significant edges when compression is needed or it is imposed by real-time constraints. In terms of efficiency, since computing the limiting CTQWs require the estimation of all the eigenvectors and eigenvalues of the Laplacian, if we constrain that task to a $K \times K$ matrix with $K \ll N$, as we do in the *indirect approach*, we will exploit all the benefits of the local-to-global behavior of limiting quantum walks provided that enough compression iterations can be performed.

Compression Through Graph Regularization The Szémeredi Regularity Lemma [16] is a fundamental result in extremal graph theory. In our context, this lemma states, in conjunction to the Key Lemma, that every large graph can

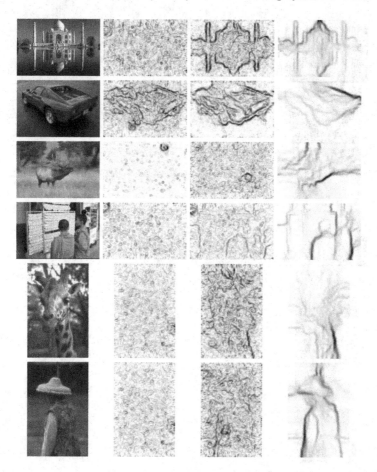

Fig. 3. Edge-detection results with *direct decompression*. First column: images from BSDS500. Second column: edges from $K = 1000$ and $t = 10$. Third column: edges from $K = 1000$ and $t = 20$. Fourth column: crisp-boundaries without compression.

be compressed in such a way that the so called *reduced graph* retains the global properties of the original graph.

More precisely, let $G = (V, E)$ a graph with $N = |V|$ vertices and $E \subseteq V \times V$ edges, and let $X, Y \subset V$ two disjoint subsets of vertices of G. The *edge density* $d(X, Y)$ associated with the pair X, Y is defined as

$$d(X, Y) = \frac{e(X, Y)}{|X||Y|}, \tag{8}$$

where $e(X, Y)$ is the number of edges between vertices of X and vertices of Y.

Given a constant $\epsilon > 0$, a pair (A, B) of disjoint vertex sets $A, B \subseteq V$ is ϵ-regular if for every $X \subseteq A$ and $Y \subseteq B$ satisfying

$$|X| > \epsilon|A| \quad \text{and} \quad |Y| > \epsilon|B| \tag{9}$$

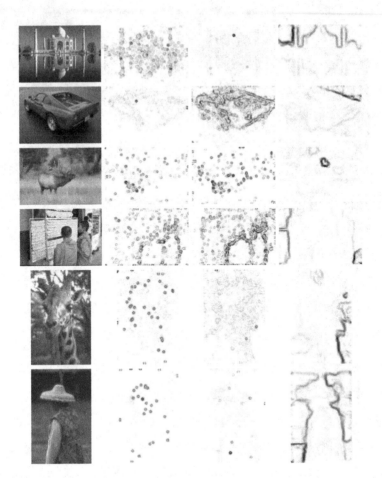

Fig. 4. Edge-detection results with *indirect decompression*. First column: images from BSDS500. Second column: edges from $K = 1000$ and $t = 10$. Third column: edges from $K = 1000$ and $t = 20$. Fourth column: edges from quantum walks for $\alpha = 0.1$ without compression.

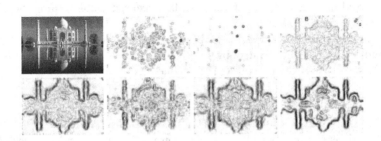

Fig. 5. Edge-detection results from *indirect reconstruction*. From top-down/left-right: input image, $(K = 1000, t = 10)$, $(K = 1000, t = 40)$, $(K = 2000, t = 10)$, $(K = 2000, t = 40)$, $(K = 3000, t = 10)$, $(K = 3000, t = 40)$ and $(K = 1000, t = 100)$

we have

$$|d(X,Y) - d(A,B)| < \epsilon, \tag{10}$$

meaning that in a ϵ-regular pair the edges are distributed quasi-uniformly. On the other hand, a partition of V into pairwise disjoint classes $C_0, C_1, \ldots, C_K$ is said *equitable* if all the classes C_i, with $(1 \leq i \leq N)$, have the same cardinality. Equitability is technically possible because the so called exceptional set C_0, which may be empty, exists. According to that, an equitable partition $C_0, C_1, \ldots, C_K$ is called ϵ-regular if $|C_0| < \epsilon|V|$ (the size of the exceptional set is a small fraction of the number of vertices) and all but at most ϵK^2 of the pairs (C_i, C_j) are ϵ-regular $(1 \leq i, j \leq N)$ (a small number of pairs are allowed to break the regularity condition).

The Szémeredi Regularity Lemma states that for every $\epsilon > 0$ and for every positive integer t, there is an integer $Q = (\epsilon, t)$ such that every graph with $N > Q$ vertices has an ϵ-regular partition into $K+1$ classes, where $t \leq K \leq Q$. In other words, for every ϵ the existence of a ϵ-regular partition is ensured.

In terms of graph compression, the lemma drives our attention to the $K+1$ classes (one of them is the exceptional set). Each of these classes $C_1, C_2, \ldots, C_K$ can be associated with a vertex of a new graph called the *reduced graph* R. In addition to ϵ let us define a density bound d. Then, given vertices C_i and C_j, we will have the edge (C_i, C_j) in R if the pair (C_i, C_j) is ϵ-regular and its density is greater than d.

The so called *Key Lemma* (see more details in [18]) states that given $d > \epsilon > 0$, a reduced graph R and a positive integer m, we can construct a graph G following these steps:

1. Replace every vertex of R by m vertices.
2. Replace the edges of R with regular pairs of density at least d.

Therefore, for the reduced graph R we have a formal mechanism to expand it to a more complex partitioned graph G which respects the edge-density bounds. Since R and G share many structural properties, it is possible to use the reduced graph R as an efficient proxy of G which is desirable when N is very large.

Due to space limitations we do not describe here how to obtain a ϵ-regular partition, but basically all existing methods rely on a refinement from an original partition until ϵ-regularity is satisfied [19]. See more details in [20] where an explicit connection between the lemma and clustering (an evolution to that described in [18]) is made. The key point here is to focus on an affinity/dissimilarity version of the lemma. The concept of density is defined in terms of the weights W_{ij} as follows:

$$d(A,B) = \frac{\sum_{i \in |A|} \sum_{j \in |B|} W_{ij}}{|A||B|} \tag{11}$$

However, finding regular partitions is different from finding clusters, since:

- Size equality of the resulting classes is an important requirement for regular pairs that is not imposed to clustering algorithms.

– The Szemerédi Regularity Lemma does not impose that items in the same class must be similar. It is more focused on inter-class relationships that on intra-class ones.

In our experiments, we have analyzed the combined use of the Szemerédi Regularity Lemma for compression and the Key Lemma for decompression. In Fig. 6, we show the results obtained through this combination. In all cases, the compression starts with a random partition. We show two regimes for ϵ: 0.51 and 0.71. The dimension of the compressed similarity matrix $\hat{W}$ depends always on ϵ. For $\epsilon \in [0.51, 0.71]$ we have always $K = 4 \times 4$, which is the minimal dimension of the compressed matrix. In general, effective/reliable values of ϵ are constrained to a small range ($\epsilon \approx 0.5$)-second column. Below 0.5 we usually obtain

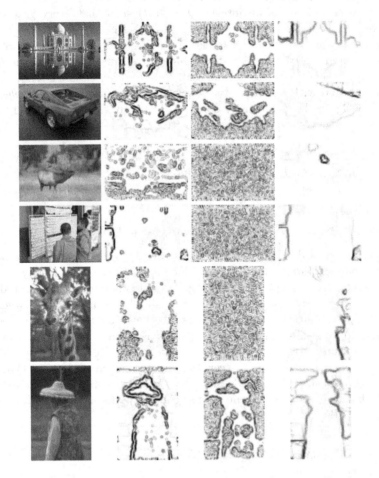

Fig. 6. Edge-detection results with *Szemerédi Regularity Lemma + Key Lemma*. First column: images from BSDS500. Second column: edges for $d = 0.44$ and $\epsilon = 0.51$. Third column: edges for $d = 0.44$ and $\epsilon = 0.71$. Fourth column: edges from quantum walks for $\alpha = 0.1$ without compression.

unstructured contrast both in the background and in the foreground. When ϵ is close to 0.5 we tend to approximate the real edges, but they appear frequently fragmented. For higher values of ϵ (for instance $\epsilon = 0.71$-third column) an interesting phenomenon occurs: the background is noisy whereas the foreground is clean whenever the segmentation problem is easy to solve (we obtain bad results when textured backgrounds arise). Since ϵ defines to what extent the regularity requirement is relaxed, we have that $\epsilon \approx 0.5$ provides the best possible trade-off. The threshold d, which determines the minimal density for declaring an edge in the reconstruction/decompression, is not critical although some images are better segmented than others. This is not the case of L, which defines the number of partitions per iteration (the rate of re-partitioning if the ϵ−regularity condition is not satisfied): for $L \neq 2$ we always obtain bad segmentation results (very noisy and unstructured edge maps, due to the fact that the dimension of $\hat{\mathbf{W}}$ drops to $K = 4 \times 4$ when $\epsilon \geq 0.51$).

Regarding the effect of introducing an indirect step through CTQWs, we have that this is useless in this case. This is due to the fact that the similarity matrices obtained through Szemerédi + Key Lemma are so noisy that limiting quantum walks are unable to recover the original edge map.

We have also done tests by starting with a deterministic partition. Doing that not only increases significantly the processing time, but produces very blurred edge maps. This is why we only show results obtained with an initial random partition.

Regarding running time we have the following averaged times: without compression we need 2 hours per image, using the factorization the running time is reduced to 2 minutes per image, and using the Szemerédi + Key Lemma we achieve 38 secs per image. Therefore, compression is a critical step for improving the efficiency of low-frequency edge detection. However, our experiments show that an ideal method for similarity compression/decompression should include features of both factorization and regularization.

4 Conclusions

In this paper we have investigated the impact of continuous-time quantum walks in compressing similarities for edge detection through spectral clustering. We found that an ideal method for similarity compression/decompression should include features of both factorization and regularization. Future work includes the development of an information-theoretic interpretation of coherent transport and the development of classifiers for predicting close-to-human edges. However, beyond the particular application domain of edge detection explored in the paper, our future developments are addressed to understand to what extend limiting quantum walks can be combined with compression-decompression approaches so that the structure of the similarity space is well understood.

Acknowledgements. Funding. F. Escolano and M. Curado: Project TIN2012-32839 (Spanish Gov.). E. R. Hancock: Royal Society Wolfson Research Merit Award.

References

1. Canny, J.: A computational approach to edge detection. IEEE Trans. Pattern Anal. Mach. Intell. **8**(6), 679–698 (1986)
2. Martin, D.R., Fowlkes, C., Malik, J.: Learning to detect natural image boundaries using local brightness, color, and texture cues. IEEE Trans. Pattern Anal. Mach. Intell. **26**(5), 530–549 (2004)
3. Dollar, P., Tu, Z., Belongie, S.: Supervised learning of edges and object boundaries. In: Proceedings of the 2006 IEEE Computer Society Conference on Computer Vision and Pattern Recognition. CVPR 2006, vol. 2, pp. 1964–1971. IEEE Computer Society, Washington, DC (2006)
4. Lim, J.J., Zitnick, C.L., Dollár, P.: Sketch tokens: a learned mid-level representation for contour and object detection. In: 2013 IEEE Conference on Computer Vision and Pattern Recognition, Portland, OR, USA, June 23–28, pp. 3158–3165 (2013)
5. Isola, P., Zoran, D., Krishnan, D., Adelson, E.H.: Crisp boundary detection using pointwise mutual information. In: Fleet, D., Pajdla, T., Schiele, B., Tuytelaars, T. (eds.) ECCV 2014, Part III. LNCS, vol. 8691, pp. 799–814. Springer, Heidelberg (2014)
6. Arbelaez, P., Maire, M., Fowlkes, C., Malik, J.: Contour detection and hierarchical image segmentation. IEEE Trans. Pattern Anal. Mach. Intell. **33**(5), 898–916 (2011)
7. Zhou, X., Belkin, M., Srebro, N.: An iterated graph laplacian approach for ranking on manifolds. In: Proceedings of the 17th ACM SIGKDD International Conference on Knowledge Discovery and Data Mining, San Diego, CA, USA, August 21–24, pp. 877–885 (2011)
8. Shi, J., Malik, J.: Normalized cuts and image segmentation. IEEE Trans. Pattern Anal. Mach. Intell. **22**(8), 888–905 (2000)
9. Qiu, H., Hancock, E.R.: Clustering and embedding using commute times. IEEE Trans. Pattern Anal. Mach. Intell. **29**(11), 1873–1890 (2007)
10. Grady, L.: Random walks for image segmentation. TPAMI **28**(11), 1768–1783 (2006)
11. Bai, L., Rossi, L., Torsello, A., Hancock, E.R.: A quantum jensen-shannon graph kernel for unattributed graphs. Pattern Recogn. **48**(2), 344–355 (2015)
12. Rossi, L., Torsello, A., Hancock, E.R., Wilson, R.C.: Characterizing graph symmetries through quantum jensen-shannon divergence. Phys. Rev. E **88**, 032806 (2013)
13. Mülken, O., Blumen, A.: Continuous-time quantum walks: models for coherent transport on complex networks. Phys. Rep. **502**(2–3), 37–87 (2011)
14. Stone, M.: On one-parameter unitary groups in hilbert space. Ann. Math. **33**(3), 643–648 (1932)
15. Farhi, E., Gutmann, S.: Quantum computation and decision trees. Phys. Rev. A **58**, 915–928 (1998)
16. Szemerédi, E.: Regular partitions of graphs. In: Colloques Internationaux CNRS 260-Problèmes Combinatoires et Théorie des Graphes, Orsay, pp. 399–401 (1976)

17. Nourbakhsh, F., Bulò, S.R., Pelillo, M.: A matrix factorization approach to graph compression. In: 22nd International Conference on Pattern Recognition, ICPR 2014, Stockholm, Sweden, August 24–28, pp. 76–81. IEEE (2014)
18. Sperotto, A., Pelillo, M.: Szemerédi's regularity lemma and its applications to pairwise clustering and segmentation. In: Yuille, A.L., Zhu, S.-C., Cremers, D., Wang, Y. (eds.) EMMCVPR 2007. LNCS, vol. 4679, pp. 13–27. Springer, Heidelberg (2007)
19. Alon, N., Duke, R.A., Lefmann, H., Rödl, V., Yuster, R.: The algorithmic aspects of the regularity lemma. J. Algorithms 16(1), 80–109 (1994)
20. Nourbakhsh, F.: Algorithms for graph compression: theory and experiments. Ph.D. thesis, Dipartamento di Scienze Ambientali, Infomatica e Statisitica, Universitá Ca'Foscari, Venice, IT (2015)

Introducing Negative Evidence in Ensemble Clustering Application in Automatic ECG Analysis

David G. Márquez[1]([✉]), Ana L.N. Fred[2], Abraham Otero[3],
Constantino A. García[1], and Paulo Félix[1]

[1] Centro de Investigación en Tecnoloxías da Información (CITIUS),
University of Santiago de Compostela, 15706 Santiago de Compostela, Spain
david.gonzalez.marquez@usc.es
[2] Instituto de Telecomunicações, Instituto Superior Técnico,
1049-001 Lisboa, Portugal
[3] Department of Information Technologies, University San Pablo CEU,
28668 Boadilla del Monte, Madrid, Spain

Abstract. Ensemble clustering generates data partitions by using different data representations and/or clustering algorithms. Each partition provides independent evidence to generate the final partition: two instances falling in the same cluster provide evidence towards them belonging to the same final partition.

In this paper we argue that, for some data representations, the fact that two instances fall in the same cluster of a given partition could provide little to no evidence towards them belonging to the same final partition. However, the fact that they fall in different clusters could provide strong negative evidence of them belonging to the same partition.

Based on this concept, we have developed a new ensemble clustering algorithm which has been applied to the heartbeat clustering problem. By taking advantage of the negative evidence we have decreased the misclassification rate over the MIT-BIH database, the gold standard test for this problem, from 2.25 % to 1.45 %.

Keywords: Clustering ensembles · Evidence accumulation · Heartbeat clustering · Heartbeat representation · Hermite functions · ECG

1 Introduction

Clustering is defined as the task of grouping together similar objects into groups called clusters. This process is one of the steps in exploratory data analysis and due to its usefulness has been addressed by researchers in many fields. The appropriate clustering algorithm and parameter settings (including parameters such as the distance function to use, a density threshold or the number of expected clusters) depend on the individual data set and intended use of the results. Therefore, we can not claim that a given algorithm will always perform better

© Springer International Publishing Switzerland 2015
A. Feragen et al. (Eds.): SIMBAD 2015, LNCS 9370, pp. 54–69, 2015.
DOI: 10.1007/978-3-319-24261-3_5

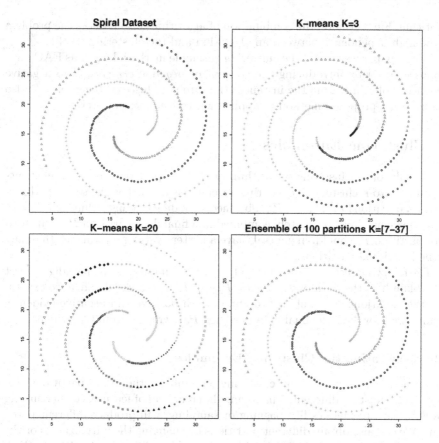

Fig. 1. (a) shows the three natural partitions present in the dataset. (b) and (c) show two versions of the K-means algorithm with K = 3 and K = 20, respectively. (d) shows the result of the combination in a single partition of 100 different partitions created by K-means algorithm using different values for K in a range between 7 and 37.

than others [3]. Furthermore, different clustering solutions may seem equally plausible without prior knowledge about the underlying data distributions. Part of the data analysis process is selecting the best clustering algorithm for the given data based on the information available on the problem. This is done by applying and tuning several algorithms in an iterative process to determine the best choice. This process is time-consuming and prone to error.

Inspired by the work in classifier combination, clustering combination approaches have been developed [1,6,7,11,22] and have emerged as a powerful method to improve the robustness and the stability of the clustering results. By combining the strengths of many individual algorithms we can improve the overall performance. Figure 1 shows how combining the results of 100 partitions created by the K-means algorithm, which is only able to create globular shape partitions, the three natural non-globular partitions are discovered. These natural partitions could never be discovered in a single execution of the K-means algorithm. Furthermore, the combination of algorithms also reduces the problem of the high dependence between an algorithm and the clustering results.

In this paper we extend the clustering ensemble method, known as EAC, first proposed in [7] by introducing the concept of *negative evidence*. The negative evidence is obtained from the instances that are not clustered together. We also illustrate the proposed method in application to heartbeat clustering.

2   Clustering Ensembles

The result of a clustering algorithm is a data partition P of n elements organized into k clusters. A clustering ensemble is defined as the set of m different data partitions $P_1, P_2, \ldots, P_m$, obtained with different algorithms or different data representations, ultimately combined in a final data partition P_*. This final data partition P_* should, in general, have a better overall performance than any of the individual partitions.

The following sections present our algorithm built on the EAC paradigm. First we explain how the data partitions $P_1, P_2, \ldots, P_m$ are created. Then we explain how the partitions are combined to obtain both positive and negative evidence. Finally, we show how the final data partition P_* is created from the evidence.

2.1   Generating the Clustering Ensembles

To harness the potential of clustering ensembles, the data partitions P_1, $P_2, \ldots, P_m$ must be different. Employing different sets of features, or perturbing the data with techniques like bagging or sampling, will produce different partitions. We can also obtain different partitions by changing the initialization or the parameters of the clustering algorithm, or by using different algorithms. With the combination of several data partitions the particular quirks of each one can be abstracted in order to find the best partition that summarizes all the results.

Among the various clustering methods, the K-means algorithm, which minimizes the squared-error criteria, is one of the simplest algorithms. Its simplicity is one of its biggest advantages, making it computationally efficient and fast. Its reduced number of parameters (typically only the number of clusters) is another strong point. Its major limitation is the inability to identify clusters with arbitrary shapes, ultimately imposing hyperspherical shaped clusters on the data. By combining the results of several K-means executions this limitation can be overcome [8].

In this work we shall use K-means to generate each data partition. We use this method due to its simplicity and small computational cost, but any other partitioning clustering algorithm may be used. To obtain different partitions we shall run the algorithm with random initializations and different values for the number of clusters. The number of clusters k in each execution will be determined at random in a range given by

$$k \in [\sqrt{n}/2, \sqrt{n}] \tag{1}$$

being n the number of instances in the data.

2.2   Combining the Data Partitions

In the literature there are several methods to combine data partitions in ensemble clustering. In this work we shall adopt the evidence accumulation method proposed in [7] and we shall expand it by introducing the concept of negative evidence. One of its advantages is that it can combine data partitions with different number of clusters.

The evidence accumulation method gathers the evidence in C, a $n x n$ matrix, using a voting mechanism. For each data partition, the co-occurrence of a pair of instances i and j in the same cluster will be stored as a vote. The underlying assumption is that instances belonging to the same "natural" cluster are more likely to be assigned to the same cluster in the different data partitions $P_1, P_2, \ldots, P_m$.

The final evidence matrix built from the m partitions will be calculated as follows:

$$C_{i,j} = \frac{n_{ij}}{m},\qquad(2)$$

where n_{ij} is the number of times the instances i and j are assigned to the same cluster in the $P_1, P_2, \ldots, P_m$ partitions.

There are some scenarios where the fact that two instances fall in the same cluster of a given partition provides little information about their natural grouping. This weak evidence could introduce noise in the combination of the partitions, worsening the results. However, in these scenarios the fact that two instances fall into different clusters could provide useful evidence against grouping those instances. As we shall argue later, this is the case for some of the features that permit the identification of some arrhythmia types. We shall call this evidence *negative evidence*.

We shall gather this negative evidence in a $n x n$ matrix C^- that is built as follows:

$$C_{i,j}^- = -\frac{o_{ij}}{m},\qquad(3)$$

where o_{ij} is the number of times the instances i and j are assigned to different clusters among the $P_1^*, P_2^*, \ldots, P_m^*$ partitions. Is important to note that the partitions from which we shall gather the negative evidence cannot be the same partitions used for gathering positive evidence. In fact, the partitions used to gather negative evidence $P_1^*, P_2^*, \ldots, P_m^*$ should be generated with different clustering algorithms or data features, more attuned to obtain this type of evidence. Futhermore, negative evidence can only be used in conjunction with positive evidence; negative evidence only indicates which instances should be in different clusters, but not which instances should be in the same cluster.

Finally, positive and negative evidence matrices are combined into a single evidence matrix, E, that will be used to generate the final partition:

$$E = C + C^-.\qquad(4)$$

2.3   Extracting the Final Data Partition

The last step of our clustering ensemble algorithm is extracting from the matrix E the final data partition P_*. To this end we shall apply a clustering algorithm. The average-link hierarchical clustering algorithm was developed for clustering correlation matrices, such as our evidence matrix [20]. Out of the several algorithms tried, this one has shown the best performance.

Most of the clustering ensemble methods rely on a user-specified number of clusters to build the final data partition P_*. In [8] an alternative method is proposed: the use of a lifetime criterion to determine the number of clusters. In an agglomerative algorithm, such as the average-link, each instance starts in its own cluster. In each iteration the closest pair of clusters are merged until only one cluster remains. The k-cluster lifetime value is defined as the absolute difference between the thresholds on the dendogram that lead to the identification of k clusters. This value is calculated for all the possible values of k (i.e., all possible number of clusters). The number of clusters that yields the highest lifetime value will be the one selected for the final data partition.

3   Application to Heartbeat Clustering

Cardiovascular diseases are the first cause of death in the world and are projected to remain the single leading cause of death for the foreseeable future [16]. The analysis of the electrocardiogram (ECG) is an important tool for the study and diagnosis of heart diseases. However, this analysis is a tedious task for the clinicians due to the large amount of data, especially in long recordings such as Holter recordings. For example, a 72-hour Holter recording contains approximately 300,000 heartbeats per lead. The recording can have up to 12 leads. In these cases, the amount of data generated makes necessary the use of automatic tools that support the clinicians. Furthermore, a disadvantage of the visual interpretation of the ECG is the strong dependence of the results on the cardiologist who performs the interpretation.

Although the detection of the heartbeat is a problem solved satisfactorily, its classification based on its origin and propagation path in the myocardium is still an open problem. This task, often referred to as arrhythmia identification, is of great importance for the interpretation of the electrophysiological function of the heart and subsequent diagnosis of the patient condition.

In the literature several approaches have been developed by estimating the underlying mechanisms using a set of labeled heartbeats [5]. However, this approach entails a strong dependence on the pattern diversity present in the training set. Inter-patient and intra-patient differences show that it can not be assumed that a classifier will yield valid results on a new patient, or even for the same patient throughout time. Furthermore, class labels only provide gross information about the origin of the heartbeats in the cardiac tissue, loosing all the information about their conduction pathways. This approach does not distinguish the multiple morphological families present in a given class, as in multifocal arrhythmias.

Heartbeat clustering aims at grouping together in a cluster those heartbeats that show similar properties. The possible differences for heartbeats of the same class are preserved with this method. If the clustering algorithm was successful, the cardiologist just has to inspect a few heartbeats of each cluster to perform an interpretation of all the heartbeats that have fallen into that cluster. There is no clustering method that has shown a significant advantage in the problem of heartbeat clustering. Here we propose the use of the clustering ensembles technique described above, to group the heartbeats according to their different types.

3.1 ECG Database

In this work we used the MIT-BIH Arrhythmia Database [17], which includes a wide range of arrhythmias and can be considered the gold standard test database for automatic detection of arrhythmias [4,5,13,24]. This database is composed by 48 two-channel ambulatory ECG recordings of 30 min. A lead is a recording of the electrical activity of the heart. Different leads record this activity from different positions in the patient's body, providing slightly different information about the heart. The recordings were digitized at 360 Hz and annotated by two or more cardiologists. Each heartbeat is annotated with its position in time and the type of heartbeat (16 different types). The leads used are the modified limb lead II (MLII) and the modified leads V1, V2, V3, V4 and V5.

3.2 Preprocessing

Before extracting the features that will represent each heartbeat the ECG signal was filtered. We applied a Wavelet filter to eliminate the baseline drift [2]. The low frequency component of the signal was reconstructed using the coefficients of the Discrete Wavelet Transform (DWT) and subtracted from the original signal, removing the baseline drift. To eliminate the noise of the high frequencies a low-pass Butterworth filter was applied with a cutoff frequency of 40 Hz.

3.3 Heartbeat Representation

The choice of data representation has a great impact on the performance of clustering algorithms. In ECG analysis we can find several options. One is using the samples of the digital signal as the feature vector. This representation has the problem of the high dimensionality of the feature vectors and the sensitivity to noise [21]. Another approach is representing the heartbeat by features such as heights and lengths of the waves that make up the beat, which are the same features used by clinicians when reasoning about the beat. However, it is hard to obtain a robust segmentation of the beat to measure those features [14]. The last main approach in the literature is using a liner combination of basis functions to represent the heartbeat [23]. The interpretability of the feature vector is lost with this representation, but its advantages are being compact and robust in the presence of noise. Hermite functions are the most widely used basis function for the representation of heartbeats [9,10,12,13,18]. They have the advantages of being orthonormal and that the shape of the functions is similar to the shape of the heartbeat.

To obtain the Hermite representation we start by extracting an excerpt of 200 ms around the beat annotation of the database. This size is enough to fit the QRS complex leaving out the P and T waves. Once the QRS has been taken into account, the T wave provides little additional information for arrhythmia detection, therefore it is not generally represented in the feature vector. The P wave provides useful information, but the difficulty in identifying it normally leads to trying to obtain information similar to that provided by the P wave from the distance between consecutive heartbeats [5,13].

Hermite functions converge to zero at $\pm\infty$. To achieve this behavior in the ECG, a padding of 100 ms zeros is added on each side of the 200 ms signal excerpt. The resulting window $x[l]$ of 400 ms is represented as:

$$x[l] = \sum_{n=0}^{N-1} c_n(\sigma)\phi_n[l,\sigma] + e[l],$$
$$l = -\left\lfloor \frac{W \cdot f_s}{2} \right\rfloor, -\left\lfloor \frac{W \cdot f_s}{2} \right\rfloor + 1, \ldots, \left\lfloor \frac{W \cdot f_s}{2} \right\rfloor, \tag{5}$$

being N the number of Hermite functions used, W the window size in seconds and f_s the sampling frequency. $\phi_n[l,\sigma]$ is the n-th discrete Hermite function obtained by sampling at f_s the n-th continuous Hermite function $\phi(t,\sigma)$, c_n are the coefficients of the linear combination, $e[l]$ is the error between $x[l]$ and the Hermite representation, and σ controls the width of the Hermite function enabling it to adjust to the width of the QRS. The Hermite functions $\phi_n[l,\sigma]$, $0 \leq n < N$, are defined as:

$$\phi_n[l,\sigma] = \frac{1}{\sqrt{\sigma 2^n n! \sqrt{\pi}}} e^{-(l \cdot T_s)^2/2\sigma^2} H_n(l \cdot T_s/\sigma), \tag{6}$$

where T_s is the inverse of the sampling frequency.

The Hermite polynomial $H_n(x)$ can be obtained recursively:

$$H_n(x) = 2x H_{n-1}(x) - 2(n-1)H_{n-2}(x), \tag{7}$$

with $H_0(x) = 1$ and $H_1(x) = 2x$.

The N coefficients of the linear combination $c_n(\sigma)$, $0 \leq n < N$, and σ compose our representation of the heartbeat. Figure 2 illustrates how heartbeats can be reconstructed from Hermite functions. We can always increase the accuracy of the representation using more functions but, after a certain point, we will start to model noise instead of the QRS complex.

For a given σ the coefficients $c_n(\sigma)$ can be calculated by minimizing the summed square error of the Hermite functions:

$$\sum_l (e[l])^2 = \sum_l \left(x[l] - \sum_{n=0}^{N-1} c_n(\sigma)\,\phi_n[l,\sigma] \right)^2. \tag{8}$$

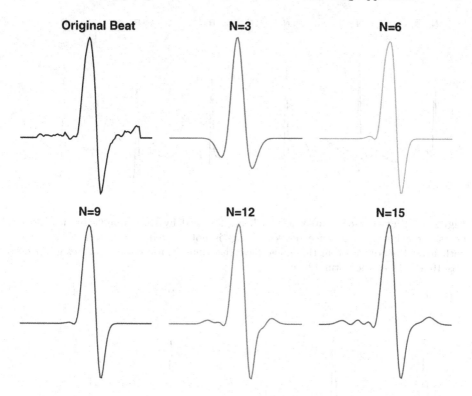

Fig. 2. Original beat and Hermite approximation with N = 3, 6, 9, 12 and 15.

The minimum of the square error is easily calculated thanks to the orthogonality property:

$$c_n(\sigma) = \boldsymbol{x} \cdot \boldsymbol{\phi}_n(\sigma), \tag{9}$$

where the vectors are defined as $\boldsymbol{x} = \{x[l]\}$ and $\boldsymbol{\phi}_n(\sigma) = \{\phi_n[l, \sigma]\}$.

An iterative stepwise increment of σ was done by recomputing (9) and (8) for each step and selecting the σ that minimizes the error.

To identify arrhythmias that do not affect the morphology of the QRS we generate two rhythm features from the heartbeat position annotations of the database:

$$R_1[i] = R[i] - R[i-1], \tag{10}$$

$$R_2[i] = u(\alpha) \cdot \alpha,$$
$$\alpha = (R_1[i+1] - R_1[i]) - (R_1[i] - R_1[i-1]), \tag{11}$$

where $R[i]$ is the time of occurrence of the i-th beat, and $u(x)$ is the Heaviside step function. In this work we shall use 16 Hermite functions to represent the heartbeat, a number high enough to represent most of the QRS complexes accurately and low enough to not model noise [15]. The representation of each

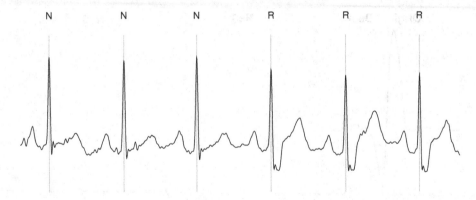

Fig. 3. The figure shows three normal beats followed by three bundle branch block beats. Note how the distance between beats is not altered at any time. The three pathological beats shown in the image have the same values for the features given by Eqs. 10 and 11 as the normal beats.

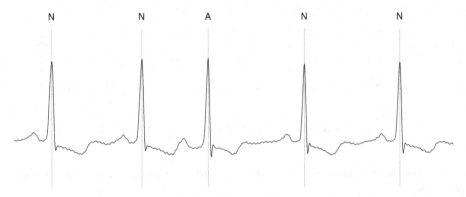

Fig. 4. The third beat is a premature atrial beat. It is morphologically identical to the other four normal beats shown in the image. The fact that the distance between the atrial beat and the preceding and subsequent beat is different than the distance between normal beats is key to identify this arrhythmia.

heartbeat will be made up by 36 features, 16 Hermite coefficients for each one of the two leads, one sigma value per lead, and the two rhythm features given by (10) and (11).

4 Experimental Results

We shall use three different strategies for ensemble generation. The first strategy is the classical approach in machine learning of putting together all the information (Hermite parameters extracted from the two ECG leads and the features given by (10) and (11)) in the same feature vector. Based on this feature vector we generate the data partitions $P_1, P_2, \ldots, P_m$.

The second strategy relies on the hypothesis that generating data partitions on different types of features yields better results than using all the features. Each lead in the ECG is recording the electrical activity from a different view point of the heart. This makes some configurations more suited to detect certain pathologies. Furthermore, the rhythm features present a completely different information, with another frame of reference such as the distance between beats instead of the electrical activity. By dividing the information in several sets we can take advantage of these differences and improve the clustering results. Based on these assumptions, the information is split in three different representations: one Hermite representation is obtained from each lead and a third one is obtained from the rhythm features. In this strategy the three representations will be used separately to generate data partitions that provide positive evidence.

In heartbeat clustering, the fact that two beats have approximately the same distance to the next beat and the previous beat doesn't mean that they are of the same type (see Fig. 3). However, two heartbeats with considerably different distances to the next beat and the previous beat are most likely of different types (see Fig. 4). In the third strategy, based on this knowledge, we will use the same configuration that in the second strategy, but in this case the partition generated from the rhythm features will be used to generate negative evidence.

In the first strategy 100 data partitions are generated using the complete feature set with the K-means algorithm as is explained in Sect. 2.1. In the second strategy 100 data partitions are generated for each one of the three sets of features, making a total of 300 data partitions. The evidence in the data partitions is gathered in the matrices C_{S1} and C_{S2} for the first and the second strategy, respectively. In these strategies we are not using the negative evidence.

In the third strategy we will also generate 100 partitions for each of the two Hermite representations extracted from each ECG leads. These partitions provide positive evidence. However, in this case the 100 data partitions corresponding to the rhythm features will be treated as negative evidence (see Eq. 3). To obtain the final matrix for this strategy we shall combine the evidence obtained from the Hermite representation of each ECG lead, C_{S3}, and the evidence obtained from the rhythm features, C_{S3}^{-}, into a final matrix E_{S3} (see Eq. 4).

The final partitions for each strategy are generated from their respective evidence matrices by applying the average-link method. We ran a test in which the lifetime criterion was used to determine the number of partitions. An additional test with a fixed number of partitions (25) was also run. This second test will allow us to compare our results with the most referenced work in heartbeat clustering [13], where 25 clusters per recording were used.

To validate our results, we shall consider that each cluster belongs to the beat type of the majority of its heartbeats. All the heartbeats of a different type than their cluster are considered errors. In practice, this mapping between clusters and beat types could be obtained just by having a cardiologist label one beat of each cluster. Table 1 shows the results for the different strategies using this procedure to count the errors. This table contains the number of errors, when using a fixed

Table 1. Results of the clustering for the three strategies. For each strategy we have the number of errors using a fixed number of 25 clusters (25C) and using the lifetime criterion. In the second case we also show the number of clusters chosen by this criterion.

Record	1 Strategy			2 Strategy			3 Strategy		
	25C	Lifetime		25C	Lifetime		25C	Lifetime	
	Errors	Errors	Clusters	Errors	Errors	Clusters	Errors	Errors	Clusters
100	33	33	5	6	33	2	6	33	6
101	3	3	7	0	3	5	0	3	5
102	7	47	6	13	58	4	12	30	12
103	1	1	15	0	1	2	0	0	80
104	251	257	11	309	351	4	235	230	35
105	11	12	10	5	5	5	7	5	43
106	2	10	9	1	28	7	1	1	24
107	0	1	9	1	1	3	1	1	29
108	11	16	9	9	9	2	9	9	20
109	4	9	14	2	10	2	3	2	28
111	0	0	11	0	0	2	0	0	17
112	2	2	7	1	2	3	2	2	26
113	0	0	11	0	0	2	0	0	64
114	12	16	12	11	16	4	9	9	36
115	0	0	4	0	0	3	0	0	37
116	2	2	13	0	2	2	1	1	24
117	1	1	7	0	0	7	0	0	56
118	96	96	12	58	100	2	45	7	188
119	0	0	7	0	0	2	0	0	28
121	1	1	12	0	1	2	0	0	27
122	0	0	8	0	0	8	0	0	11
123	0	0	6	0	0	2	0	0	81
124	36	43	9	41	41	4	41	41	11
200	129	130	15	117	531	14	53	52	86
201	48	54	7	50	65	4	48	49	10
202	37	42	12	17	56	2	19	19	31
203	81	82	19	286	385	2	76	59	171
205	14	14	9	13	15	6	14	14	18
207	187	196	20	52	318	5	130	23	76
208	107	109	17	120	449	3	105	143	6
209	181	298	5	106	162	3	66	136	3
210	32	37	17	30	71	2	33	18	120
212	0	0	11	3	4	4	2	2	57
213	112	351	8	90	396	3	102	103	15

(Continued)

Table 1. *(Continued)*

Record	1 Strategy			2 Strategy			3 Strategy		
	25C	Lifetime		25C	Lifetime		25C	Lifetime	
	Errors	Errors	Clusters	Errors	Errors	Clusters	Errors	Errors	Clusters
214	6	6	14	4	5	12	4	4	31
215	4	5	20	9	26	3	7	4	100
217	34	50	10	65	69	10	58	58	29
219	11	12	9	11	18	3	9	9	6
220	94	94	3	4	94	2	6	5	35
221	1	3	8	1	1	6	1	1	31
222	389	389	10	328	421	2	288	156	183
223	116	125	17	108	265	3	106	62	59
228	3	3	14	3	4	7	3	3	12
230	0	0	9	0	0	3	0	0	25
231	2	2	5	2	2	5	2	2	5
232	388	398	12	80	89	15	68	97	22
233	19	20	18	32	35	3	17	17	57
234	2	50	5	1	50	2	1	1	15
Total	2470	3020	508	1989	4192	203	1590	1411	2091
%	2.25	2.75		1.81	3.81		1.45	1.28	

Table 2. P-values of the Wilcoxon test of significance

	1 Strategy vs 2 Strategy	1 Strategy vs 3 Strategy	2 Strategy vs 3 Strategy
25 Clusters	0.0820593	0.0006947	0.0402501
lifetime criterion	0.0046556	0.0000204	0.0000028

number of 25 clusters, and the number of errors and the corresponding number of clusters, when using the lifetime criterion, for each recording of the MIT-BIH Arrhythmia Database. We can divide the number of errors by the number of heartbeats in the database (109966 heartbeats) to obtain the error percentage. The results for the fixed number of clusters execution are 2.25 %, 1.81 % and 1.45 % for the first, second and third strategies, respectively. Using the lifetime criterion the results are 2.75 %, 3.81 % and 1.28 %, respectively.

Normality was tested for the number of misclassification errors in each of the strategies and rejected using a Shapiro-Wilk test [19]. A non-parametric Wilcoxon test was used to determine the significance of the differences between strategies. For a fixed number of clusters the p-values were 0.08, <0.01 and 0.04 for strategy 1 vs. strategy 2, strategy 1 vs. strategy 3, and strategy 2 vs.

strategy 3, respectively. When using the lifetime criterion the p-values were <0.01 in all comparisons (see Table 2).

5   Discussion

The improvement between the first and the second strategy, from 2.25 % to 1.81 % (p-value = 0.08) with the fixed number of clusters, suggests that the idea of splitting the information of each channel and the rhythm features has merit and should be studied further. This idea is particularly interesting to process 12-lead ECG. Usually the 12 leads are available in the clinical routine and they all are used in the diagnosis of the patient. However, up to date, to avoid an explosion on the size of the feature vectors representing the heartbeat, typically only one or two leads are used when trying to identify arrhythmias. Each lead provides a different perspective on the electrical signal and an automatic solution would benefit of combining them. Furthermore, some ECG leads may be misplaced, disconnected or may present noise. A solution that can combine the 12 leads would be more robust and accurate than the normal approach of using only one or two leads.

When the lifetime criterion is used, the error increases from 2.75 % to 3.81 % (p-value = 0.004) between the first and the second strategies. At the same time, the total number of clusters created goes down from 508 to 203 clusters, an average of 10.5 and 4.2 clusters per recording, respectively. A small number of clusters is desired because it means that the cardiologist will have to do less work to interpret the results. However here it comes at the expense of a large increase in the error.

Using a fixed number of clusters, the misclassification error between the second strategy and the third strategy decreases from 1.81 % to 1.45 % (p-value = 0.04). The only difference is the treatment of the information from the rhythm features. This result supports our previous assumption that the use of some representations as negative evidence can improve the results: the use of the rhythm features as negative evidence results in a lower misclassification error than using them as positive evidence.

When using the lifetime criterion, the misclassification error between the second strategy and the third strategy decreases from 3.81 % to 1.28 % (p-value <0.01). But the lifetime criterion creates 2091 clusters (an average of 43.56 clusters per recording). This proliferation of clusters in some cases, such as in recording 222, may be due to the noise and artifacts present in the recordings. Especially for the third strategy, the results using the lifetime criterion are unsatisfactory due to the high number of groups generated. Some adjustments should be done to control the proliferation of the clusters, or a different criterion should be used to determine the optimum number of clusters.

In [13] a clustering algorithm based on Self Organizing Maps (SOM) is used with a fixed number of 25 clusters. There are some differences between this paper and our work. Lagerholm et al. used their own annotations which may be slightly different from the database annotations that we are using, and they don't use a high frequency noise filter. Nevertheless, the differences are small enough that a comparison between their results and our results with the fixed number of clusters is relevant. The best result obtained by Lagerholm et al. was an error rate of 1.51 % for the complete MIT-BIH database. In our case in the first and second strategy we obtain worse error rates 2.25 % and 1.81 %. However, using the negative evidence in the third strategy our error rate, 1.45 %, is slightly lower.

6   Conclusions

In traditional clustering ensembles algorithms evidence is accumulated only from the instances that belong to the same partition. We argue that for some data representations the fact that two instances belong to the same partition may provide little or no information. However these data representations need not to be useless; on the contrary: the fact that two instances belong to different partitions created from those representations can provide useful evidence towards the instances belonging to different clusters in the final partition.

In this paper we have introduced the concept of negative evidence to gather evidence from the instances that do not belong to the same data partitions. Based on this concept, we have designed a new ensemble clustering algorithm that exploits both positive and negative evidence to create the final partition. We have applied this algorithm to the problem of heartbeat clustering. Our hypothesis was that the information derived from the distance from one beat to previous and next beats would not be useful for generating positive evidence, but may be used to generate negative evidence. When we apply our algorithm over the MIT-BIH database the misclassification error fall from 1.81 % to 1.45 % when the number of clusters was fixed to 25 and from 3.81 % to 1.28 % when the number of clusters was selected by the lifetime criterion just by using the information extracted from the distance between beats to generate negative evidence instead of positive evidence. These results demonstrate the usefulness of the negative evidence and encourage further research on this concept.

As a future work, we would also like to study the applicability of the clustering ensembles to the 12-lead ECG and to develop further the concept of negative evidence, including other potential applications.

Acknowledgments. This work was supported by the University San Pablo CEU under the grant PPC12/2014. David G. Márquez is funded by an FPU Grant from the Spanish Ministry of Education (MEC) (Ref. AP2012-5053). Constantino A. García acknowledges the support of Xunta de Galicia under "Plan I2C" Grant program (partially cofunded by The European Social Fund of the European Union).

References

1. Bakker, B., Heskes, T.: Clustering ensembles of neural network models. Neural Netw. **16**(2), 261–269 (2003)
2. Blanco-Velasco, M., Weng, B., Barner, K.E.: ECG signal denoising and baseline wander correction based on the empirical mode decomposition. Comput. Biol. Med. **38**(1), 1–13 (2008)
3. Celebi, M.E.: Partitional Clustering Algorithms. Springer, Cham (2014)
4. de Chazal, P., O'Dwyer, M., Reilly, R.B.: Automatic classification of heartbeats using ECG morphology and heartbeat interval features. IEEE Trans. Biomed. Eng. **51**(7), 1196–1206 (2004)
5. de Chazal, P., Reilly, R.B.: A patient-adapting heartbeat classifier using ECG morphology and heartbeat interval features. IEEE Trans. Biomed. Eng. **53**(12 Pt 1), 2535–2543 (2006)
6. Dudoit, S., Fridlyand, J.: Bagging to improve the accuracy of a clustering procedure. Bioinformatics **19**(9), 1090–1099 (2003)
7. Fred, A.: Finding Consistent Clusters in Data Partitions. In: Kittler, J., Roli, F. (eds.) MCS 2001. LNCS, vol. 2096, pp. 309–318. Springer, Heidelberg (2001)
8. Fred, A.L., Jain, A.K.: Combining multiple clusterings using evidence accumulation. IEEE Trans. Pattern Analy. Mach. Intell. **27**(6), 835–850 (2005)
9. García, C.A., Otero, A., Vila, X., Márquez, D.G.: A new algorithm for wavelet-based heart rate variability analysis. Biomed. Signal Proces. Control **8**(6), 542–550 (2013)
10. Gil, A., Caffarena, G., Márquez, D.G., Otero, A.: Hermite Polynomial Characterization of Heartbeats with Graphics Processing Units. In: IWBBIO 2014 (2014)
11. Hong, Y., Kwong, S., Chang, Y., Ren, Q.: Unsupervised feature selection using clustering ensembles and population based incremental learning algorithm. Pattern Recogn. **41**(9), 2742–2756 (2008)
12. Jane, R., Olmos, S., Laguna, P.: Adaptive Hermite models for ECG data compression: performance and evaluation with automatic wave detection. In: Computers in Cardiology (1993)
13. Lagerholm, M., Peterson, C., Braccini, G., Edenbrandt, L., Sörnmo, L.: Clustering ECG complexes using Hermite functions and self-organizing maps. IEEE Trans. Biomed. Eng. **47**(7), 838–848 (2000)
14. Madeiro, J.P., Cortez, P.C., Oliveira, F.I., Siqueira, R.S.: A new approach to QRS segmentation based on wavelet bases and adaptive threshold technique. Med. Eng. Phys. **29**(1), 26–37 (2007)
15. Márquez, D.G., Otero, A., Félix, P., García, C.A.: On the Accuracy of Representing Heartbeats with Hermite Basis Functions. In: BIOSIGNALS 2013, pp. 338–341 (2013)
16. Mathers, C.D., Loncar, D.: Projections of global mortality and burden of disease from 2002 to 2030. PLoS Med. **3**(11), e442 (2006)
17. Moody, G., Mark, R.: The impact of the MIT-BIH arrhythmia database. IEEE Eng. Med. Biol. Mag. **20**(3), 45–50 (2001)
18. Park, K., Cho, B., Lee, D., Song, S., Lee, J., Chee, Y., Kim, I., Kim, S.: Hierarchical support vector machine based heartbeat classification using higher order statistics and Hermite basis function. In: 2008 Computers in Cardiology, pp. 229–232. IEEE, September 2008
19. Rodríguez-Fdez, I., Canosa, A., Mucientes, M., Bugarín, A.: STAC: a web platform for the comparison of algorithms using statistical tests (2015). http://tec.citius.usc.es/stac

20. Sokal, R.R.: A statistical method for evaluating systematic relationships. Univ. Kans. Sci. Bull. **38**, 1409–1438 (1958)
21. Sörnmo, L., Laguna, P.: Bioelectrical signal processing in cardiac and neurological applications. Elsevier Academic Press, New York (2005)
22. Topchy, A.P., Jain, A.K., Punch, W.F.: A mixture model for clustering ensembles. In: SDM, pp. 379–390. SIAM (2004)
23. Young, T.Y., Huggins, W.H.: On the representation of electrocardiograms. IEEE Trans. Bio-Med. Electron. **10**(3), 86–95 (1963)
24. Zhang, Z., Dong, J., Luo, X., Choi, K.S., Wu, X.: Heartbeat classification using disease-specific feature selection. Comput. Biol. Med. **46**, 79–89 (2014)

Dissimilarity Representations
for Low-Resolution Face Recognition

Mairelys Hernández-Durán[1]([✉]), Veronika Cheplygina[2,3],
and Yenisel Plasencia-Calaña[1,3]

[1] Advanced Technologies Application Center, La Habana, Cuba
{mhduran,yplasencia}@cenatav.co.cu
[2] Biomedical Imaging Group Rotterdam, Erasmus Medical Center,
Rotterdam, The Netherlands
[3] Pattern Recognition Laboratory, Delft University of Technology,
Delft, The Netherlands
v.cheplygina@tudelft.nl

Abstract. Low-resolution face recognition is a very difficult problem. In this setup, the training database or gallery contains high-resolution images, but the image to be recognized is of low resolution. Thus we are dealing with a resolution mismatch problem for training and test images. Standard face recognition methods fail in this setting, which suggests that current feature representation approaches are not adequate to cope with this problem. Therefore, we propose the use of dissimilarity representations based on different strategies, which differ in how images with different resolutions are compared, to solve the resolution mismatch problem. Experiments on four standard face datasets demonstrate that a strategy based on first down-scaling and afterwards up-scaling training images while up-scaling test images outperforms all the other approaches.

Keywords: Dissimilarity space · Low-resolution face recognition · Super-resolution · Prototype selection

1 Introduction

Face recognition has been studied for decades due to its wide range of applications. Although face recognition has achieved high recognition accuracy under controlled environments, in low-resolution face recognition (LR FR) systems the results are still unsatisfactory. Nowadays, there is a growing interest in real applications such as video protection and surveillance in which subjects are far away from the camera. In such scenarios, the face image sizes tend to be small and the images do not have a good definition of facial features. Moreover, discriminatory features present in the facial images used for distinguishing one person from another are lost due to the decrease in resolution, resulting in unsatisfactory performance. As a result, low-resolution (LR) images affect the performance of traditional face recognition systems. LR FR aims at recognizing face images with LR and variations such as pose and illumination. In LR FR the gallery contains

© Springer International Publishing Switzerland 2015
A. Feragen et al. (Eds.): SIMBAD 2015, LNCS 9370, pp. 70–83, 2015.
DOI: 10.1007/978-3-319-24261-3_6

high resolution images while the test images are of low resolution, causing the so-called dimensional mismatch [1,2].

Current approaches mainly include feature vector representations to allow a good discrimination between different faces for addressing LR FR. Methods such as the nearest neighbour (1-NN) and the bicubic interpolation are the simplest ways to increase resolution for an input LR image [3].

In [4] the authors propose a 1-NN approach for producing super-resolution images from ordinary images and videos. Sparse representation [5] and metric learning [6], are some of the feature methods for LR FR with the advantages of low computational complexity and lower requirement of training samples, making them more suitable for real applications. However, it is difficult to find a good feature representation in LR FR because most of the effective features used in high-resolution face recognition such as texture and color may fail in LR case. As a consequence, most of the successful approaches cannot be efficiently applied to LR case [3].

A representation based on dissimilarities between objects [7,8] is an alternative to the feature-based representation. A dissimilarity-based representation is advantageous in situations where it is difficult to define sufficiently discriminative features, but it is easier to define dissimilarities. More specifically, the dissimilarity space (DS) approach is very attractive due to its efficiency and easy possibility to map new test objects compared to the Pseudo-Euclidean space representation [7].

Based on the success of previous works [7], we used the dissimilarity representation approach to tackle our problem. Intuitively, the proximity information is more important for discriminating between the classes than the composition and features of each object independently [9]. Particularly, we believe that a dissimilarity space representation can be suitable for LR FR because in the context of comparisons with the prototype objects we can compensate the noise introduced by the low resolution as well as the lack of information in such low resolution images. By using the differences with the prototype images for creating the representations we may be able to emphasize relevant information for discrimination among the classes, which, otherwise, by only analyzing the image, may be difficult to express in a feature representation. Furthermore, a dissimilarity representation has been used for other difficult problems as well such as: small sample size situations [10] or problems where the results of the 1-NN on features are still unsatisfactory [8,11].

In this work, we present an alternative to feature-based representations for LR FR based on the DS representation. We compare the proposed dissimilarity representation with feature representations for LR FR and also for very low-resolution face recognition. Three different strategies are tested based on original or up-scaled test images, and original or down-scaled training images to address the mismatch problem between training and test images. The comparisons show that the dissimilarity space representation outperforms the feature representation and that the low-high strategy, where the training images are down-scaled and then up-scaled while the test images are up-scaled, is the best way to cope with the mismatch problem. In particular, the linear discriminant classifier (LDC) in the dissimilarity space is very promising.

The paper is organized as follows. Section 2 presents the related work on LR FR and the dissimilarity representation. Section 3 presents our proposed reduced dissimilarity space to cope with classification of LR and very low-resolution images. Experiments and discussion are presented in Sect. 4, and concluding remarks are provided in Sect. 5.

2   Related Work

The purpose of LR FR is to recognize faces from small size or poor quality images (e.g. face inside a 32×20 pixels image) which can also present challenging facial variations such as pose, illumination, and expression. The LR of the test images causes a dimensional mismatch when having to deal with high resolution training images. Three main research lines have been considered to cope with the problem: interpolation [12,13], down-scaling [14] and unified feature space [15]. The first approach has limitations associated to the scale factor and it is more suitable for synthesizing generic objects or scenes instead of faces. The second approach allows to match in the LR domain by down-sampling the training set, but it represents a reduction of the information useful for the recognition process. In the third approach, although it seems feasible to cope with the mismatch problem, it is not easy to find an optimal inter-resolution space.

Several methods have been used for recognizing faces from LR images. Super resolution (SR) is one of the most frequently employed techniques for dealing with this problem. SR methods recover the lost information during the image formation process by including a-priori information about the image. SR methods produce a reconstructed high-resolution image from a low-resolution one by making assumptions about the image structure or content. The first SR techniques based on reconstruction represent an intuitive approach to improve a face image, but are aimed mostly at a visual improvement, and are not designed from a pattern recognition point of view.

Recently, Zou and Yuen [14] proposed the very low recognition problem, where the resolution of the face images to be recognized is lower than 16×12 pixels. Hennings et al. included facial features as prior information into an SR method named Simultaneous Super-Resolution and Recognition (S2R2) [2] to improve the results. They showed that when faces are of very low-resolution, the approach of matching in the low-resolution domain is better than applying SR. Li et al. [15] proposed the coupled locality preserving mappings method to include robust features in a unified feature space for increasing the discriminability in the recognition process. Nevertheless, finding a resolution-robust feature representation is still far from being a solved problem.

An alternative solution is a dissimilarity representation between objects based on the general idea proposed in [7], in which dissimilarities are considered as the connection between perception and higher-level knowledge, thus being an important factor in the process of human recognition and categorization. The dissimilarity representation is also able to deal with several problems related to the feature vector representation. A feature-based description may be difficult to find or can be inefficient for the learning task. Furthermore, the dimensionality of the feature vector is usually larger than the number of images, commonly known as the curse of dimensionality. Another advantageous property of this representation is the possibility to learn from small sample sizes [10].

The dissimilarity-based approach has successfully been used for multiple tasks such as person re-identification [16] and object classification [17]. In [16], Satta et al. convert a given appearance-based re-identification method into a dissimilarity-based one and show a reduction in both the processing time and the memory requirements. In [18], Orozco et al. use a dissimilarity-based method for face recognition which was derived by applying the eigenface transformation and, afterwards, the Euclidean distance between the eigenface representations.

Our present work differs from these works in several aspects. The application considered in this paper is very different from previous applications as we have to transform the images first to cope with the resolution mismatch problem, i.e., we propose different strategies to be able to compare test images with training images. We also propose the use of a reduced dissimilarity space by using prototype selection, including an analysis of its benefits at test time. We show experimentally that one of our proposals is very promising, and that a small dimensionality of the DS is sufficient to achieve a good discrimination among the classes.

3 Proposed Approach: Reduced Dissimilarity Space

3.1 Dissimilarity Space and Prototype Selection

Dissimilarity representations have been studied in a number of problems [18–20], however their application for LR FR has not been studied so far. We believe that this type of relational representation can cope with the poor discriminability of standard feature representations when using LR images. Let X be the space of objects, let $R = \{r_1, r_2, ..., r_k\}$ be the set of prototypes such that $R \in X$, and let $d : X \times X \to \mathbb{R}^+$ be a suitable dissimilarity measure for the problem. For a training set $T = \{x_1, x_2, ..., x_l\}$ such that $T \in X$, a mapping $\phi_R^d : X \to \mathbb{R}^k$ defines the embedding of training and test objects in the DS by the dissimilarities with the prototypes:

$$\phi_R^d(x_i) = [d(x_i, r_1) \ d(x_i, r_2) \ ... \ d(x_i, r_k)]. \tag{1}$$

In a problem where training, prototype, and test images have the same resolution it is straightforward to apply the approach. However, in our setup, test images are of LR, so we need to decide how to deal with the resolution mismatch problem. We compare three different strategies to cope with the resolution mismatch between training, prototype, and test images:

- Low-resolution test images, down-scaled training images (low) and down-scaled prototypes

- up-scaled low-resolution test images, down-scaled and then up-scaled training images (low-high), and high-resolution prototypes
- up-scaled low-resolution test images, high-resolution training images (high), and high-resolution prototypes

The same training set can be used as the set of prototypes. However, for training sets of moderate to large size, a selection of the best set of prototypes is needed to find a trade-off between classification accuracy and computational efficiency. This can be achieved by selecting a reduced set of prototypes which has similar performance to using the whole set.

To select the reduced set of prototypes we need a search strategy with a suitable criterion. Different approaches have been previously studied for this purpose (see [8,19]). Recently, a genetic algorithm (GA) was proposed in [21], which showed to be very fast and accurate in selecting a good set of prototypes. It proposes a number of improvements to the simple GA such as the use of indexes for codifying the prototypes instead of binary chromosomes, and an early stopping criterion which was shown to be adequate for this type of problem. In addition, only scalable criteria are considered for the fitness function to evaluate each solution (set of prototypes), therefore the method is fast and scalable. We will use the supervised prototype selection strategy from [21] to find an adequate set of prototypes for a given or desired cardinality of the DS.

The GA can also be used for feature selection by using a slightly different selection criterion. The criterion for selecting prototypes is based on maximizing matching labels between the prototypes and their nearest neighbours. Therefore, for selecting features, it is replaced by a criterion minimizing the nearest neighbour error in the training set for a feature set of a given cardinality.

3.2   Considerations at Test Time

We want to remark the advantages of a reduced dissimilarity space (RDS) by prototype selection in comparison with a RDS by feature extraction as well as the advantages over a reduced feature space (RFS) by feature selection or by feature extraction.

Suppose we have these spaces with the same dimensionality. The problem of a feature space with selected features is that we lose the information contained in the discarded features, especially in problems where the majority of the features are informative. Even if only the selected features are informative, due to the nature of the representation (such as a histogram), all features might need to be extracted before discarding the non-informative ones. In contrast, once the prototypes were selected to create a RDS, for a new test object we only need to measure the dissimilarities with the selected prototypes. Besides, a small set of prototypes is often enough to represent the data properly which is not the case for handcrafted feature representations [22].

Feature extraction methods, both in a feature space or a DS, present even stronger disadvantages in terms of computing time at test time. These methods always require the computation of the full set of features (or alternatively dissimilarities with the large set of prototypes) before applying the transformation to a reduced space, which is performed by expensive floating-point multiplications of the test object representation with elements from a mapping or projection matrix. These costs are not adequate for deployment in real-world scenarios [22].

4   Experiments and Discussion

This section presents the experimental comparison, results and discussion of different feature-based and dissimilarity based strategies for the classification of LR images where the gallery is composed by high resolution images.

4.1   Databases Description

Four different standard face datasets were used for the experiments. In each case, the test images were obtained by down-scaling the original images using a bicubic interpolation. All images were geometrically normalized by the center of the eyes to a LR size of 10×12 pixels or 24×30 pixels during experiments. A bicubic interpolation was also applied in the up-scaling process to obtain high resolution images of 64×80 pixels.

Olivetti Research Database (ORL) [23]. The ORL database contains 400 grayscale images of 40 individuals, 10 images per person. Some images are taken with a certain time difference. They present variations in facial expression (including opening and closing the eyes), illumination changes, different details on the face (with and without glasses) and a slight difference in scale. Figure 1 shows examples of variations on this database.

Fig. 1. Some examples of ORL database

Yale Database [24]. The Yale database contains images with variations in lighting condition (left-light, center-light, right-light), facial expression (normal, happy, sad, sleepy, surprised, and wink), and with/without glasses. Figure 2 shows example images with some variations for the individuals. During the experiments we used a subset of the database, which consists of 200 images belonging to 10 subjects with different variations. Some subsets were removed because they have strong differences in lighting conditions and addressing this problem is not the purpose in this work.

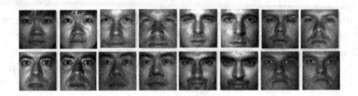

Fig. 2. Some examples of Yale database

Essex Database [25]. The database contains single light source images with racial diversity, and variations with glasses, beards, and so forth. The images are captured from a fixed distance with different orientation and different facial expression. The database consists of images of 153 individuals (20 images each). Each image has plain green background with no head scale but with very minor variation in head turn, tilt and slant. Some example images are shown in Fig. 3.

During the experiments we used a subset of the database which consists of 720 images in total belonging to 20 different subjects having 36 images per person with different variations. Some subsets were removed to focus on the low-resolution problem.

Fig. 3. Some examples of Essex database

Labeled Faces in the Wild (LFW) [26]. It contains 13233 labelled faces of 5749 people. For 1680 people two or more faces are available. The data is challenging, as the faces are detected in images "in the wild", taken from Yahoo! News. The faces present some variations including changes in scale, pose, background, hairstyle, clothing, expression, image resolution, focus, and others. During the experiments we used a subset of the database consisting of 3 832 images belonging to 178 classes, by selecting the classes with 8 or more images. Some example images are shown in Fig. 4.

The characteristics of the datasets are summarized in Table 1.

4.2 Experimental Setup

We randomly divided the datasets into two sets for training and testing of equal size five times, ensuring that each class is equally represented in each set. The classifiers as well as the prototype selectors are trained using the training set and classification errors are computed for the test set. The average error values are reported.

Fig. 4. Some examples of LFW database

Table 1. Characteristics of the datasets used for the experiments

Datasets	# Classes	# Obj in total
ORL	40	400
Yale	10	200
Essex	36	720
LFW	178	3832

We consider two different representation spaces: a feature space (feat) and a dissimilarity space (DS). Furthermore, we consider two different classifiers: the linear discriminant classifier (LDC), which assumes equal covariance matrices for the classes, and the 1-NN.

In order to obtain the feature representation, we compute local binary patterns on local blocks of the geometrically normalized images. Histograms were computed on each block and concatenated. Chi square distances are used for the 1-NN classifiers as well as for creating the DS. Note that, in our case, the dissimilarity measure was computed on top of a feature representation, therefore we suffer from the cost of first computing the feature representation. However, a dissimilarity representation can also be computed by directly matching the images if we have a good dissimilarity measure for this purpose.

As it would be convenient to compute the dissimilarity measure by matching the images directly, we reviewed the literature to find good (dis)similarity measures for this purpose. However, we found that such measures are not as heavily used for face recognition as feature-based measures. This happens because several conditions affect facial images such as differences in pose, illumination, expression, and other capturing conditions, which directly affect image matching measures such as correlation. Unfortunately, despite several attempts to create good illumination and pose normalization methods to improve the original images so they can be used for direct matching, it is easier to use features that intrinsically deal with these problems such as the local binary patterns histograms that we used as base for computing the dissimilarities. The definition of such a measure that is able to deal with the mentioned problems directly is still an open issue.

In general, our motivations behind the use of dissimilarities on top of features for the experiments are: first, we can perform a fair comparison between the feature representation and the dissimilarity representation since it was computed on top of the same feature representation, second, the Chi square distance measure on top of the local binary patterns histograms have shown very good performances in previous works for face recognition [27]. Therefore, it is a good starting point for our research.

Different DSs are created for each of the strategies and classifiers. However, as a baseline, the results of the 1-NN and LDC in the feature space are shown only for the best performing resolution strategy in the DS.

As parameters for the GA for prototype selection we used very similar parameters to [21]:

- 40 chromosomes for the population
- 30 generations reached or 10 generations without change in the fitness value as stopping criteria
- Reproduction probability equal to 0.5
- Mutation probability equal to 0.02

For the feature representation the same GA was used for feature selection to compare the feature space and DS space with the same dimensionality. The criterion used for feature selection is an equivalent version to the one used for prototype selection, the minimization of the 1-NN error on the training set.

4.3   Results and Discussion

Figures 5, 6, 7 and 8 show error rates for different numbers of prototypes in the DS or features in the feature space. For the 1-NN all the features are used. For both baseline classifiers the training set used is consistent with the one used for the different DS. Note that the 1-NN with the up-scaled images (1-NN low-high feat) correspond to a variant of baseline in LR FR, the so-called super resolution.

From the results we can see that the DS representation outperforms the feature representations. We think that LR images benefit from the relational

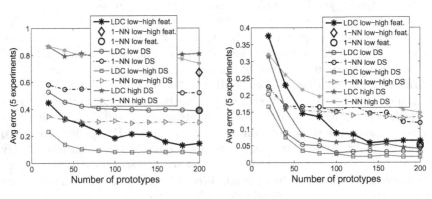

(a) using 10x12 pixels as low-resolution size

(b) using 24x30 pixels as low-resolution size

Fig. 5. Experimental results in ORL database

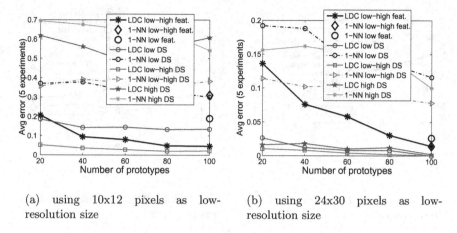

(a) using 10x12 pixels as low-resolution size

(b) using 24x30 pixels as low-resolution size

Fig. 6. Experimental results in Yale database

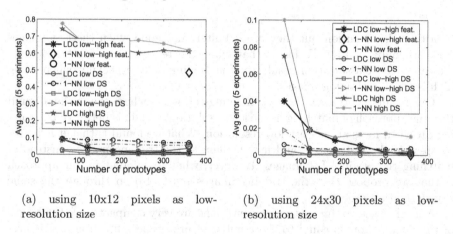

(a) using 10x12 pixels as low-resolution size

(b) using 24x30 pixels as low-resolution size

Fig. 7. Experimental results in Essex database

representation since features alone may not capture relevant information for discrimination. Comparisons with other objects can provide relevant information for discrimination since small details only present in high resolutions are not as influential as in a feature representation. The LR and high-resolution strategies perform poorly, while the best performing strategy is the low-high one. Especially the classification results with the LDC in the DS for this strategy are very promising.

The low-high strategy focuses on making the gallery images resemble the condition of the test images, since they are down-scaled and then up-scaled in the same way as the test images. In higher resolutions, the feature representation is able to capture the relevant information which is not possible for the LR case. Therefore, original high-resolution training images may be useful for comparing

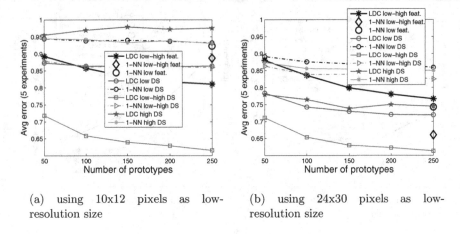

(a) using 10x12 pixels as low-resolution size

(b) using 24x30 pixels as low-resolution size

Fig. 8. Experimental results in LFW database

high to high resolution but they are definitely not good when the test images were originally of LR. We found that while the resolution of the test images increases, the classification results in the DS improve, especially when using high resolution training images.

Our results contradict those of Hennings et al. [2] where the authors found that the approach of matching in the low-resolution domain is better than applying SR when faces are of very low-resolution. What we found is that it is better to up-scale the test images and match them to the training images, instead of matching the original LR images. However, what is different in our approach is that we propose that the training images must also go through the same transformation process.

Note that the dissimilarity representations are very compact since the length of the final vectors is equal to the number of prototypes, and from the figures it can be seen than a small set of prototypes (e.g. cardinality equal to 200) is usually sufficient to obtain a good representation. This makes the approach suitable for large-scale and real-time recognition systems. This is also beneficial for representing a new test object since it implies that at test time only the dissimilarities with the small set of prototypes need to be measured. Note that we do not compare feature extraction methods because they would require the computation of dissimilarities with all the prototypes before performing the reduction for incoming test objects. This poses an extra computational cost that is avoided by our proposal.

5   Conclusions

In this paper we presented the reduced dissimilarity space (RDS) as an alternative representation for low-resolution face recognition. Different dissimilarity-based representations were compared with feature-based representations.

We found that using the down-scaled gallery and prototype images is counterproductive, while the strategies that up-scale the test images perform the best. However, there was a large difference between using the gallery or training images in their original high resolution and transforming them by first down-scaling and afterwards up-scaling them again. The proposed transformation outperformed using the gallery images in their original resolution. This is interesting since previous approaches focused on finding the best transformation for the low-resolution test images to resemble the high resolution images from the gallery, while we propose to also transform the gallery images to resemble the low-resolution test images.

The experiments showed that more discriminative information for classification can be obtained if the LR images are analyzed in the context of dissimilarities with other images. Note that, as our approach only assumes general dissimilarity measures, it can be used with any user-defined or learned metric. Dissimilarity measures computed directly on the images are desirable, however we did not find such a measure in the literature with good results and adopted an established dissimilarity for face recognition. In addition, our approach produces very compact representations which are suitable for large-scale and real-time recognition systems.

Future studies will be devoted to study metric learning approaches to create more discriminative dissimilarity measures or to improve the representation in the dissimilarity space. Furthermore, extending the dissimilarity space with additional dissimilarity measures [28] or prototypes from outside the training set [29] could be of interest. We believe that a learned representation using the dissimilarity representation as a starting point could improve the results even further. The design of robust measures for matching the images directly is also an interesting open issue.

References

1. Choi, J.Y., Ro, Y.M., Plataniotis, K.N.: Feature subspace determination in video-based mismatched face recognition. In: 8th IEEE International Conference on Automatic Face & Gesture Recognition, FG 2008, pp. 1–6. IEEE (2008)
2. Hennings-Yeomans, P.H., Baker, S., Kumar, B.V.: Simultaneous super-resolution and feature extraction for recognition of low-resolution faces. In: IEEE Conference on Computer Vision and Pattern Recognition, CVPR 2008, pp. 1–8. IEEE (2008)
3. Wang, Z., Miao, Z., Wu, Q.J., Wan, Y., Tang, Z.: Low-resolution face recognition: a review. Visual Comput. **30**(4), 359–386 (2014)
4. Zhu, S., Han, M., Gong, Y.: Super resolution using gaussian regression, US Patent 7,941,004, 10 May 2011
5. Wright, J., Yang, A.Y., Ganesh, A., Sastry, S.S., Ma, Y.: Robust face recognition via sparse representation. IEEE Trans. Pattern Anal. Mach. Intell. **31**(2), 210–227 (2009)
6. Li, B., Chang, H., Shan, S., Chen, X.: Coupled metric learning for face recognition with degraded images. In: Zhou, Z.-H., Washio, T. (eds.) ACML 2009. LNCS, vol. 5828, pp. 220–233. Springer, Heidelberg (2009)

7. Pekalska, E., Duin, R.P.W.: The Dissimilarity Representation for Pattern Recognition: Foundations and Applications (Machine Perception and Artificial Intelligence). World Scientific Publishing Co. Inc, River Edge (2005)
8. Pekalska, E., Duin, R.P.W., Paclík, P.: Prototype selection for dissimilarity-based classifiers. Pattern Recogn. **39**(2), 189–208 (2006)
9. Plasencia-Calaña, Y., García-Reyes, E., Orozco-Alzate, M., Duin, R.P.W.: Prototype selection for dissimilarity representation by a genetic algorithm. In: Proceedings of the 20th International Conference on Pattern Recognition, ICPR 2010, Washington, DC, USA, pp. 177–180. IEEE Computer Society (2010)
10. Orozco-Alzate, M., Duin, R.P.W., Castellanos-Domínguez, G.: A generalization of dissimilarity representations using feature lines and feature planes. Pattern Recogn. Lett. **30**(3), 242–254 (2009)
11. Pekalska, E., Duin, R.P.: Dissimilarity representations allow for building good classifiers. Pattern Recogn. Lett. **23**(8), 943–956 (2002)
12. Wolberg, G.: Digital Image Warping, vol. 10662. IEEE computer society press, Los Alamitos (1990)
13. Baker, S., Kanade, T.: Hallucinating faces. In: 2000 Proceedings of Fourth IEEE International Conference on Automatic Face and Gesture Recognition, pp. 83–88. IEEE (2000)
14. Zou, W.W., Yuen, P.C.: Very low resolution face recognition problem. IEEE Trans. Image Process. **21**(1), 327–340 (2012)
15. Li, B., Chang, H., Shan, S., Chen, X.: Low-resolution face recognition via coupled locality preserving mappings. IEEE Signal Process. Lett. **17**(1), 20–23 (2010)
16. Satta, R., Fumera, G., Roli, F.: Fast person re-identification based on dissimilarity representations. Pattern Recogn. Lett. **33**(14), 1838–1848 (2012)
17. Carli, A., Castellani, U., Bicego, M., Murino, V.: Dissimilarity-based representation for local parts. In: 2010 2nd International Workshop on Cognitive Information Processing (CIP), pp. 299–303. IEEE (2010)
18. Orozco-Alzate, M., Castellanos-Domínguez, C.: Nearest feature rules and dissimilarity representations for face recognition problems. Face Recognition; International Journal of Advanced Robotic Systems, Vienna, Austria, pp. 337–356 (2007)
19. Bunke, H., Riesen, K.: Graph classification based on dissimilarity space embedding. In: da Vitoria Lobo, N., Kasparis, T., Roli, F., Kwok, J.T., Georgiopoulos, M., Anagnostopoulos, G.C., Loog, M. (eds.) SSPR & SPR 2008. LNCS, vol. 5342, pp. 996–1007. Springer, Heidelberg (2008)
20. Li, Y., Duin, R.P., Loog, M.: Combining multi-scale dissimilarities for image classification. In: Proceedings of the 2012 21th International Conference on Pattern Recognition, ICPR 2012. IEEE Computer Society (2012)
21. Plasencia-Calaña, Y., Orozco-Alzate, M., Méndez-Vázquez, H., García-Reyes, E., Duin, R.P.W.: Towards scalable prototype selection by genetic algorithms with fast criteria. In: Fränti, P., Brown, G., Loog, M., Escolano, F., Pelillo, M. (eds.) S+SSPR 2014. LNCS, vol. 8621, pp. 343–352. Springer, Heidelberg (2014)
22. Chen, D., Cao, X., Wen, F., Sun, J.: Blessing of dimensionality: High-dimensional feature and its efficient compression for face verification. In: Proceedings of the 2013 IEEE Conference on Computer Vision and Pattern Recognition, CVPR 2013, Washington, DC, USA, pp. 3025–3032. IEEE Computer Society (2013)
23. Samaria, F.S., *t, F.S.S., Harter, A., Site, O.A.: Parameterisation of a stochastic model for human face identification (1994)
24. Belhumeur, P.N., Hespanha, J.P., Kriegman, D.J.: Eigenfaces vs. fisherfaces: recognition using class specific linear projection. In: Buxton, B.F., Cipolla, R. (eds.) ECCV 1996. LNCS, vol. 1064, pp. 43–58. Springer, Heidelberg (1996)

25. Spacek., L.: Essex face recognition data. http://cswww.essex.ac.uk/mv/allfaces/index.html
26. Huang, G.B., Ramesh, M., Berg, T., Learned-Miller, E.: Labeled faces in the wild: A database for studying face recognition in unconstrained environments. Technical Report 07–49, University of Massachusetts, Amherst (2007)
27. Ahonen, T., Hadid, A., Pietikäinen, M.: Face recognition with local binary patterns. In: Pajdla, T., Matas, J.G. (eds.) ECCV 2004. LNCS, vol. 3021, pp. 469–481. Springer, Heidelberg (2004)
28. Plasencia-Calaña, Y., Cheplygina, V., Duin, R.P.W., García-Reyes, E.B., Orozco-Alzate, M., Tax, D.M.J., Loog, M.: On the informativeness of asymmetric dissimilarities. In: Hancock, E., Pelillo, M. (eds.) SIMBAD 2013. LNCS, vol. 7953, pp. 75–89. Springer, Heidelberg (2013)
29. Dinh, V.C., Duin, R.P.W., Loog, M.: A study on semi-supervised dissimilarity representation. In: International Conference on Pattern Recognition, pp. 2861–2864. IEEE (2012)

Deep Metric Learning Using Triplet Network

Elad Hoffer[✉] and Nir Ailon

Department of Computer Science, Technion Israel Institute of Technology,
Haifa, Israel
ehoffer@tx.technion.ac.il, nailon@cs.technion.ac.il

Abstract. Deep learning has proven itself as a successful set of models for learning useful semantic representations of data. These, however, are mostly implicitly learned as part of a classification task. In this paper we propose the *triplet network* model, which aims to learn useful representations by distance comparisons. A similar model was defined by Wang et al. (2014), tailor made for learning a ranking for image information retrieval. Here we demonstrate using various datasets that our model learns a better representation than that of its immediate competitor, the Siamese network. We also discuss future possible usage as a framework for unsupervised learning.

Keywords: Deep learning · Metric learning · Representation learning

1 Introduction

For the past few years, deep learning models have been used extensively to solve various machine learning tasks. One of the underlying assumptions is that deep, hierarchical models such as convolutional networks create useful representation of data [1,10], which can then be used to distinguish between available classes. This quality is in contrast with traditional approaches requiring engineered features extracted from data and then used in separate learning schemes. Features extracted by deep networks were also shown to provide useful representation [20,24] which can be, in turn, successfully used for other tasks [19].

Despite their importance, these representations and their corresponding induced metrics are often treated as side effects of the classification task, rather than being explicitly sought. There are also many interesting open questions regarding the intermediate representations and their role in disentangling and explaining the data [2]. Notable exceptions where explicit metric learning is preformed are the *Siamese Network* variants [3,5,9], in which a contrastive loss over the metric induced by the representation is used to train the network to distinguish between similar and dissimilar *pairs* of examples. A contrastive loss favours a small distance between pairs of examples labeled as similar, and large distances for pairs labeled dissimilar. However, the representations learned by these models provide sub-par results when used as features for classification, compared with other deep learning models including ours. Siamese networks

© Springer International Publishing Switzerland 2015
A. Feragen et al. (Eds.): SIMBAD 2015, LNCS 9370, pp. 84–92, 2015.
DOI: 10.1007/978-3-319-24261-3_7

are also sensitive to calibration in the sense that the notion of similarity vs dissimilarity requires context. For example, a person might be deemed similar to another person when a dataset of random objects is provided, but might be deemed dissimilar with respect to the same other person when we wish to distinguish between two individuals in a set of individuals only. In our model, such a calibration is not required. In fact, in our experiments here, we have experienced hands on the difficulty in using Siamese networks.

We follow a similar task to that of [4]. For a set of samples $\mathbb{P}$ and a chosen rough similarity measure $r(x, x')$ given through a training oracle (e.g. how close are two images of objects semantically) we wish to learn a similarity function $S(x, x')$ induced by a normed metric. Unlike [4]'s work, our labels are of the form $r(x, x_1) > r(x, x_2)$ for triplets x, x_1, x_2 of objects. Accordingly, we try to fit a metric embedding and a corresponding similarity function satisfying:

$$S(x, x_1) > S(x, x_2), \quad \forall x, x_1, x_2 \in \mathbb{P} \quad \text{for which } r(x, x_1) > r(x, x_2).$$

In our experiment, we try to find a metric embedding of a multi-class labeled dataset - meaning that our similarity function is the same-class indicator. We will always take x_1 to be of the same class as x and x_2 of a different class, although in general more complicated choices could be made. Accordingly, we will use the notation x^+ and x^- instead of x_1, x_2. We focus on finding an L_2 embedding, by learning a function $F(x)$ for which $S(x, x') = \|F(x) - F(x')\|_2$. Inspired from the recent success of deep learning, we will use a deep network as our embedding function $F(x)$.

We call our approach a *triplet network*. A similar approach was proposed in [23] for the purpose of learning a ranking function for image retrieval. Compared with the single application proposed in [23], we make a comprehensive study of the triplet architecture which is, as we shall argue below, interesting in and of itself. In fact, we shall demonstrate below that the triplet approach is a strong competitor to the Siamese approach, its most obvious competitor.

2 The Triplet Network

A *Triplet network* (inspired by "Siamese network") is comprised of 3 instances of the same feed-forward network (with shared parameters). When fed with 3 samples, the network outputs 2 intermediate values - the L_2 distances between the embedded representation of two of its inputs from the representation of the third. If we will denote the 3 inputs as x, x^+ and x^-, and the embedded representation of the network as $Net(x)$, the one before last layer will be the vector:

$$TripletNet(x, x^-, x^+) = \begin{bmatrix} \|Net(x) - Net(x^-)\|_2 \\ \|Net(x) - Net(x^+)\|_2 \end{bmatrix} \in \mathbb{R}_+^2 \ .$$

In words, this encodes the pair of distances between each of x^+ and x^- against the *reference* x (Fig. 1).

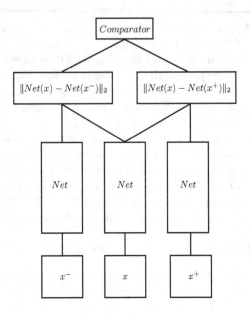

Fig. 1. Triplet network structure

2.1 Training

Training is preformed by feeding the network with samples where, as explained above, x and x^+ are of the same class, and x^- is of different class. The network architecture allows the task to be expressed as a 2-class classification problem, where the objective is to correctly classify which of x^+ and x^- is of the same class as x. We stress that in a more general setting, where the objective might be to learn a metric embedding, the label determines which example is *closer* to x. Here we simply interpret "closeness" as "sharing the same label". In order to output a comparison operator from the model, a SoftMax function is applied on both outputs - effectively creating a ratio measure. Similarly to traditional convolutional-networks, training is done by simple Stochastic Gradient Descent on a negative-log-likelihood loss with regard to the 2-class problem. We later examined that better results are achieved when the loss function is replaced by a simple Mean Squared Error on the soft-max result, compared to the $(0,1)$ vector, so that the loss is

$$Loss(d_+, d_-) = \|(d_+, d_- - 1)\|_2^2 = const \cdot d_+^2$$

where

$$d_+ = \frac{e^{\|Net(x) - Net(x^+)\|_2}}{e^{\|Net(x) - Net(x^+)\|_2} + e^{\|Net(x) - Net(x^-)\|_2}}$$

and

$$d_- = \frac{e^{\|Net(x) - Net(x^-)\|_2}}{e^{\|Net(x) - Net(x^+)\|_2} + e^{\|Net(x) - Net(x^-)\|_2}} .$$

We note that $Loss(d_+, d_-) \to 0$ iff $\frac{\|Net(x) - Net(x^+)\|}{\|Net(x) - Net(x^-)\|} \to 0$, which is the required objective. By using the same shared parameters network, we allow the back-propagation algorithm to update the model with regard to all three samples simultaneously.

3 Tests and Results

The Triplet network was implemented and trained using the Torch7 environment [7].

3.1 Datasets

We experimented with 4 datasets. The first is *Cifar10* [11], consisting of 60000 32×32 color images of 10 classes (of which 50000 are used for training only, and 10000 for test only). The second dataset is the original *MNIST* [12] consisting of 60000 28×28 gray-scale images of handwritten digits 0–9, and a corresponding set of 10000 test images. The third is the *Street-View-House-Numbers (SVHN)* of [18] consisting of 600000 32×32 color images of house-number digits 0–9. The fourth dataset is *STL10* of [6], similar to Cifar10 and consisting of 10 object classes, only with 5000 training images (instead of 50000 in Cifar) and a bigger 96×96 image size.

It is important to note that no data augmentation or whitening was applied, and the only preprocessing was a global normalization to zero mean and unit variance. Each training instance (for all four datasets) was a uniformly sampled set of 3 images, 2 of which are of the same class (x and x^+), and the third (x^-) of a different class. Each training epoch consisted of 640000 such instances (randomly chosen each epoch), and a fixed set of 64000 instances used for test. We emphasize that each test instance involves 3 images from the set of test images which was excluded from training.

3.2 The Embedding Net

For Cifar10 and SVHN we used a convolutional network, consisting of 3 convolutional and 2×2 max-pooling layers, followed by a fourth convolutional layer. A *ReLU* non-linearity is applied between two consecutive layers. Network configuration (ordered from input to output) consists of filter sizes $\{5,3,3,2\}$, and feature map dimensions $\{3,64,128,256,128\}$ where a 128 vector is the final embedded representation of the network. Usually in convolutional networks, a subsequent fully-connected layer is used for classification. In our net this layer is removed, as we are interested in a feature embedding only.

The network for STL10 is identical, only with stride=3 for the first layer, to allow the bigger input size. The network used for MNIST was a smaller version consisting of smaller feature map sizes $\{1,32,64,128\}$.

3.3 Results

Training on all datasets was done by SGD, with initial learning-rate of 0.5 and a learning rate decay regime. We used a momentum value of 0.9. We also used the dropout regularization technique with $p = 0.5$ to avoid over-fitting. After training on each dataset for 10–30 epochs, the network reached a fixed error over the triplet comparisons. We then used the embedding network to extract features from the full dataset, and trained a simple 1-layer network model on the full 10-class classification task (using only training set representations). The test set was then measured for accuracy. These results (Table 1) are comparable to state-of-the-art results with deep learning models, without using any artificial data augmentation [8,14,25]. Noteworthy is the STL10 dataset, in which the TripletNet achieved the best known result for non-augmented data. We conjecture that data augmentation techniques (such as translations, mirroring and noising) may provide similar benefits to those described in previous works.

We also note that similar results are achieved when the embedded representations are classified using a linear SVM model or KNN classification with up to 0.5 % deviance from the results in Table 1. Another side-affect noticed, is that the representation seems to be sparse - about 25 % non-zero values. This is very helpful when used later as features for classification both computationally and with respect to accuracy, as each class is characterised by only a few non zero elements.

Table 1. Classification accuracy (no data augmentation)

Dataset	TripletNet	SiameseNet	Best known result (no data augmentation)
Mnist	99.54±0.08 %	97.9±0.1 %	99.61 % [13,16]
Cifar10	87.1±0.07 %	-	90.22 % [13]
SVHN	95.37±0.08 %	-	98.18 % [13]
STL10	70.67±0.1 %	-	67.9 % [15]

3.4 2d Visualization of Features

In order to examine our main premise, which is that the network embeds the images into a representation with meaningful properties, we use PCA to project the embedding into 2d euclidean space which can be easily visualized (Figs. 2, 3 and 4). We can see a significant clustering by semantic meaning, confirming that the network is useful in embedding images into the euclidean space according to their content. Similarity between objects can be easily found by measuring the distance between their embedding and, as shown in the results, can reach high classification accuracy using a simple subsequent linear classifier

3.5 Comparison with Performance of the Siamese Network

The Siamese network is the most obvious competitor for our approach. Our implementation of the Siamese network consisted of the same embedding network, but with the use of a contrastive loss between a pair of samples, instead of three (as explained in [5]). The generated features were then used for classification using a similar linear model as was used for the TripletNet method. We measured lower accuracy on the MNIST dataset compared to results gained using the TripletNet representations Table 1.

We have tried a similar comparison for the other three datasets, but unfortunately could not obtain any meaningful result using a Siamese network. We conjecture that this might be related to the problem of context described above, and leave the resolution of this conjecture to future work.

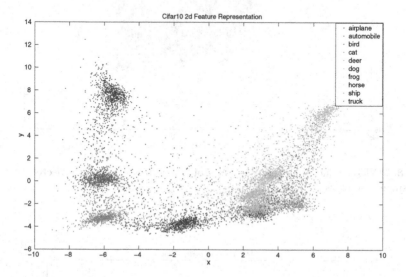

Fig. 2. CIFAR10 - Euclidean representation of embedded test data, projected onto top two singular vectors

4   Future Work

As the Triplet net model allows learning by comparisons of samples instead of direct data labels, usage as an unsupervised learning model is possible. Future investigations can be performed in several scenarios:

- **Using Spatial Information.** Objects and image patches that are spatially near are also expected to be similar from a semantic perspective. Therefore, we could use geometric distance between patches of the same image as a rough similarity oracle $r(x, x')$, in an unsupervised setting.
- **Using Temporal Information.** The same is applicable to time domain, where two consecutive video frames are expected to describe the same object, while a frame taken 10 min later is less likely to do so. Our Triplet net may provide a better embedding and improve on past attempts in solving classification tasks in an unsupervised environment, such as that of [17].

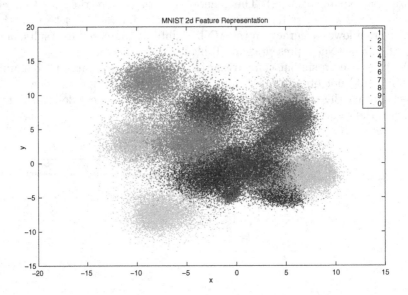

Fig. 3. MNIST - Euclidean representation of embedded test data, projected onto top two singular vectors

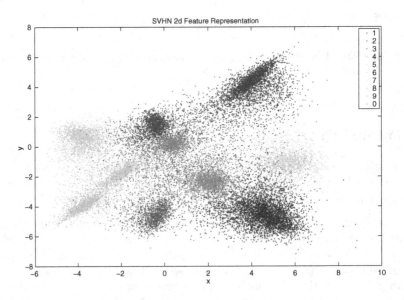

Fig. 4. SVHN - Euclidean representation of embedded test data, projected onto top two singular vectors

It is also well known that humans tend to be better at accurately providing comparative labels. Our framework can be used in a crowd sourcing learning environment. This can be compared with [22], who used a different approach. Furthermore, it may be easier to collect data trainable on a Triplet network, as comparisons over similarity measures are much easier to attain (pictures taken at the same location, shared annotations, etc).

5   Conclusions

In this work we introduced the *Triplet network* model, a tool that uses a deep network to learn useful representation explicitly. The results shown on various datasets provide evidence that the representations that were learned are useful to classification in a way that is comparable with a network that was trained explicitly to classify samples. We believe that enhancement to the embedding network such as Network-in-Network model [14], Inception models [21] and others can benefit the Triplet net similarly to the way they benefited other classification tasks. Considering the fact that this method requires to know only that two out of three images are sampled from the same class, rather than knowing what that class is, we think this should be inquired further, and may provide us insights to the way deep networks learn in general. We have also shown how this model learns using only comparative measures instead of labels, which we can use in the future to leverage new data sources for which clear out labels are not known or do not make sense (e.g. hierarchical labels).

Acknowledgements. We gratefully acknowledge the support of NVIDIA Corporation with the donation of the Titan-Z GPU used for this research. This research was additionally supported by the Israel Science Foundation (ISF) grant No. 1271/13, and by the ISF-UGC India-Israel joint research program grant No. 1932/14.

References

1. Bengio, Y.: Learning Deep Architectures for AI (2009). ISSN 1935–8237
2. Bengio, Y.: Deep learning of representations: looking forward. In: Dediu, A.-H., Martín-Vide, C., Mitkov, R., Truthe, B. (eds.) SLSP 2013. LNCS, vol. 7978, pp. 1–37. Springer, Heidelberg (2013)
3. Bromley, J., Bentz, J.W., Bottou, L., Guyon, I., LeCun, Y., Moore, C., Säckinger, E., Shah, R.: Signature verification using a time delay neural network. Int. J. Pattern Recogn. Artif. Intell. **7**(04), 669–688 (1993)
4. Chechik, G., Sharma, V., Shalit, U., Bengio, S.: Large scale online learning of image similarity through ranking. J. Mach. Learn. Res. **11**, 1109–1135 (2010)
5. Chopra, S., Hadsell, R., LeCun, Y.: Learning a similarity metric discriminatively, with application to face verification. In: Proceedings of the IEEE Computer Society Conference on Computer Vision and Pattern Recognition, vol. 1, pp. 539–546 (2005). ISBN 0769523722
6. Coates, A., Ng, A.Y., Lee, H.: An analysis of single-layer networks in unsupervised feature learning. In: International Conference on Artificial Intelligence and Statistics, pp. 215–223 (2011)

7. Collobert, R., Kavukcuoglu, K., Farabet, C.: Torch7: A matlab-like environment for machine learning. In: BigLearn, NIPS Workshop, number EPFL-CONF-192376 (2011)
8. Goodfellow, I.J., Warde-Farley, D., Mirza, M., Courville, A., Bengio, Y.: Maxout networks (2013). arXiv preprint arXiv:1302.4389
9. Hadsell, R., Chopra, S., LeCun, Y.: Dimensionality reduction by learning an invariant mapping. In: 2006 IEEE computer society conference on Computer vision and pattern recognition, vol. 2, pp. 1735–1742. IEEE (2006)
10. Hinton, G.E.: Learning multiple layers of representation (2007). ISSN 13646613
11. Krizhevsky, A. Hinton, G.: Learning multiple layers of features from tiny images. Computer Science Department, University of Toronto, Technical report (2009)
12. LeCun, Y., Bottou, L., Bengio, Y., Haffner, P.: Gradient-based learning applied to document recognition. Proc. IEEE **86**(11), 2278–2324 (1998)
13. Lee, C.-Y., Xie, S., Gallagher, P., Zhang, Z., Tu, Z.: Deeply-supervised nets (2014). arXiv preprint arXiv:1409.5185
14. Lin, M., Chen, Q., Yan, S.: Network in network. CoRR, abs/1312.4400 (2013). http://arxiv.org/abs/1312.4400
15. Lin, T.-H. Kung, H.T.: Stable and efficient representation learning with nonnegativity constraints. In Proceedings of the 31st International Conference on Machine Learning (ICML 2014), pp. 1323–1331 (2014)
16. Mairal, J., Koniusz, P., Harchaoui, Z., Schmid, C.: Convolutional kernel networks. In: Advances in Neural Information Processing Systems, pp. 2627–2635 (2014)
17. Mobahi, H., Collobert, R., Weston, J.: Deep learning from temporal coherence in video. In: Proceedings of the 26th Annual International Conference on Machine Learning, pp. 737–744. ACM (2009)
18. Netzer, Y., Wang, T., Coates, A., Bissacco, A., Wu, B., Ng, A.Y.: Reading digits in natural images with unsupervised feature learning (2011)
19. Razavian, A.S., Azizpour, H., Sullivan, J., Carlsson, S.: CNN Features off-the-shelf: an Astounding Baseline for Recognition (2014). Arxiv http://arxiv.org/abs/1403.6382
20. Sermanet, P., Eigen, D., Zhang, X., Mathieu, M., Fergus, R., LeCun, Y.: OverFeat : Integrated Recognition, Localization and Detection using Convolutional Networks, pp. 1–15 (2013). arXiv preprint arXiv:1312.6229, http://arxiv.org/abs/1312.6229
21. Szegedy, C., Liu, W., Jia, Y., Sermanet, P., Reed, S., Anguelov, D., Erhan, D., Vanhoucke, V., Rabinovich, A.: Going deeper with convolutions. CoRR, abs/1409.4842 (2014). http://arxiv.org/abs/1409.4842
22. Tamuz, O., Liu, C., Belongie, S., Shamir, O., Kalai, A.: Adaptively learning the crowd kernel. In: Getoor, L., Scheffer, T. (eds.) Proceedings of the 28th International Conference on Machine Learning (ICML-11), ICML 2011, pp. 673–680. ACM, New York (2011). ISBN 978-1-4503-0619-5
23. Wang, J., Song, Y., Leung, T., Rosenberg, C., Wang, J., Philbin, J., Chen, B., Wu. Y.: Learning fine-grained image similarity with deep ranking In: CVPR (2014)
24. Zeiler, M.D., Fergus, R.: Visualizing and Understanding Convolutional Networks (2013). arXiv preprint arXiv:1311.2901, http://arxiv.org/abs/1311.2901
25. Zeiler, M.D., Fergus, R.: Stochastic pooling for regularization of deep convolutional neural networks (2013). arXiv preprint arXiv:1301.3557

Cluster Merging Based on Dominant Sets

Jian Hou[1][✉], Chunshi Sha[2], Hongxia Cui[1], and Lei Chi[2]

[1] School of Information Science and Technology, Bohai University, Jinzhou, China
dr.houjian@gmail.com
[2] School of Engineering, Bohai University, Jinzhou, China

Abstract. As an important unsupervised learning approach, clustering is widely used in pattern recognition, information retrieval and image analysis, etc. In various clustering approaches, graph based clustering has received much interest and obtain impressive success in application recently. However, existing graph based clustering algorithms usually require as input some parameters in one form or another. In this paper we study the dominant sets clustering algorithm and present a new clustering algorithm without any parameter input. We firstly use histogram equalization to transform the similarity matrices of data. This transformation is shown to make the clustering results invariant to similarity parameters effectively. Then we merge clusters based on the ratio between intra-cluster and inter-cluster similarity. Our algorithm is shown to be effective in experiments on seven datasets.

1 Introduction

Clustering is an important unsupervised learning approach and widely used in various fields, including pattern recognition, information retrieval and image analysis, etc. Generally, existing clustering algorithms fall into five categories, i.e., partitioning based, density based, model based, grid based and hierarchical clustering. Some popular algorithms of these categories include k-means, BIRCH, DBSCAN [1], EM and CLIQUE [2], etc. Some recent developments in these fields include [3–6].

Among various kinds of clustering algorithms, graph based clustering has attracted much interest and achieved impressive success in application in recent years, and the popular works in this domain include [7,8]. Graph based clustering algorithms capture the pairwise relations among data with a graph and then represent the graph by a pairwise similarity matrix. With the similarity matrix as input, these algorithms try to find a partitioning of the graph where each part corresponds to a cluster. In the following we briefly review three types of graph based clustering algorithms. Spectral clustering performs dimension reduction by making use of the eigen-decomposition of the similarity matrix and then clusters data in smaller dimensions. The normalized cuts algorithm [7], as one type of spectral clustering, has been commonly used in data clustering and image segmentation. Different from spectral clustering, the affinity propagation algorithm [8] identifies the exemplars and members of clusters by

A. Feragen et al. (Eds.): SIMBAD 2015, LNCS 9370, pp. 93–102, 2015.
DOI: 10.1007/978-3-319-24261-3_8

means of passing affinity messages among data iteratively. Affinity propagation algorithms have been successfully applied to human faces clustering and gene detection, etc. The third type is the so-called dominant sets (DSets) clustering [9], which is based on a graph-theoretic concept of a cluster. DSets clustering extracts clusters sequentially and determines the number of clusters automatically. DSets clustering has been successfully used in such various domains as image segmentation [9,10], object detection [11], object classification [12] and human activity analysis [13], etc.

However, all the three graph based clustering algorithms mentioned above require parameters input explicitly or implicitly. With the normalized cuts algorithm we must determine the number of clusters beforehand. The affinity propagation algorithm requires the preference values of all data to be specified. Though DSets clustering does not require any parameter input explicitly, we have found that its clustering results are influenced by the similarity parameter σ in building the similarity matrix. Here σ denotes the regulation parameter in $s(x,y) = exp(-d(x,y)/\sigma)$, where $s(x,y)$ is the similarity between two data items x and y, and $d(x,y)$ is the distance. In other words, with these algorithms the clustering results are parameter dependent. In order to obtain satisfactory clustering results, we must determine the proper value of related parameter(s) beforehand, which is not easy in many cases. While correlation clustering [14] is an parameter-independent approach, in this paper we focus on dominant sets clustering.

In order to solve the parameter dependence problem, we study the influence of σ's on DSets clustering results. As a result, we proposed to use histogram equalization to transform similarity matrices before they are used in clustering [15]. This transformation is shown to transform similarity matrices from different σ's to be nearly identical, and therefore make the clustering results invariant to σ's effectively. However, we also found that this transformation causes over-segmentation in some cases, and harms the clustering quality. In [15] we used a cluster extension process to solve this problem. However, the cluster extension involves some parameters which are determined mainly based on experience. In this paper we present a cluster merging process based on similarity ratio of intra-cluster and inter-cluster similarities. This merging process does not involve any parameters, and make our cluster algorithm independent of any parameter tuning process.

The remaining of this paper is organized as follows. In Sect. 2 we introduce the DSets clustering briefly and analyze its advantages and problems. Then we present our solution to the existing problems in Sect. 3 and experimental validation in Sect. 4. Finally, Sect. 5 concludes this paper.

2   Dominant Sets

In order to help understand the method in this paper, we firstly introduce the concept of dominant sets briefly, and refer interested read to [9,16] for details.

Dominant sets clustering is based on a graph-theoretic concept of a cluster [9]. Let's say that we have n data to be clustered and their pairwise similarity matrix is $A = (a_{pq})$. Obviously these data can be represented as an undirected edge-weighted graph $G = (V, E, w)$ with no self-loops, where V, E and w represent the vertex set, the edge set and the weight function, respectively. With a non-empty subset $D \subseteq V$ and $p \in D, q \notin D$, the weight of p with respect to D is defined in [9] as

$$w_D(p) = \begin{cases} 1, & \text{if} \quad |D| = 1, \\ \sum\limits_{k \in D \setminus \{p\}} \phi_{D \setminus \{p\}}(k, p) w_{D \setminus \{p\}}(k), & \text{otherwise} \end{cases} \quad (1)$$

where $\phi_D(p, q)$ is defined by

$$\phi_D(p, q) = a_{pq} - \frac{1}{n} \sum_{k \in D} a_{pk} \quad (2)$$

From the definition, we see that $w_D(p)$ reflects the relation between two similarities, i.e., the average similarity between p and $D \setminus \{p\}$, and the overall similarity in $D \setminus \{p\}$. This relation can be described as follows. A positive $w_D(p)$ indicates that p is very similar to $D \setminus \{p\}$ and D has larger internal coherency than $D \setminus \{p\}$. In contrast, a negative $w_D(p)$ means that adding p into the set $D \setminus \{p\}$ will reduce the internal coherency inside $D \setminus \{p\}$.

With the total weight of D defined as $W(D) = \sum_{p \in S} w_D(p)$, we are able to present the formal definition of dominant sets. A non-empty subset $D \subseteq V$ such that $W(T) > 0$ for any non-empty $T \subseteq D$ is called a dominant set if the following conditions are satisfied:

1. $w_D(p) > 0$, for all $p \in D$.
2. $w_{D \cup p}(p) < 0$, for all $p \notin D$.

In this definition the first condition guarantees that a dominant sets is internally coherent, and the second one implies that the internal coherency will be destroyed if the dominant set is enlarged. These two conditions together define a dominant set as a maximally, locally coherent subset of data. This further implies high similarity within dominant sets and low similarity between dominant sets, and enable a dominant set to be regarded as a cluster.

It is showed in [9,16] that a dominant set can be extracted with a game dynamics, e.g., the Replicator Dynamics or the Infection and Immunization Dynamics [17]. The clustering can then be accomplished by extracting clusters (dominant sets) sequentially, and the number of clusters is determined automatically.

DSets clustering uses only the pairwise similarity matrix of data as input, therefore it does not require any parameter to be determined beforehand explicitly. However, the similarity of two data items is usually in the form of $s(x, y) = exp(-d(x, y)/\sigma)$, and different σ's lead to different similarity matrices. While we were expecting DSets clustering results to be invariant to σ's, experiments indicate that this is not the case. In fact, we report the DSets clustering results with different σ's on seven datasets in Fig. 1(a), where F-measure is used

Table 1. The datasets used in experiments.

	Number of points	Feature dimension	Ground truth number of clusters
Aggregation	788	2	7
Compound	399	2	6
Pathbased	300	2	3
Jain	373	2	2
Flame	240	2	2
Wine	178	13	3
Iris	150	4	3

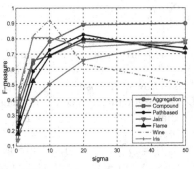

(a) Without histogram equalization.

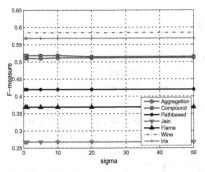

(b) With histogram equalization

Fig. 1. The clustering quality of 8 datasets with different σ's. (a) The similarity matrices are used in clustering without being transformed by histogram equalization. (b) The similarity matrices are transformed by histogram equalization before being used in clustering.

to evaluate the clustering quality. The seven datasets include Aggregation [18], Compound [19], Pathbased [20], Jain [21], Flame [22] and two UCI datasets Wine and Iris. The seven datasets are described compactly in Table 1. Before building the similarity matrices, we scale each attribute in the data vector to the range [0,1]. It is evident from Fig. 1(a) that different σ's cause significant variance in the clustering results.

3 Cluster Merging

In order to remove the influence of σ's on the DSets clustering results, we proposed to use histogram equalization to transform similarity matrices before they are used in clustering. In order to apply histogram equalization to a similarity matrix, we need to quantize the similarity matrix in order to build a histogram. Since a very large σ enable all the similarity values in a similarity matrix to be very large, and a very small σ results in near-zero similarity values, we prefer

Table 2. The comparison of clustering results after histogram equalization and the best results without histogram equalization. In the table we use "histeq" to denote histogram equalization.

	The best without histeq	After histeq
Aggregation	0.90	0.51
Compound	0.78	0.52
Pathbased	0.83	0.42
Jain	0.78	0.27
Flame	0.80	0.37
Wine	0.92	0.58
Iris	0.81	0.57

a small bin in the quantization step to differentiate between different similarity values. In this paper we quantize the similarity range $[0,1]$ to 50 bins, and this option is found to make dominant sets clustering results invariant to σ in the range from $0.5\overline{d}$ to $50\overline{d}$. In experiments the histogram equalization transformation is shown to transform similarity matrices from different σ's to be nearly identical, and therefore generate almost the same clustering results, as shown in Fig. 1(b).

However, we also observe that this transformation harms the clustering quality in some cases. If we compare Fig. 1(a) to (b), we find that after histogram equalization transformation, the cluster qualities are inferior to the best ones before histogram equalization transformation, i.e., the peaks of curves in Fig. 1(a). In fact, the quantitative comparison is reported in Table 2. Our explanation for this observation is as follows. Based on the definition of a dominant set, one data item must be similar enough to all the data inside a cluster in order to be admitted into the cluster. Since histogram equalization maximizes the overall contrast of similarity values inside a similarity matrix, this transformation potentially enlarges the similarity differences and results in a large number of small clusters, i.e., over-segmentation. In fact, we demonstrate the DSets clustering results after histogram equalization in Fig. 2, where the over-segmentation effect is quite evident.

In order to remove over-segmentation effect and improve the clustering quality, [15] proposed to use a cluster extension process. However, the algorithm involves some parameter which are determined mainly based on experiments, and this make the algorithm less attractive in application.

Since the histogram equalization process tends to cause over-segmentation in DSets clustering results, in this paper we propose to use a cluster merging process to solve this problem. This merging decision is made based the very definition of clustering and no parameters are involved. Specifically, we define a clustering quality evaluation measure based on the intra-cluster and inter-cluster similarities, and then refine the clustering results in an iterative process. The details is described as follows.

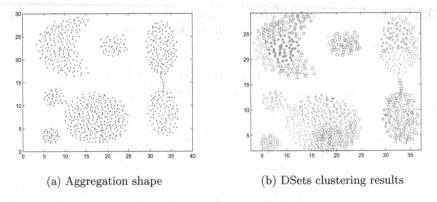

(a) Aggregation shape   (b) DSets clustering results

Fig. 2. The Aggregation shape data set and DSets clustering results after histogram equalization.

The basic requirement of good clustering results can be stated as high intra-cluster and low inter-cluster similarities. Starting from this point, we define the clustering quality evaluation measure as the overall ratio between intra-cluster and inter-cluster similarities. Specifically, for each cluster c_i, we find its nearest neighbor c_{in} so that

$$S_{inter}(c_i, c_{in}) = \max_{j=1,\cdots,N, j\neq i} S_{inter}(c_i, c_j) \tag{3}$$

$$S_{inter}(c_i, c_j) = \sum_{u\in c_i, v\in c_j} \frac{s(u,v)}{n_i * n_j} \tag{4}$$

where N is the number of clusters and n_i is the size of cluster c_i. In order to reflect the neighboring relationship between two clusters, in implementation we calculate $S_{inter}(c_i, c_j)$ as the average of the largest $\frac{n_i * n_j}{2}$ inter-cluster similarity values.

With Eq. (4) as the definition of inter-cluster similarity, we define the intra-cluster similarity of a cluster c_i as

$$s_{intra}(c_i) = \sum_{u,v\in c_i, u\neq v} \frac{s(u,v)}{n_i * (n_i - 1)} \tag{5}$$

With one cluster c_i and its nearest neighbor c_{in}, the ratio between intra-cluster and inter-cluster similarity is defined as

$$r(c_i, c_{in}) = \frac{s_{intra}(c_i) + s_{intra}(c_{in})}{s_{inter}(c_i, c_{in})} \tag{6}$$

The overall ratio is then defined as

$$RATIO = \frac{\sum_{i=1}^{N} r(c_i, c_{in}) * (n_i + n_{in})}{\sum_{i=1}^{N} (n_i + n_{in})} \tag{7}$$

where n_{in} is the size of cluster c_{in}.

Then we merge clusters in such a way to maximize the overall ratio of intra-cluster and inter-cluster similarities. This part is implemented as follows

1. Use DSets clustering algorithm to obtain a set of clusters.
2. Calculate the ratio of intra-cluster and inter-cluster similarities with Eq. (7), denoted as $RATIO_0$.
3. For each cluster c_i, find its nearest neighbor c_{in} with Eq. (3).
4. For each pair of clusters (c_i, c_{in}), calculate the new ratio of intra-cluster and inter-cluster similarities if they are merged.
5. Find the pair of clusters with the largest ratio $RATIO_1$. If the ratio gain $RATIO_1 - RATIO_0$ is larger than zero, accept the merging, and set $RATIO_0 = RATIO_1$.
6. Go to step 3, until the ratio gain is smaller than zero.

4   Experiments

In this section we use experiments to validate the effectiveness of the proposed algorithm. The experiments are conducted on the same seven datasets as in Sect. 2. As all these datasets have ground truth clustering results, we use F-measure to evaluate the clustering quality.

In the first step we test if the algorithm are still invariant to σ's. With the same experimental setups as in Sect. 2, we report the clustering quality measured by F-measure of our algorithm in Fig. 3. It is evident to see that with our algorithm, the clustering qualities are almost invariant to σ's completely.

We then compare our algorithm with the original DSets clustering algorithm and also the normalized cuts algorithm. With the original DSets algorithm we

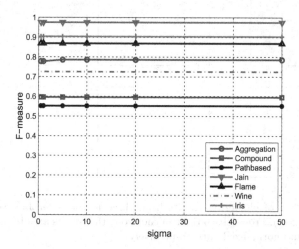

Fig. 3. The clustering results on 7 datasets with different σ's, using our algorithm.

Table 3. Clustering quality (F-measure) comparison of different clustering algorithms on seven datasets.

	DSets	Normalized cuts	Ours
Aggregation	0.51	**0.81**	0.78
Compound	0.52	0.59	**0.60**
Pathbased	0.42	**0.73**	0.55
Jain	0.27	0.88	**0.97**
Flame	0.37	0.84	**0.87**
Wine	0.58	**0.97**	0.73
Iris	0.57	0.89	**0.90**
mean	0.46	**0.82**	0.77

also apply histogram equalization to the similarity matrices in order to remove the influence of σ's. Since normalized cuts algorithm requires as input the number of clusters, we assign the ground truth number of clusters to this algorithm. The comparison is reported in Table 3. From the table we see that our algorithm outperforms the original DSets algorithm significantly. This shows that the cluster merging step is effective. Besides, our algorithm also performs better than or comparably to normalized cuts algorithm. Since the normalized cuts algorithm benefits from the ground truth number of clusters and our algorithm involves no user-defined parameters, we believe that the comparison validates the effectiveness of our algorithm.

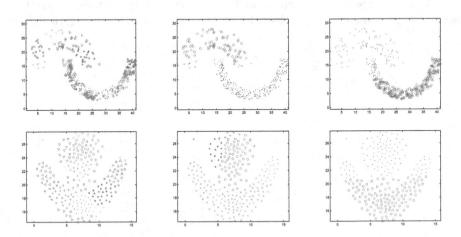

Fig. 4. Illustration of clustering results from three methods on Jain (top row) and Flame (bottom row). From left to right in each row, the results are obtained by DSets, our algorithm and normalized cuts, respectively.

Noticing that as a clustering quality evaluation criterion, F-measure does not always coincide with human judgement, we show in Fig. 4 the clustering results of three methods on the datasets Jain and Flame. From the comparison in Fig. 4 we see that the clustering results of our method is more close to ground truth than the other two methods, consistent with the comparison of clustering quality evaluated by F-measure.

5   Conclusion

In this paper we study the influence of similarity matrices on dominant sets clustering results and present a new clustering algorithm. We firstly use histogram equalization to transform the similarity matrices before they are used in clustering. This transformation is shown to remove the dependence of clustering results on similarity matrices effectively. However, we also observe over-segmentation in clustering results after the transformation. Therefore we define an internal clustering quality evaluation measure based on the ratio of intra-cluster and inter-cluster similarities. We then merge the over-segmented clusters in order to maximize the clustering quality. Experiments on seven datasets indicate that our algorithm has little dependence on any parameters, and the clustering quality is comparable to that of the state-of-the-art algorithms. These results enable us to believe that our work is a useful step forward in exploring a totally nonparametric clustering algorithm.

Acknowledgement. This work is supported in part by National Natural Science Foundation of China under Grant No. 61473045 and No. 41371425, and by the Program for Liaoning Innovative Research Team in University under Grant No. LT2013023.

References

1. Ester, M., Kriegel, H.P., Sander, J., Xu, X.W.: A density-based algorithm for discovering clusters in large spatial databases with noise. In: International Conference on Knowledge Discovery and Data Mining, pp. 226–231 (1996)
2. Agrawal, R., Gehrke, J., Gunopulos, D., Raghavan, P.: Automatic subspace clustering of high dimensional data. In: International Conference on Knowledge Discovery and Data Mining, pp. 517–521 (2005)
3. Panagiotakis, C., Grinias, I., Tziritas, G.: Natural image segmentation based on tree equipartition, bayesian flooding and region merging. IEEE Trans. Image Process. **20**, 2276–2287 (2011)
4. Couprie, C., Grady, L., Najman, L., Talbot, H.: Power watersheds: A new image segmentation framework extending graph cuts, random walker and optimal spanning forest. In: IEEE International Conference on Computer Vision, pp. 731–738 (2009)
5. Panagiotakis, C., Papadakis, H., Grinias, E., Komodakis, N., Fragopoulou, P., Tziritas, G.: Interactive image segmentation based on synthetic graph coordinates. Pattern Recogn. **46**, 2940–2952 (2013)

6. Zhao, Y., Nie, X., Duan, Y., Huang, Y., Luo, S.: A benchmark for interactive image segmentation algorithms. In: IEEE Workshop on Person-Oriented Vision, 33–38 (2011)

7. Shi, J., Malik, J.: Normalized cuts and image segmentation. IEEE Trans. Pattern Anal. Mach. Intell. **22**, 167–172 (2000)

8. Brendan, J.F., Delbert, D.: Clustering by passing messages between data points. Science **315**, 972–976 (2007)

9. Pavan, M., Pelillo, M.: Dominant sets and pairwise clustering. IEEE Trans. Pattern Anal. Mach. Intell. **29**, 167–172 (2007)

10. Hou, J., Xu, E., Liu, W.X., Xia, Q., Qi, N.M.: A density based enhancement to dominant sets clustering. IET Comput. Vision **7**, 354–361 (2013)

11. Yang, X.W., Liu, H.R., Laecki, L.J.: Contour-based object detection as dominant set computation. Pattern Recogn. **45**, 1927–1936 (2012)

12. Hou, J., Pelillo, M.: A simple feature combination method based on dominant sets. Pattern Recogn. **46**, 3129–3139 (2013)

13. Hamid, R., Maddi, S., Johnson, A.Y., Bobick, A.F., Essa, I.A., Isbell, C.: A novel sequence representation for unsupervised analysis of human activities. Artif. Intell. **173**, 1221–1244 (2009)

14. Bansal, N., Blum, A., Chawla, S.: Correlation clustering. Mach. Learn. **56**, 89–113 (2004)

15. Hou, J., Xu, E., Chi, L., Xia, Q., Qi, N.M.: Dset++: a robust clustering algorithm. In: International Conference on Image Processing, pp. 3795–3799 (2013)

16. Pavan, M., Pelillo, M.: A graph-theoretic approach to clustering and segmentation. In: IEEE International Conference on Computer Vision and Pattern Recognition, pp. 145–152 (2003)

17. Rota Bulò, S., Pelillo, M., Bomze, I.M.: Graph-based quadratic optimization: a fast evolutionary approach. Comput. Vis. Image Underst. **115**, 984–995 (2011)

18. Gionis, A., Mannila, H., Tsaparas, P.: Clustering aggregation. ACM Trans. Knowl. Discov. Data **1**, 1–30 (2007)

19. Zahn, C.T.: Graph-theoretical methods for detecting and describing gestalt clusters. IEEE Trans. Comput. **20**, 68–86 (1971)

20. Chang, H., Yeung, D.Y.: Robust path-based spectral clustering. Pattern Recogn. **41**, 191–203 (2008)

21. Jain, A.K., Law, M.H.C.: Data clustering: a user's dilemma. In: Pal, S.K., Bandyopadhyay, S., Biswas, S. (eds.) PReMI 2005. LNCS, vol. 3776, pp. 1–10. Springer, Heidelberg (2005)

22. Fu, L., Medico, E.: Flame, a novel fuzzy clustering method for the analysis of dna microarray data. BMC Bioinf. **8**, 1–17 (2007)

An Adaptive Radial Basis Function Kernel for Support Vector Data Description

André E. Lazzaretti[1]([⊠]) and David M.J. Tax[2]

[1] Institute of Technology for Development, Avenida Comendador Franco 1341,
Curitiba, Paraná, Brazil
`lazzaretti@lactec.org.br`
[2] Pattern Recognition Laboratory, Delft University of Technology, Mekelweg 4,
2628 CD Delft, The Netherlands
`D.M.J.Tax@tudelft.nl`

Abstract. For one-class classification or novelty detection, the metric of the feature space is essential for a good performance. Typically, it is assumed that the metric of the feature space is relatively isotropic, or flat, indicating that a distance of 1 can be interpreted in a similar way for every location and direction in the feature space. When this is not the case, thresholds on distances that are fitted in one part of the feature space will be suboptimal for other parts. To avoid this, the idea of this paper is to modify the width parameter in the Radial Basis Function (RBF) kernel for the Support Vector Data Description (SVDD) classifier. Although there have been numerous approaches to learn the metric in a feature space for (supervised) classification problems, for one-class classification this is harder, because the metric cannot be optimized to improve a classification performance. Instead, here we propose to consider the local pairwise distances in the training set. The results obtained on both artificial and real datasets demonstrate the ability of the modified RBF kernel to identify local scales in the input data, extracting its general structure and improving the final classification performance for novelty detection problems.

Keywords: Gaussian kernel · Kernel machines · Metric learning · Novelty detection · Radial Basis Function Kernel · Support Vector Data Description

1 Introduction

The most appropriate way to define the similarity between pairs of examples in a dataset is a recurrent subject in pattern recognition problems [2]. There are different metrics that can be chosen, but finding (or even building) a good metric for a specific problem is generally difficult. In particular, for datasets that have different scales [3–5,8], it is expected that known and outlier classes are composed by examples with different pairwise distances (scales), as presented in Fig. 1. In this dataset, pairs of examples at the bottom left have lower pairwise distances, when compared to other regions in the input space.

© Springer International Publishing Switzerland 2015
A. Feragen et al. (Eds.): SIMBAD 2015, LNCS 9370, pp. 103–116, 2015.
DOI: 10.1007/978-3-319-24261-3_9

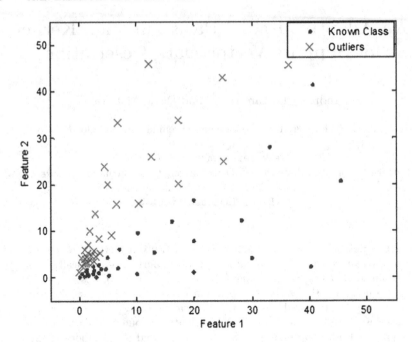

Fig. 1. Dataset with different scales (pairwise distances) in known and novelty (outlier) classes, which are linearly separable in this case.

For standard one-class classifiers [14], such datasets are particularly challenging, once they can lead to different types of errors for different solutions. To illustrate the problem, let us consider the case of the Support Vector Data Description classifier [12] applied to the dataset presented in Fig. 1. The result for two different scales are presented in Fig. 2, a large scale and a small scale.

For relatively low pairwise distance values (i.e. examples located around the origin), it is possible to discriminate between the known and novelty examples well with the *low-scale* solution. This is not true for the *high-scale* solution, that misclassifies many outliers that are genuine target objects. On the other hand, for relatively high pairwise distance values that occur in the top right part of the scatter plot, the *high-scale* description is more suitable. There, the *low-scale* solution rejects most of the target examples unnecessarily.

Additionally, Fig. 2 presents the result for the SVDD with negative examples [12]. In this formulation, examples from the outlier (negative) class are used during the training stage to improve the description (i.e. to obtain a tighter boundary around the data, in areas where outlier objects are present). Such result highlights that, for one-class classification, the scaling problem is even more important, because objects from the outlier class cannot fix (adjust) the boundary, as one can observe in Fig. 2 for low pairwise distance values. As a general conclusion, one can state that the SVDD with standard RBF kernel is not able to extract different scales in datasets, even when the outliers are used in the training stage.

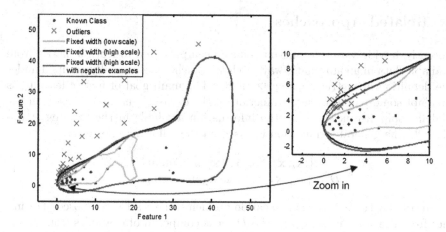

Fig. 2. Standard SVDD with two different scales applied in the dataset presented in Fig. 1.

Such limitation could suggest the use of a preprocessing stage with the aim of extracting scale structures in the dataset, e.g. unsupervised metric learning (ML) algorithms. Some ML methods based on pairwise similarity information have been proposed for novelty detection problems [11,18,22,23]. However, as we present in Sect. 2, most of them typically fits a single Mahalanobis metric on the dataset and, because of that, they are not locally adaptive. Accordingly, there is no guarantee that standard unsupervised metric learning algorithms can improve the one-class classification description for standard one-class classifiers.

Based on what we present so far, the idea of this paper is to introduce an adaptive local scale approach in the Radial Basis Function kernel for Support Vector Data Description, in order to adapt (rescale) the similarity measure in the feature space for different scales that may be present in the dataset – a local scale approach, derived from the empirical distances in the training set. The SVDD classifier has been selected due to the flexibility in the representation of similarities in feature space. Also, the RBF kernel allows a direct modification to incorporate local concepts in the similarity measure, following the general idea presented in [21].

Note that this adaptive local scale approach is not restricted to the SVDD classifier and it can be extended to any kernel-based methods, e.g. the Parzen density classifier, or the one-class Support Vector Machine [10]. The important contribution is that there is not one Mahalanobis metric for the whole feature space that is being trained, but a local adjustment of the metric is proposed.

The paper is organized as follows: Sect. 2 contains some of the most used metric learning methods for one-class classification problems and its main limitations. In Sect. 3, theoretical aspects related to standard SVDD are presented. Section 4 presents the proposed method, emphasizing the advantages of a local representation in the feature space for the SVDD classifier. In Sect. 5, the results obtained for artificial and real datasets are presented. Finally, in Sect. 6, conclusions are summarized and future work is outlined.

2   Related Approaches

Recently, a wide variety of methods have been proposed to learn a metric from available data in an automatic way. Such approaches are normally grouped under the definition of metric learning [2,19,20]. The main goal of metric learning is to adapt some pairwise metric function to the dataset – normally based on the Mahalanobis distance – using the information available in the training examples [2]. The general formulation is based on the following relations:

$$S = \{(\mathbf{x}_i, \mathbf{x}_j) : \mathbf{x}_i \text{ and } \mathbf{x}_j \text{ are similar}\},$$
$$D = \{(\mathbf{x}_i, \mathbf{x}_j) : \mathbf{x}_i \text{ and } \mathbf{x}_j \text{ are dissimilar}\}. \tag{1}$$

In standard supervised classification problems, the S set is composed of examples from the same class, whilst the D set is composed of examples from different classes. The learning process, from the metric learning perspective, involves minimizing distances in the S set and, simultaneously, maximizing distances between dissimilar examples (D set). At the end of the training stage, one can obtain a new metric for the problem of interest, which is more similar to the distance characteristics in the input data. It is also possible to extend metric learning methods to learn multiple locally linear transformations, as presented in [19]. With a new metric, standard distance-based algorithms (e.g. k-nearest-neighbors) can be used to perform classification tasks. Usually, final classification performances increase with the new metric, as presented in [7,19].

In the particular case of kernel machines, e.g. Support Vector Machine (SVM) with RBF kernels (SVM-RBF), the most popular Mahalanobis metric learning algorithms as preprocessing stage normally do not lead to relevant improvements for SVM-RBF classification [21]. In such cases, the most appropriate method is based on the combination between learning a Mahalanobis metric with the training of the RBF kernel parameters. This is equivalent to adapt the kernel function, or the similarity measure, in the feature space [16]. With the metric learning applied directly in the feature space, it is possible to obtain a satisfactory improvement in the final classification performance, as presented in [21]. It is noteworthy that the approach proposed in [21] is similar to the idea of the present work: adapt the metric directly in the feature space. However, different scales are not discussed in that paper.

In unsupervised problems, such as novelty detection, the distance function learning problems are ill-posed with no well-defined optimization criteria, mainly because the D set is not available during the training stage [23]. One possible way to overcome such limitation is to minimize distances in the S set, including a constraint to prevent the solution from being achieved by shrinking the entire space to a single point [1]. The most common solution for this problem is presented in the Relevant Component Analysis (RCA) [11].

RCA is a linear transform that assigns large weights to relevant dimensions and low weights to irrelevant dimensions of the dataset. It is also possible to use the kernel version of the RCA transform, as presented in [15], or other variations discussed in [22,23]. When the number of *chunklets*[1] in the RCA or kernel-RCA is equal to one[2], the final solution is equivalent to the standard whitening transform [1] and its corresponding kernel version [13], respectively. Some of the advantages of RCA and kernel-RCA for novelty detection problems are presented in [18], and consequently, in [13].

When the RCA and the kernel-RCA are applied to the dataset presented in Fig. 1, one obtains the result shown in Fig. 3. For both mappings, only known examples are used to learn the new metric. In the test stage, the learned metric is used to embed known and unknown (outlier) examples. For the sake of visualizing the kernel-RCA representation, we apply kernel-Principal Component Analysis (PCA) [9] based on the learned kernel matrix to embed the points in a two-dimensional space [22].

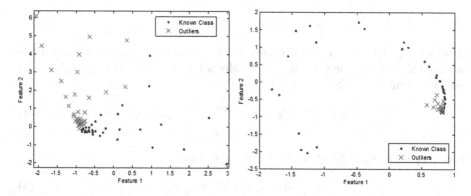

Fig. 3. Linear RCA (left) and Kernel-RCA (right) applied to the dataset presented in Fig. 1.

In the linear RCA, the different local scales are still preserved in the new representation. It appears that RCA does not adapt to the nonlinear charac- teristics in the original dataset. As for the kernel-RCA, a similar result can be observed, mainly for known examples. In this case, the similarity measure is also affected by different scales in the dataset. Thus, both RCA and kernel-RCA are not the most appropriate solution to cope with different scales in novelty detec- tion problems, as they preserve most of the pairwise distance characteristics in the mapped space – i.e. they are not locally adaptive. Based on this fact, Sects. 3 and 4 present one possible way to modify the metric directly in the feature space, in order to adapt the selected one-class classifier (SVDD) in different scales in the dataset.

---

[1] A *chunklet* is defined as a set of points where all data points have an identical but unknown class label.

[2] This is normally the case in novelty detection problems, where the known class corresponds to one single *chunklet*.

3   Support Vector Data Description

For a given input class, with N examples and features $(\mathbf{x}_1, ..., \mathbf{x}_N)$, we assume that there is a closed surface (hypersphere) that surrounds it. The hypersphere is characterized by its center $\mathbf{a}$ and radius R. In the original formulation, the SVDD model contains two terms. The first term (R^2) is related to the structural risk and the second term penalizes objects located at a large distance from the edge of the hypersphere, keeping the trade-off between empirical and structural risks. The minimization problem can defined as:

$$\varepsilon(R, \mathbf{a}, \boldsymbol{\xi}) = R^2 + C_1 \sum_i \xi_i, \tag{2}$$

grouping almost all patterns within the hypersphere:

$$\|\mathbf{x}_i - \mathbf{a}\|^2 \leq R^2 + \xi_i, \ \xi_i \geq 0, \ \forall i, \tag{3}$$

in which C_1 gives the trade-off between the volume of the description and the errors. This optimization problem is usually solved through its Lagrangian dual problem, which consists of maximizing:

$$L = \sum_i \alpha_i (\mathbf{x}_i \cdot \mathbf{x}_i) - \sum_{i,j} \alpha_i \alpha_j (\mathbf{x}_i \cdot \mathbf{x}_j), \tag{4}$$

with respect to α_i, subject to the following constraint:

$$0 \leq \alpha_i \leq C_1, \ \ \forall i. \tag{5}$$

The center of the hypersphere may be computed using the expression:

$$\mathbf{a} = \sum_i \alpha_i \Phi(\mathbf{x}_i). \tag{6}$$

Through Lagrange multiplier constraint analysis, it is possible to establish the location of a given pattern with respect to the edges of the hypersphere. That is, a pattern may be located within the edge, on the edge, or outside the edge of the hypersphere (novelty). The patterns located on the edge of the hypersphere with nonzero α_i are called support vectors, since they are responsible for the characterization of the hypersphere.

The main feature of the SVDD model is the representation of the input data in a high-dimensional space without the need of large additional computational effort [14]. This representation allows more flexible descriptors of the input data, following the same general idea of Support Vector Machines [17].

In order to develop the hypersphere in feature space, it is necessary to perform a mapping $\Phi(\mathbf{x})$ to the new space. Therefore, Eq. 4 can be rewritten:

$$L = \sum_i \alpha_i K(\mathbf{x}_i, \mathbf{x}_i) - \sum_{i,j} \alpha_i \alpha_j K(\mathbf{x}_i, \mathbf{x}_j). \tag{7}$$

In this representation, a new pattern $\mathbf{z}$ is classified as a novelty if:

$$\sum_i \alpha_i K(\mathbf{z}, \mathbf{x}_i) < \frac{1}{2}\left[1 + \sum_{i,j} \alpha_i \alpha_j K(\mathbf{x}_i, \mathbf{x}_j) - R^2\right]. \tag{8}$$

Finally, the radius of the hypersphere can be calculated by the distance between $\mathbf{a}$ and one of the unbounded support vectors $\mathbf{x}_s$:

$$R^2 = K(\mathbf{x}_s, \mathbf{x}_s) - 2\sum_i \alpha_i K(\mathbf{x}_i, \mathbf{x}_s) + \sum_{i,j} \alpha_i \alpha_j K(\mathbf{x}_i, \mathbf{x}_j). \tag{9}$$

The RBF kernel, which is the selected kernel in this work, is given by:

$$K(\mathbf{x}_i, \mathbf{x}_j) = \exp\left(\frac{-\|\mathbf{x}_i - \mathbf{x}_j\|^2}{\sigma^2}\right), \tag{10}$$

where σ represents the kernel parameter (width).

4   Proposed Method

The final solution for the SVDD classifier with the RBF kernel is highly dependent on different scales in the dataset. In general, the similarity measure provided by the RBF kernel reflects distance characteristics in the dataset: the higher the distance between pairs of examples in the input space, the lower the similarity measure in the feature space. In novelty detection problems, such representation is highly suitable when target class contains similar pairwise distances. However, one may have a target class with different pairwise distances, as presented in Fig. 1. In such cases, a fixed-σ solution does not fit different scales in the dataset, as presented in Fig. 4.

From Fig. 4, one can conclude that the most appropriate description should combine different kernel parameters (σ). For lower scales, lower σ values reduce the number of outliers that are accepted. As for higher scales, descriptions with relatively higher σ values can include all target examples. One possible way to do so, is to modify the RBF kernel in such way that similarity measures can be normalized for different scales in the target class. The purpose of this paper is to use the following modified RBF kernel:

$$K(\mathbf{x}_i, \mathbf{x}_j) = \exp\left(\frac{-\|\mathbf{x}_i - \mathbf{x}_j\|^2}{\sigma(\mathbf{x}_i, \mathbf{x}_j)^2}\right), \tag{11}$$

where $\sigma(\mathbf{x}_i, \mathbf{x}_j)$ is the normalization factor for each pair of examples $\mathbf{x}_i$ and $\mathbf{x}_j$. The computation of $\sigma(\mathbf{x}_i, \mathbf{x}_j)$ contains two different parts and it characterizes the local scale of both $\mathbf{x}_i$ and $\mathbf{x}_j$:

$$\sigma(\mathbf{x}_i, \mathbf{x}_j) = \lambda\left[\frac{\eta(\mathbf{x}_i) + \eta(\mathbf{x}_j)}{2}\right] + (1 - \lambda)\sigma_0. \tag{12}$$

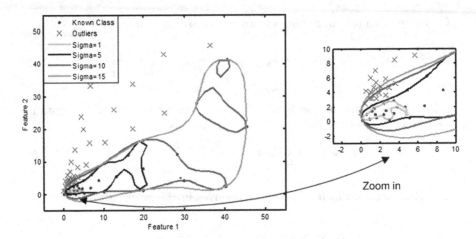

Fig. 4. Standard SVDD with different values of σ, applied in the dataset from Fig. 1. Descriptions with lower σ values are more suitable for lower scales (bottom left), while descriptions with higher σ values, all target examples are accepted.

The first part $\eta\left(\mathbf{x}\right)$ defines the local scale as the average of the distances between $\mathbf{x}$ and its K nearest neighbors:

$$\eta\left(\mathbf{x}\right) = \frac{1}{K}\sum_{k=1}^{K}NN_k\left(\mathbf{x}\right), \tag{13}$$

where $NN_k(\mathbf{x})$ is the distance between $\mathbf{x}$ and the k nearest neighbor. The second part, defined here as σ_0, is a global regularization factor. It is defined as the average among all K nearest neighbor distances in the training set (with N examples), providing a general idea of the pairwise distances in the dataset:

$$\sigma_0 = \frac{1}{N}\sum_{i=1}^{N}\eta(\mathbf{x}_i). \tag{14}$$

By modifying the regularization parameter λ, one can control the influence of the local and global factors in the final description. This is an important step, mainly because it is possible to avoid severe overfitting in the training stage, by increasing the σ_0 factor. There may be some cases where the amount of training data is not relevant enough to extract local scales and, when we increase the local factor, we tend to lose the general structure of the dataset (overfitting in this case). In this work, the parameters (σ and λ) are selected by cross-validation.

In the test stage, we have to compute the similarity measure between the new test point $\mathbf{z}$ and the support vectors $\mathbf{x}_s$: $K(\mathbf{z}, \mathbf{x}_s)$. To do so, the training data is used as a reference for $\eta\left(\mathbf{z}\right)$ and $\eta\left(\mathbf{x}_s\right)$ calculation.

The final description with the modified RBF kernel, here defined as *Adaptive Width*, is presented in Fig. 5. As one can observe, the final description with the

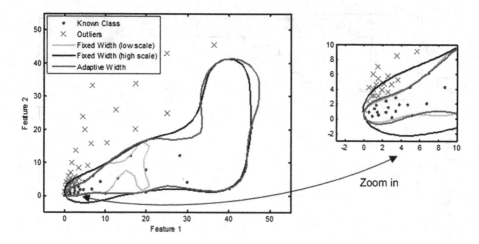

Fig. 5. Comparison between SVDD with fixed and adaptive widths.

Adaptive Width fits the target data in different scales: it does not accept outliers in lower scales and all target points are included in the description – in other words, it captures the structure in the data in different scales.

The main drawback of k-nearest-neighbors-based methods is that one has to retain the training set to perform the classification in the test stage. For large datasets, the prediction can be strongly affected by this issue. However, our main objective with the proposed procedure is imbalanced datasets, with just a few examples in the target class. In such cases, SVDD-based methods normally present a better overall performance for novelty detection problems, especially when we compare to density-based methods, because the SVDD formulation allows to fit the model on a relatively small set of examples [12].

5   Results

5.1   Artificial Dataset

In order to present the main contribution of the *Adaptive Width* in the RBF kernel for SVDD, we start by presenting the results for the artificial dataset shown in Fig. 1. Results are obtained using five times 10-fold stratified cross-validation and the Area Under the Curve (AUC) for the Receiver Operating Characteristic (ROC) curve is used as a reference for classification performance comparison [6]. The training and test sets for known and outliers classes are generated using the same data distribution[3]. The average results are summarized in Fig. 6.

By comparing the ROC curves for the three different descriptions, it is noteworthy that the *Adaptive Width* increases the number of targets accepted (true

---

[3] The artificial dataset can be generated using uniform random distribution in two-dimensional space, followed by a logarithmic (or even polynomial) operation.

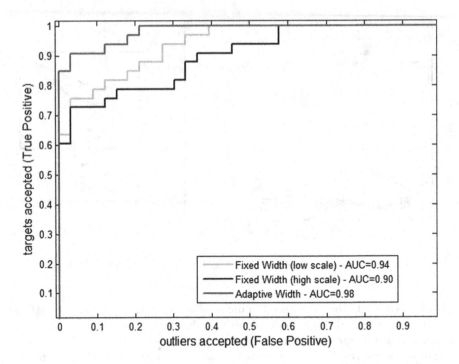

Fig. 6. ROC curve and the corresponding AUC for three different descriptions with fixed and adaptive width.

positive rate) and also decreases the number of outliers accepted (false positive rate) for different thresholds. The improvement is reflected in the final AUC.

5.2 Real Dataset

In addition to the tests with the artificial dataset, we have performed some novelty detection experiments on four different real-world data sets from the University of California at Irvine (UCI) Machine Learning Repository[4] and the Delft pump dataset presented in [24]. Table 1 shows the main characteristics of each selected data set, such as the number of features, the number of target objects and the number of outlier objects.

Additionally, the following division was applied for each dataset, in order to obtain target and outlier classes:

- *Wisconsin Breast Cancer*: Target class is malignant cancer and the outlier class is benign;
- *Glass Identification*: *Vehicle Windows Float Processed* class is used as target class and all other five classes are outliers;

---

[4] The selected data sets, arranged for novelty detection problems, are available at http://homepage.tudelft.nl/n9d04/occ/index.html.

Table 1. Dataset characteristics.

Dataset	Number of features	Number of target objs	Number of outlier objs
Wisconsin Breast Cancer (UCI)	9	241	458
Glass Identification (UCI)	9	17	197
Liver-disorders (UCI)	6	200	145
SPECTF heart (UCI)	44	254	95
Delft Pump	64	137	463

- *Liver-disorders*: Disorder absence is used as target class and disorder present is used as outlier class;
- *SPECTF (Single Proton Emission Computed Tomography) heart*: Abnormal patients are used as target class and normal patients are used as outlier class;
- *Delft Pump*: Details of the *Delft Pump* dataset can be found in [24].

As presented before, the effectiveness of the proposed *Adaptive Width* can be measured indirectly by measuring the performance improvement of the novelty detection problem. In this work, the AUC is used for performance comparison. Also, we compare the proposed method with the standard SVDD and the SVDD with the Relevant Component Analysis as the preprocessing stage.

In the SVDD, we have to optimize the regularization parameter (C_1) and the width of the Gaussian kernel (σ). The regularization parameter C_1 is related to the percentage of positive (target) samples (F_p) which are rejected during training. The relationship is presented below:

$$C_1 = \frac{1}{N_p F_p},\tag{15}$$

where N_p is the number of positive (target) examples. With that relationship, we can directly use the percentage factor F_p in the SVDD formulation. In this work, it was selected from the set $\{0.01, 0.02, 0.05\}$. Also, σ is selected among the following set of discrete values: $\{\sigma_0/8, \sigma_0/4, \sigma_0/2, \sigma_0, 2\sigma_0, 4\sigma_0, 8\sigma_0\}$.

As for the SVDD with the *Adaptive Width*, we have to select the second regularization parameter λ and the number of neighbors K. The λ is optimized from the set $\{0.2, 0.5, 0.8\}$ and the number of neighbors is chosen from $\{3, 5, 7\}$.

In all experiments, 80 % of the examples are used to train each classifier. In order to adjust the parameters, a ten-fold cross-validation is used. Once the classifier is trained and adjusted, the final test is done using the remaining examples.

The average AUC results are summarized in Table 2. The experiment was repeated 50 times independently on each data set, with different training-test set distributions, randomly selected and fixed for all classifiers.

The results indicate that SVDD with the *Adaptive Width* achieves the best AUC results for *Delft Pump* and *Glass Identification* data sets. Such result indicates that different scales may be present in those data sets. It is important to

Table 2. AUC for real datasets.

Dataset	Standard SVDD	RCA and SVDD	SVDD with adaptive width
Wisconsin Breast Cancer	**0.97 (0.01)**	0.51 (0.02)	**0.97 (0.01)**
Glass Identification	0.81 (0.12)	0.78 (0.26)	**0.84 (0.12)**
Liver-disorders	0.52 (0.04)	**0.60 (0.12)**	**0.60 (0.10)**
SPECTF heart	**0.66 (0.21)**	0.50 (0.07)	**0.66 (0.32)**
Delft Pump	0.92 (0.05)	0.80 (0.08)	**0.94 (0.02)**

emphasize that this statement is based on the Wilcoxon rank-sum test. Additionally, the SVDD with the *Adaptive Width* method produces comparable results for all other data sets, without compromising the classification performance, as one can observe with RCA and SVDD for the *Wisconsin Breast Cancer*, *Glass Identification* and *Delft Pump* data sets.

In the *Wisconsin Breast Cancer* and *SPECTF heart* data sets, different scales may not be present, as the results for the Standard SVDD and the proposed approach are statistically equivalent. On the other hand, even with local scales, the amount of available training data may not be enough to represent local structures in the feature space. In such cases, one could argue that there is no need to use the proposed approach during the training stage. However, due to the complexity in finding different scales in high dimensional data sets *a priori*, the proposed method is one possible way to check if relatively low performances are related to different scales in the dataset, by evaluating the improvements in the representation of the target-class boundary.

6   Conclusions

This paper presented an adaptive local scale approach in the Radial Basis Function kernel for Support Vector Data Description. This approach is especially useful for the problem of one-class classification, because in one-class classification the outliers are mainly determined by the distance to the target class. Furthermore, in one-class classification, standard metric learning approaches are unsuitable because no supervised information is available.

Our proposed approach adapts the similarity measure in the feature space for different scales that may be present in the dataset, by modifying the width parameter (σ) in the RBF kernel. The different scales are derived from the pairwise distances that are observed in the target class. The proposed method contains two factors: the first is related to the local scale and the other to the global scale. When the amount of training data is not sufficient to extract local scales reliably, one has to regularize by the global scale factor (σ_0) – this avoids the overfitting problem that the local factor may impose.

Experimental results on artificial and real data sets show that the proposed method yields significantly better overall AUC for different one-class classification problems, both better than the fixed scale Support Vector Data Description results, and better than the results using the Relevant Component Analysis (RCA) as a preprocessing stage. We compared the proposed method to RCA, as the RCA is a metric learning approach that can deal with unsupervised data. Additionally, the proposed method does not compromise the classification performance, as one can observe in some cases with the RCA and SVDD.

In the sequence of this work, we intend to apply the proposed method to different real-world datasets and extend the *Adaptive Width* approach to other novelty detectors, e.g. Parzen density classifier. In addition, we will investigate some possibilities to overcome the k-nearest-neighbor rule in the estimation of η. With this rule, we have to retain the training set during the prediction stage. The idea is to avoid storing the entire training set, by replacing it with a simpler representation, maintaining the adaptive local scale idea.

Acknowledgment. This work was partially supported by the Coordination for Improvement of Higher Education Personnel (CAPES – Brazil).

References

1. Bar-Hillel, A., Weinshall, D.: Learning a mahalanobis metric from equivalence constraints. J. Mach. Learn. Res. **6**, 937–965 (2005)
2. Bellet, A., Habrard, A., Sebban, M.: A survey on metric learning for feature vectors and structured data. CoRR abs/1306.6709, p. 59 (2013)
3. Benoudjit, N., Verleysen, M.: On the kernel widths in radial basis function networks. Neural Process. Lett. **18**(2), 139–154 (2003)
4. Chang, H., Yeung, D.Y.: Locally linear metric adaptation for semi-supervised clustering. In: Proceedings of the Twenty-First International Conference on Machine Learning. pp. 153–160 (2004)
5. Chang, Q., Chen, Q., Wang, X.: Scaling gaussian RBF kernel width to improve SVM classification. In: International Conference on Neural Networks and Brain, pp. 19–22 (2005)
6. Fawcett, T.: An introduction to ROC analysis. Pattern Recogn. Lett. **27**, 861–874 (2006)
7. Kedem, D., Tyree, S., Weinberger, K.Q., Louis, S., Lanckriet, G.: Non-linear metric learning. In. In Proceedings of Advances in Neural Information Processing Systems, vol. 25, pp. 1–9 (2012)
8. Rabaoui, A., Davy, M., Rossignol, S., Lachiri, Z., Ellouze, N.: Improved one-class SVM classifier for sounds classification. In: IEEE Conference on Advanced Video and Signal Based Surveillance, pp. 1–6 (2007)
9. Schölkopf, B., Smola, A., Smola, E., Müller, K.R.: Nonlinear component analysis as a kernel eigenvalue problem. Neural Comput. **10**, 1299–1319 (1998)
10. Schölkopf, B., Smola, A.J.: Learning with Kernels: Support Vector Machines, Regularization, Optimization and Beyond. MIT Press, Cambridge (2001)
11. Shental, N., Hertz, T., Weinshall, D., Pavel, M.: Adjustment learning and relevant component analysis. In: Proceedings of the 7th European Conference on Computer Vision, pp. 776–792 (2002)
12. Tax, D.M.J., Duin, R.P.W.: Support vector data description. Mach. Learn. **54**, 45–66 (2004)

13. Tax, D.M.J., Juszczak, P.: Kernel whitening for one-class classification. In: First International Workshop on Pattern Recognition with Support Vector Machines, pp. 40–52 (2002)
14. Tax, D.M.J.: One-class classification. Ph.D. thesis, Technische Universiteit Delft (2001)
15. Tsang, I., Kwok, J.: Kernel relevant component analysis for distance metric learning. In: Proceedings of the IEEE International Joint Conference on Neural Networks, pp. 954–959 (2005)
16. Vapnik, V., Chapelle, O.: Bounds on error expectation for support vector machines. Neural Comput. **12**(9), 2013–2036 (2000)
17. Vapnik, V.N.: Statistical Learning Theory. Wiley, New York (1998)
18. Wang, Z., Gao, D., Pan, Z.: An effective support vector data description with relevant metric learning. In: 7th International Symposium on Neural Networks, pp. 42–51 (2010)
19. Weinberger, K.Q., Saul, L.K.: Distance metric learning for large margin nearest neighbor classification. J. Mach. Learn. Res. **10**, 207–244 (2009)
20. Xing, E.P., Ng, A.Y., Jordan, M.I., Russell, S.: Distance metric learning, with application to clustering with side-information. In: Advances in Neural Information Processing Systems, vol. 15, pp. 505–512. MIT Press, Cambridge (2002)
21. Xu, Z.E., Weinberger, K.Q., Sha, F.: Distance metric learning for kernel machines. CoRR abs/1208.3422, pp. 1–17 (2012)
22. Yeung, D.Y., Chang, H.: A kernel approach for semisupervised metric learning. IEEE Trans. Neural Netw. **18**(1), 141–149 (2007)
23. Yeung, D.Y., Chang, H., Dai, G.: A scalable kernel-based algorithm for semi-supervised metric learning. Neural Comput. **20**(11), 1138–1143 (2008)
24. Ypma, A.: Learning methods for machine vibration analysis and health monitoring. Ph.D. thesis, Technische Universiteit Delft (2001)

Robust Initialization for Learning Latent Dirichlet Allocation

Pietro Lovato[1]([✉]), Manuele Bicego[1], Vittorio Murino[2], and Alessandro Perina[2]

[1] Department of Computer Science, University of Verona,
Strada le Grazie 15, 37134 Verona, Italy
pietro.lovato@univr.it
[2] Pattern Analysis and Computer Vision (PAVIS),
Istituto Italiano di Tecnologia (IIT), Via Morego 30, 16163 Genova, Italy

Abstract. Latent Dirichlet Allocation (LDA) represents perhaps the most famous topic model, employed in many different contexts in Computer Science. The wide success of LDA is due to the effectiveness of this model in dealing with large datasets, the competitive performances obtained on several tasks (e.g. classification, clustering), and the interpretability of the solution provided. Learning the LDA from training data usually requires to employ iterative optimization techniques such as the Expectation-Maximization, for which the choice of a good initialization is of crucial importance to reach an optimal solution. However, even if some clever solutions have been proposed, in practical applications this issue is typically disregarded, and the usual solution is to resort to random initialization.

In this paper we address the problem of initializing the LDA model with two novel strategies: the key idea is to perform a repeated learning by employ a topic splitting/pruning strategy, such that each learning phase is initialized with an informative situation derived from the previous phase.

The performances of the proposed splitting and pruning strategies have been assessed from a twofold perspective: *i)* the log-likelihood of the learned model (both on the training set and on a held-out set); *ii)* the coherence of the learned topics. The evaluation has been carried out on five different datasets, taken from and heterogeneous contexts in the literature, showing promising results.

Keywords: Topic models · LDA · Split · Prune · Expectation-Maximization

1 Introduction

Topic models represent an important and flexible class of probabilistic tools, originally introduced in the Natural Language Processing community [5,6,20]. Their main goal is to describe text documents, based on word counts, abstracting the *topics* the various documents are speaking about. Recently, the importance

© Springer International Publishing Switzerland 2015
A. Feragen et al. (Eds.): SIMBAD 2015, LNCS 9370, pp. 117–132, 2015.
DOI: 10.1007/978-3-319-24261-3_10

of topic models has drastically grown beyond text, and they have been exported as a versatile tool to model and solve a huge variety of tasks in different contexts [1,8,21,25,30,34,36]. Their wide usage is motivated by the competitive performances obtained in very different fields, by their expressiveness and efficiency, and by the interpretability of the solution provided [9]. Among others, Latent Dirichlet Allocation (LDA) [6] is the most cited and famous topic model. The key idea of LDA is that a document may be characterized by the presence of a small number of topics (e.g. sports, finance, politics), each one inducing the presence of some particular words that are likely to co-occur in the document; the total number of topics expected to be found in the *corpus* of documents is a fixed quantity decided beforehand. From a probabilistic point of view, a topic is a probability distribution over a fixed dictionary of words: for example, a topic about sports would involve words like "match" or "player" with high probability.

The parameters of the model are *learned* from a set of training objects: however, the learning problem is intractable [6], and is therefore tackled using approximate optimization techniques such as the variational Expectation-Maximization (EM [11,17]). The EM is an iterative algorithm that, starting from some initial values assigned to the afore-described probabilities, maximizes the log likelihood of the model until convergence is reached. The choice of such initial values is a critical issue because the EM converges to a local maximum of the log likelihood function [35], and the final estimate depends on the initialization.

From a very general point of view, different robust variants of the EM algorithm have been proposed in the past ([13,33], just to cite a few); nevertheless, in most practical applications where the LDA model is employed, this initialization problem is overlooked, with most solutions starting the EM iterations from a random solution; this is usually motivated by the already appropriate performances of the method. Only few papers explicitly addressed the EM initialization issue in the LDA case: the authors of [15] proposed to employ a clustering step using the k-means as initial solution for the EM; in [14], a method based on the SVD decomposition is proposed. These methods have been originally proposed for a slightly different topic model called PLSA [20], but can be easily adapted for LDA. More often, workarounds are employed at experimental level: in some cases, the learning is repeated several times, and average performances are reported [19]. In other cases, the learning is repeated several times, and the model with the highest log likelihood is retained [3] (also employed in other EM-based techniques, such as Gaussian mixtures clustering [26]).

In this paper we contribute to this context, by proposing two novel strategies for the initialization of the LDA training that specifically exploit the intrinsic characteristics of the LDA model and the information therein. Both approaches share the same structure: start by learning a model with an extremely small (or an extremely large) number of topics, proceeding with consecutive operations of splitting (pruning) of the topics, until the desired number of topics is reached; each learning phase is initialized with an informative situation derived from the previous phase. The pruning strategy takes inspiration from the observation that, when the number of topics is extremely large, the dependency from the initialization of the final estimate is much weaker than when the number of topics is close to the optimum [4,16,28]. On the other hand, the splitting approach exploits reasoning derived for divisive clustering algorithms, where it has been shown that such a strategy is useful when the size of the dataset is particularly high [7,12,31]. In both cases, the approach initializes these "extreme" models at random, and use the learned estimates to initialize a new model with a number of topics closer to the desired one. To choose which are the best topics to split/prune, we exploit a quantity which can be readily extracted from the learned LDA: the prior Dirichlet probability, which can be thought of a number indicating the "importance" of each individual topic. This quantity is intrinsic in the LDA formulation, and is not exploited by the methods described in [14,15].

The proposed splitting and pruning strategies have been extensively tested on 5 datasets, taken from heterogeneous applicative contexts where LDA has already been successfully employed. Benefits and merits of both techniques are discussed, as well as the situations where one seems better suited over the other. Experimental results confirm the usefulness of initializing the LDA model with the proposed approach (i) in terms of the model log likelihood (evaluated both on the training set and on a held out, testing set) and (ii) in terms of the coherence and the interpretability of the learned topics.

The remainder of the paper is organized as follows: Sect. 2 gives some background notions on the LDA model, whereas Sect. 3 details the proposed strategies of robust initialization. Sect. 4 contains the experimental evaluation, and the discussion of the obtained results. Finally, in Sect. 5 conclusions are drawn and future perspectives envisaged.

2 Background: Latent Dirichlet Allocation

In the general LDA formulation, the input is a set of D objects (e.g. documents), represented as "bag of words" vectors $\mathbf{c}^d$ [27]. The bag of words is a representation particularly suited when the object is characterized (or assumed to be characterized) by the repetition of basic, "constituting" elements w, called words. By assuming that all possible words are stored in a dictionary of size N, the bag of words vector $\mathbf{c}^d$ for one particular object (indexed by d) is obtained by counting the number of times each element w_n of the dictionary occurs in d.

In LDA, the presence of a word w_n in the object d is mediated by a latent *topic* variable, $z \in Z = \{z_1,...,z_K\}$. The joint probability of the model variables is:

$$p(w_n, z_k, \theta^d) = p(\theta^d|\alpha)p(z_k|\theta^d)p(w_n|z_k, \beta) \qquad (1)$$

In other words, the topic z_k is a probabilistic co-occurrence of words encoded by the distribution $p(w_n|z_k, \beta)$, $w = \{w_1,...,w_N\}$, where β represents, in tabular form, the probability of word w_n being "involved" in topic z_k. The variable $\theta^d_k = p(z_k|\theta^d)$ represents the proportion of topics in the object indexed by d; finally $p(\theta|\alpha)$ is a Dirichlet prior indicating the probability of selecting a particular mixture of topics: α_k can be seen as a measure of the prior "importance" of each topic. From this, the process that generates an object is defined as follows.

Table 1. Summary of the LDA distributions.

Name	Distribution	Parameter	Dimensionality
$p(\theta^d|\alpha)$	Dirichlet	α	$1 \times K$
$p(z_k|\theta^d)$	Multinomial	θ	$K \times D$
$p(w_n|z_k, \beta)$	Multinomial	β	$N \times K$

First, the proportion of topics θ that will compose the object is generated from the Dirichlet $p(\theta|\alpha)$; then, a topic z_k is drawn from the distribution $p(z|\theta)$, and from this topic a word is selected according to the probabilities in β. Finally, the process is repeated, by selecting another topic and another word, until the whole object is generated. A summary of the distributions involved in the LDA formulation, as well as their parameter dimensionality, is summarized in Table 1.

Learning the LDA model requires to estimate the parameters α and β from a set of training data, in order to maximize the likelihood $\mathcal{L}$, defined as

$$\mathcal{L} = p(D|\alpha, \beta) = \prod_{d=1}^{D} \int_{\theta^d} p(\theta^d|\alpha) \left(\sum_{k=1}^{K} \prod_{n=1}^{N} \left(p(z_k|\theta^d)p(w_n|z_k, \beta) \right)^{c_n^d} \right) \quad (2)$$

Since this function is intractable [6], such parameters are learned using a variational Expectation-Maximization algorithm (EM) [17]. The EM iteratively learns the model by minimizing a bound $\mathcal{F}$ (called the *free energy* [17]) on the negative log likelihood, by alternating the E and M-step. A detailed derivation of the EM algorithm for LDA is out of the scopes of this paper (interested readers can refer to the original LDA paper [6]): intuitively, the derivation yields the following iterative algorithm:

1. Initialize α and β
2. **E-step:** for each object in the training set, estimate the posterior probability $p(\theta, \mathbf{z} \mid \mathbf{c}^d, \alpha, \beta)$ (obtained by using Bayes' law from the likelihood formula in Eq. 2). Unfortunately, obtaining such estimate proved to be intractable [6], and so an approximate form of the posterior is estimated.
3. **M-step:** minimize the free energy bound with respect to the model parameters α and β. This corresponds to find a maximum likelihood estimate for each object, under the approximate posterior which is computed in the E-step.
4. Repeat the steps 2 and 3 until some convergence criterion (usually, a small variation in the free energy between two consecutive iterations) is met.

Summarizing, the EM is an iterative algorithm that, starting from some initial values assigned to the parameters α and β, refines their estimates by maximizing the log likelihood of the model until convergence is reached. As outlined in the introduction, the choice of such initial values is a critical issue because the EM converges to a local maximum of the free energy function [35]: the final estimate depends on the initialization.

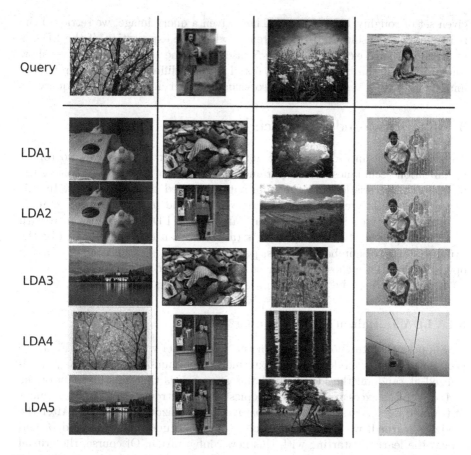

Fig. 1. The top-most row shows some query images we selected: 5 independent runs of the LDA model (initialized at random) produce very different retrieved images, presented under each query image.

Even if this problem is known, most practical systems initialize the EM iterations at random. This may lead to very poor results: let us clarify this point with a simple toy example, inspired by the framework of [8]. In that paper, the goal was to classify a query image into a scene category (e.g. mountain, forest, office): first, the LDA is learned on a training set, and each training image d is projected in the topic space through the vector θ^d. Then, the query image d_{test} is also projected in the topic space via an E-step, and its vector $\theta^{d_{\text{test}}}$ is estimated. The retrieval step can be carried out by simply showing the nearest neighbor, computed for example using the euclidean distance between $\theta^{d_{\text{test}}}$ and the training θ^d. In our simple example, we devised the same retrieval strategy on a recent dataset of images collected from Flickr[1]: in particular we learned 5 LDA models – in each case starting with a different random initialization – on a

---

[1] More details on the dataset, called PsychoFlickr, can be found in [10].

given set of roughly 10000 images. Then, given a query image, we retrieved the most similar by using the five different models; the expectation, if the LDA is well trained, is to extract in all the 5 cases the same image. In Fig. 1 we show some results: it can be immediately noted that, in different cases, the retrieved images are diverse, in some cases also visually rather unrelated to the query.

3   The Proposed Approach

As stated in the introduction, the goal of this paper is to derive two robust initialization techniques for the parameters α and β of LDA, by exploiting the intrinsic characteristics and the information derived from the model. In this section the two strategies, that we term *splitting* and *pruning*, will be detailed. Intuitively, the idea is to initialize at random the LDA model designed with an extremely small (for the splitting strategy), or an extremely large (for the pruning strategy) number of topics, performing a series of splitting or pruning operations until the chosen number of topics is reached.

In the following, the proposed initialization techniques are detailed.

3.1   LDA Initialization by Pruning

Suppose that the goal is to learn the LDA model with K topics. First, we propose to learn a model with an extremely large number of topics K_{large}, initialized at random: the idea behind this approach is that this first run of the EM, due to the excessive number of topics (at the extreme, equal to the number of training documents D), is less sensitive to initialization [4,16,28]. After the model is learned, we select a candidate topic to prune, update α and β, and repeat the learning starting with this new configuration. Of course, the crucial problem is to decide which topic to prune. To make this choice, we look at the

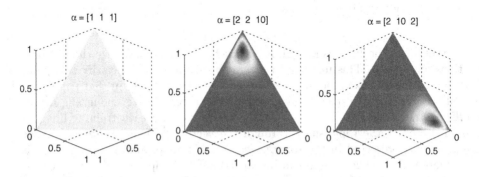

Fig. 2. Effects on the α parameter on the sampled topic proportions θ. The triangular region correspond to the simplex where the θ probability distributions live, with the edges of the triangle corresponding to the θ distribution where only one topic is present with probability 1. Note that high values of α for a particular topic k "move" the proportions θ to be concentrated towards k.

learned parameter α of the prior Dirichlet distribution. Intuitively, a high value of α_k indicates that a specific topic distribution θ – where k is highly present – is more likely to appear in the corpus of training objects. On the contrary, a low value of α_k indicates that k is overall scarcely present – Fig. 2 depicts a graphical illustration of this idea.

For the above mentioned reason, it seems reasonable to consider as the least interesting topic, i.e. the topic to prune, the topic $\hat{k}$ with the lowest corresponding α, i.e.

$$\hat{k} = \arg\min_k \alpha_k \tag{3}$$

In practice, pruning a topic $\hat{k}$ implies (i) to remove its $\alpha_{\hat{k}}$ value, and (ii) to remove the whole vector of probabilities from β, i.e. $\beta_{n,\hat{k}} = p(w_n|z_{\hat{k}})$ for each n. This is graphically pictured in the left part of Fig. 3. After the pruning, the remaining parameter vectors α and β can provide a good starting point for the learning of a new LDA, where the number of topics is decreased by one. This is reasonable because we are making simple modifications to a good solution (the model has already converged). Finally, the learning is repeated until K topics are obtained.

From a practical point of view, it is interesting to notice that it is not necessary to prune one topic at a time: the learned prior α can be used to rank topics, from the least to the most important, and an arbitrary number of unimportant topics can be pruned before repeating the learning procedure. The main advantage is that computational cost is reduced, because less LDA models have to be learned; however, this can deteriorate the quality of the final solution.

Finally, we can draw a parallelism between our approach and an agglomerative hierarchical-type clustering scheme: we start from a large number of topics and evolve by decreasing such number until the desired one is reached.

3.2   LDA Initialization by Splitting

Contrarily to the pruning approach, the idea behind the splitting strategy is to initialize at random an LDA model with an extremely small number of topics K_{small}, and proceeding by splitting one topic at a time into two new topics.

From a clustering perspective, the splitting approach can be seen as a divisive (or top-down) hierarchical-type scheme: starting from a small number of clusters, the process evolves towards a greater number of clusters. Divisive clustering algorithms proved to be particularly appropriate when the size of the data is particularly high [7,12,31], and seem therefore a promising strategy to investigate in this context. Once the first model with K_{small} topics is learned, we employed – as for the pruning strategy – the α prior in order to decide the topic to split. In particular, the idea is that a high value of α indicates an overall highly present topic in the training set. From the divisive clustering perspective, these topics are the "largest", clustering together many words and summarizing most of the objects. For this reason, we propose to split the topic $\hat{k}$ such that

$$\hat{k} = \arg\max_k \alpha_k \tag{4}$$

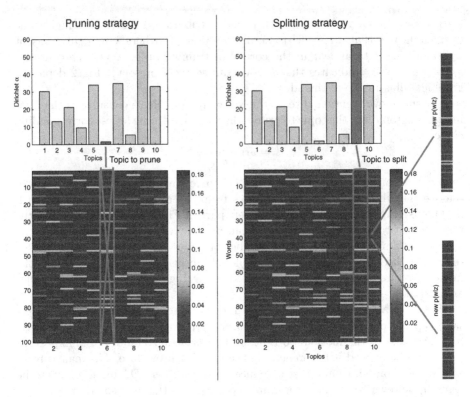

Fig. 3. (left) Summary of the pruning strategy. The top bar graph represents the learned α parameter after EM convergence. The candidate topic to prune is the one with the lowest value of α. On the bottom, the β probabilities are graphically depicted, with a brighter, red color indicating a higher probability of a particular word belonging to a particular topic (each column corresponds to a topic). This topic is pruned by simply removing the corresponding column from the β probabilities. (right) Summary of the splitting strategy. Given a learned LDA, the topic to split the one with the highest value of α. A small amount of Gaussian noise is applied to each copy of the splitted topic (Color figure online).

In practice, splitting a topic $\hat{k}$ implies to substitute the topic $\hat{k}$ with two topics $\hat{k}_1$ and $\hat{k}_2$ such that: (i) the β probability of $\hat{k}_1$ and $\hat{k}_2$ are equal to the β of $\hat{k}$ plus a small amount of Gaussian noise (a simple normalization is also applied so that such probabilities add up to 1); (ii) the α of $\hat{k}_1$ and $\hat{k}_2$ are assigned the same value of $\alpha_{\hat{k}}$. A graphical summary of the splitting strategy is depicted on the right side of Fig. 3. Finally, note that – as for the pruning strategy – more than one topic can be splitted after a learning phase for speedup purposes.

4   Experimental Evaluation

In order to evaluate our robust initialization schemes, we performed several experiments on 5 different datasets. A summary of the employed datasets is

Table 2. Summary of the employed dataset. Columns W, D and Z correspond to the number of words, documents, and topics respectively.

Dataset name	References	Type of words	N	D	Z
1. HIV gag proteins	[24]	Protein sequence	1680	204	100
2. Lung genes	[2]	Genes	12600	203	100
3. FragBag	[29]	3D protein fragments	400	2928	100
4. Flickr images	[10]	Heterogeneous image features	82	60000	50
5. Science magazine	[23]	Textual words	24000	36000	100

reported on Table 2, where for each dataset we indicated its name, the number of words N (i.e. the dictionary size), the number of objects D, and the number of topics Z we employed for learning (when available, this number corresponds to the optimal choice found by the authors of the papers in the reported references).

We took these datasets from heterogeneous applicative contexts in the literature, which involve a wide variety of tasks, ranging from classification and clustering, to feature selection and visualization. Due to this heterogeneity, quantities such as the classification error can not be employed as a general measure of performance. Therefore, we resorted to two other validation indices: the first one is based on the log-likelihood of the learned model (on both the training set and an held out testing set), the second one takes into account the coherence of the learned topics. In both cases, we divided each dataset in a training and testing set using 10-fold crossvalidation, repeating the random subdivisions 3 times. For each fold and each repetition, we employed the proposed approaches to learn the LDA on the training set[2]. For the splitting approach, we set K_{small} to 2, and the Gaussian noise variance σ to 0.01. After a preliminary evaluation, we found that this noise parameter does not influence much results, provided that it is reasonably small (we found that performances deteriorate when $\sigma \geq 0.1$). For the pruning approach, we set K_{large} equal to the number of documents for the first three datasets, whereas we set it to 1000 for the Flickr images.

We compared our strategies with the random initialization (the currently most employed method), as well as with the technique proposed in [14], where the authors propose to initialize the β distribution by performing a Latent Semantic Analysis (LSA) on the training bag of words matrix: we will refer to this initialization technique as LSA. Please note that this method has been originally designed for initializing a slightly different topic model called PLSA. Its generalization to LDA is easy, because in PLSA the Dirichlet distribution is not employed, and θ is estimated point-wise (the equivalence between PLSA and LDA has been demonstrated in [18]): however, it is not clear how to initialize α. We decided to initialize $\alpha_k = 1$ $\forall k$, this corresponding to a uniform prior over θ.

---

[2] We employed the public Matlab LDA implementation available at http://lear. inrialpes.fr/~verbeek/software.php.

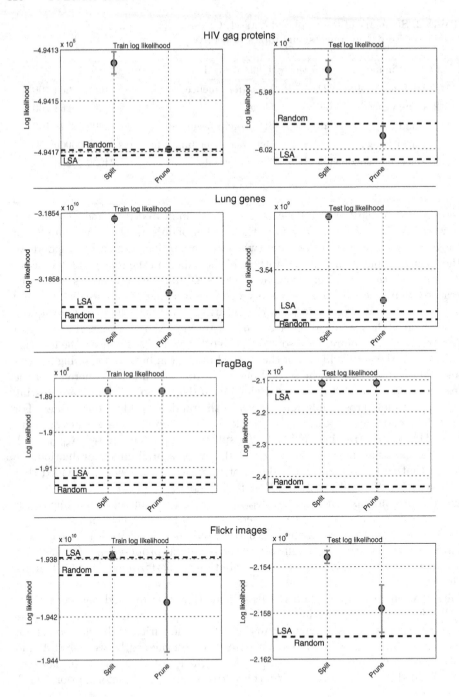

Fig. 4. Log-likelihood of the proposed methods for the different dataset. On the left, the log-likelihood of the training set. On the right, the log-likelihood evaluated on the held out testing set.

4.1   Log-Likelihood Evaluation

We firstly assessed the log-likelihood of the trained LDA models, on both a training and an held out testing set: while the log-likelihood of the training set indicates the quality of the learned model, the log-likelihood of the testing set gives insights into the generalization capability. Such log likelihoods, averaged over folds and repetitions, are shown in Fig. 4, for the first 4 datasets: the column on the left represents log-likelihoods obtained on the training set, whereas the column on the right depicts the ones obtained on the testing (held out) set. The dashed lines indicate the log-likelihood obtained with the Random and LSA methods we compared against, whereas the dots correspond to the log-likelihoods obtained with the proposed approaches. Finally, the bars correspond to the 95 % confidence intervals computed after a t-test, performed to assess if the results obtained with the proposed approaches led to a statistically significant improvement over the best-performing method (among the random and LSA initialization schemes – we highlighted statistically significant results in blue). From the figure it can be noted that the splitting scheme is on average the best one, being able to outperform other approaches in every case except one. The pruning scheme, even if reaching satisfactory results on 5 cases out of 8, seems to be slightly worse.

4.2   Coherence Evaluation

As a second measure of evaluation, we employed a measure of topic coherence to evaluate the proposed approaches. The coherence is essentially a score that is given to a single topic by measuring the degree of semantic similarity between highly probable words in the topic. Several coherence measures have been proposed in the past [22,32], and they are aimed at distinguish between topics that are semantically interpretable and topics that are artifacts of statistical inference. In this paper we adopted the internal criterion of Umass coherence [22]. We chose this in particular because it does not rely on an external corpus providing the ground-truth, which can be available in the text domain, but is absent in the other scenarios considered here. The Umass coherence defines a score based on a set of "topic words" V_k, which is created by retaining the top probable words in the topic (ranked by β probabilities). The Umass coherence of topic k is defined as

$$coherence(V_k) = \sum_{v_i, v_j \in V_k} score(v_i, v_j) \tag{5}$$

where

$$score(v_i, v_j) = \log \frac{p(v_i, v_j) + 1/D}{p(v_i)p(v_j)} \tag{6}$$

In the equation, $p(v_i, v_j)$ indicates the frequency of documents containing words v_i and v_j, and $p(v_i)$ measures the frequency of documents containing v_i. Note that the Umass computes these frequencies over the original corpus used to train the topic models: it attempts to confirm that highly probable words in the topic

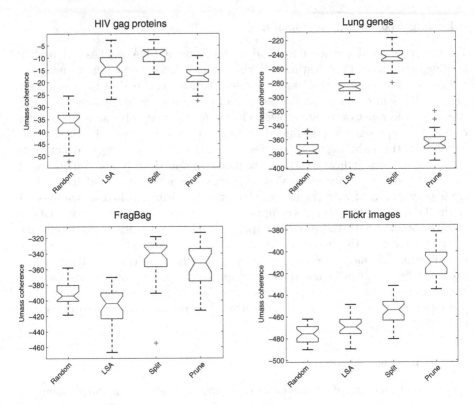

Fig. 5. Umass coherence for the different datasets and the different initialization schemes. The boxplot can be useful to assess statistical significance.

indeed co-occur in the corpus. In the end, the average coherence over the whole set of topics is reported as performance: a higher mean coherence indicates an overall better capability of the model to correctly cluster words in topics.

In our evaluation, for each fold and each repetition of each dataset, we applied the proposed approaches to learn the LDA on the training set. Then, as done before [32], we retained for each topic the top 10 words and computed the Umass coherence for all topics. Finally we averaged the coherences of all topics to get a final single score for the model. Coherence results, averaged over different folds and repetitions, are presented as boxplots in Fig. 5. Each box describes an evaluated method, and the red bar is the median coherence over the 30 repetitions (10 folds, randomly extracted 3 times). The edges of the blue box are the 25th and 75th percentiles, while the whiskers (black dashed lines) extend to the most extreme data points not considered outliers. Outliers are plotted individually with a red cross. Two medians are significantly different (at 95 % confidence) if their notches do not overlap. The splitting strategy always significantly outperforms the state of the art, thus confirming the suitability of this initialization strategy.

Concerning the pruning approach, we noticed that on the HIV and Lung datasets – while surpassing the random initialization – it is not competitive with respect to the other initialization techniques. On the contrary, on the last two datasets (FragBag and Flickr images), this strategy performs adequately well, achieving very high topic coherence on the Flickr images dataset in particular. Interestingly, we can observe that the HIV and lung datasets, due to the peculiar applicative scenario, present more words than objects, whereas the FragBag and Flickr images have a larger number of documents than words.

As a final consideration, we compared the computation times of the different initialization strategies. All the algorithms have been implemented in Matlab and run on a quad-core Intel Xeon E5440 @ 2.83GHz, with 4GB of RAM. The pruning strategy requires the largest running time, several order of magnitude greater than the other strategies. For what concerns the other strategies, it should be observed that in general results depend on the characteristics of the dataset (number of documents and number of words). In fact, when the number of documents D is fairly small (as for the HIV gag dataset), the running times of the LSA and splitting strategies are comparable with the random one: even if initializing the parameters α and β at random is almost istantaneous, more iterations are required to achieve convergence in the learning phase. For example, learning the LDA model starting from one random initialization required 158 iterations, starting from the LSA initialization required 140 iterations and starting from the splitting initialization required 134. On the contrary, when the number of documents is really high (as for the Psychoflickr dataset), then the random initialization is approximately 5 times faster. However, it may still be reasonable to raise the computational burden and adopt the splitting strategy, motivated by the quality of the solution that can be achieved (in many cases, the learning is done only once, off-line).

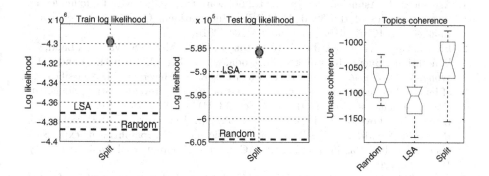

Fig. 6. Science magazine results. The first two panels depict as a dot the train and test log likelihood of the splitting strategy, which is always significantly higher than the dashed lines, corresponding to the random and LSA initialization techniques. On the right, comparison between the Umass coherence of the different approaches.

4.3 Science Magazine Dataset

An important consideration that has to be made for the pruning strategy is that, although it seems suited in several situations, it is not applicable when the number of documents is very high. This is the case of the Science magazine dataset, which we discuss separately because we evaluated only the splitting strategy. Results on this dataset are reported on Fig. 6. Also in this case, it can be noted that the splitting strategy reaches satisfactory log-likelihood values, as well as coherence scores, when compared with the other alternatives.

5 Conclusions

In this paper we proposed two novel strategies to initialize the Latent Dirichlet Allocation (LDA) topic model, that aim at fully exploiting the characteristics of the model itself. The key idea is to employ a splitting or a pruning approach, where each training session is initialized from an informative situation derived from the previous training phase. Then, in order to choose the best topic to split/prune, we leveraged the intrinsic information derived from the model: in particular, we exploit the parameter α of the Dirichlet distribution, that can be seen as a measure of the prior "importance" of each topic. The quality of the LDA model learned using our approaches has been experimentally evaluated on 5 different datasets, taken from heterogeneous contexts in the literature. Results suggested that the splitting and pruning strategies are well suited, and can boost the model in terms of its train and test log likelihood, as well as in terms of the coherence of the discovered topics.

References

1. Asuncion, H., Asuncion, A., Taylor, R.: Software traceability with topic modeling. In: Proceedings of the 32nd ACM/IEEE International Conference on Software Engineering, ICSE 2010, vol. 1, pp. 95–104 (2010)
2. Bhattacharjee, A., Richards, W., Staunton, J., Li, C., Monti, S., Vasa, P., Ladd, C., Beheshti, J., Bueno, R., Gillette, M., Loda, M., Weber, G., Mark, E., Lander, E., Wong, W., Johnson, B., Golub, T., Sugarbaker, D., Meyerson, M.: Classification of human lung carcinomas by mrna expression profiling reveals distinct adenocarcinoma subclasses. Proc. Natl. Acad. Sci. **98**(24), 13790–13795 (2001)
3. Bicego, M., Lovato, P., Perina, A., Fasoli, M., Delledonne, M., Pezzotti, M., Polverari, A., Murino, V.: Investigating topic models' capabilities in expression microarray data classification. IEEE/ACM Trans. Comput. Biol. Bioinform. **9**(6), 1831–1836 (2012)
4. Bicego, M., Murino, V., Figueiredo, M.: A sequential pruning strategy for the selection of the number of states in hidden Markov models. Pattern Recogn. Lett. **24**(9), 1395–1407 (2003)
5. Blei, D.: Probabilistic topic models. Commun. ACM **55**(4), 77–84 (2012)
6. Blei, D., Ng, A., Jordan, M.: Latent Dirichlet Allocation. J. Mach. Learn. Res. **3**, 993–1022 (2003)

7. Boley, D.: Principal direction divisive partitioning. Data Mining Knowl. Disc. **2**(4), 325–344 (1998)
8. Bosch, A., Zisserman, A., Muñoz, X.: Scene classification via pLSA. In: Leonardis, A., Bischof, H., Pinz, A. (eds.) ECCV 2006. LNCS, vol. 3954, pp. 517–530. Springer, Heidelberg (2006)
9. Chang, J., Gerrish, S., Wang, C., Boyd-graber, J., Blei, D.: Reading tea leaves: how humans interpret topic models. Adv. Neural Inf. Process. Syst. **22**, 288–296 (2009)
10. Cristani, M., Vinciarelli, A., Segalin, C., Perina, A.: Unveiling the multimedia unconscious: Implicit cognitive processes and multimedia content analysis. In: Proceedings of the 21st ACM International Conference on Multimedia, pp. 213–222 (2013)
11. Dempster, A., Laird, N., Rubin, D.: Maximum likelihood from incomplete data via the EM algorithm. J. Roy. Stat. Soc. Ser. B (Methodol.) **39**, 1–38 (1977)
12. Dhillon, I., Mallela, S., Kumar, R.: A divisive information theoretic feature clustering algorithm for text classification. J. Mach. Learn. Res. **3**, 1265–1287 (2003)
13. Elidan, G., Friedman, N.: The information bottleneck EM algorithm. In: Proceedings of the Uncertainty in Artificial Intelligence, pp. 200–208 (2002)
14. Farahat, A., Chen, F.: Improving probabilistic latent semantic analysis with principal component analysis. In: EACL (2006)
15. Fayyad, U., Reina, C., Bradley, P.: Initialization of iterative refinement clustering algorithms. In: Knowledge Discovery and Data Mining, pp. 194–198 (1998)
16. Figueiredo, M.A.T., Leitão, J.M.N., Jain, A.K.: On fitting mixture models. In: Hancock, E.R., Pelillo, M. (eds.) EMMCVPR 1999. LNCS, vol. 1654, pp. 54–69. Springer, Heidelberg (1999)
17. Frey, B., Jojic, N.: A comparison of algorithms for inference and learning in probabilistic graphical models. IEEE Trans. Pattern Anal. Mach. Intell. **27**, 1–25 (2005)
18. Girolami, M., Kabán, A.: On an equivalence between plsi and lda. In: Proceedings of the 26th Annual International ACM SIGIR Conference on Research and Development in Formaion Retrieval, pp. 433–434 (2003)
19. Hazen, T.: Direct and latent modeling techniques for computing spoken document similarity. In: 2010 IEEE Spoken Language Technology Workshop (SLT), pp. 366–371 (2010)
20. Hofmann, T.: Unsupervised learning by probabilistic latent semantic analysis. Mach. Learn. **42**(1–2), 177–196 (2001)
21. Lienou, M., Maitre, H., Datcu, M.: Semantic annotation of satellite images using Latent Dirichlet Allocation. IEEE Geosci. Remote Sens. Lett. **7**(1), 28–32 (2010)
22. Mimno, D., Wallach, H., Talley, E., Leenders, M., McCallum, A.: Optimizing semantic coherence in topic models. In: Proceedings of the Conference on Empirical Methods in Natural Language Processing, pp. 262–272 (2011)
23. Perina, A., Kim, D., Turski, A., Jojic, N.: Skim-reading thousands of documents in one minute: data indexing and visualization for multifarious search. In: Workshop on Interactive Data Exploration and Analytics, IDEA 2014 at KDD (2014)
24. Perina, A., Lovato, P., Jojic, N.: Bags of words models of epitope sets: HIV viral load regression with counting grids. In: Proceedings of International Pacific Symposium on Biocomputing (PSB), pp. 288–299 (2014)
25. Quinn, K., Monroe, B., Colaresi, M., Crespin, M., Radev, D.: How to analyze political attention with minimal assumptions and costs. Am. J. Polit. Sci. **54**(1), 209–228 (2010)

26. Roberts, S., Husmeier, D., Rezek, I., Penny, W.: Bayesian approaches to gaussian mixture modeling. IEEE Trans. Pattern Anal. Mach. Intell. **20**(11), 1133–1142 (1998)
27. Salton, G., McGill, M.: Introduction to Modern Information Retrieval. McGraw-Hill, Inc., New York (1986)
28. Segalin, C., Perina, A., Cristani, M.: Personal aesthetics for soft biometrics: a generative multi-resolution approach. In: Proceedings of the 16th International Conference on Multimodal Interaction, pp. 180–187 (2014)
29. Shivashankar, S., Srivathsan, S., Ravindran, B., Tendulkar, A.: Multi-view methods for protein structure comparison using Latent Dirichlet Allocation. Bioinformatics **27**(13), i61–i68 (2011)
30. Smaragdis, P., Shashanka, M., Raj, B.: Topic models for audio mixture analysis. In: NIPS Workshop on Applications for Topic Models: Text and Beyond, pp. 1–4 (2009)
31. Steinbach, M., Karypis, G., Kumar, V.: A comparison of document clustering techniques. In: KDD workshop on text mining. vol. 400, pp. 525–526 (2000)
32. Stevens, K., Kegelmeyer, P., Andrzejewski, D., Buttler, D.: Exploring topic coherence over many models and many topics. In: Proceedings of the 2012 Joint Conference on Empirical Methods in Natural Language Processing and Computational Natural Language Learning, pp. 952–961 (2012)
33. Ueda, N., Nakano, R.: Deterministic annealing EM algorithm. Neural Netw. **11**(2), 271–282 (1998)
34. Wang, C., Blei, D., Li, F.F.: Simultaneous image classification and annotation. In: Proceedings of IEEE Conference on Computer Vision and Pattern Recognition (CVPR), pp. 1903–1910 (2009)
35. Wu, C.: On the convergence properties of the EM algorithm. Ann. Stat. **1**(1), 95–103 (1983)
36. Yang, S., Long, B., Smola, A., Sadagopan, N., Zheng, Z., Zha, H.: Like like alike: joint friendship and interest propagation in social networks. In: Proceedings of the 20th International Conference on World Wide Web (WWW), WWW 2011, pp. 537–546 (2011)

Unsupervised Motion Segmentation Using Metric Embedding of Features

Yusuf Osmanlıoğlu[1]([✉]), Sven Dickinson[2], and Ali Shokoufandeh[1]

[1] Department of Computer Science, Drexel University, Philadelphia, USA
{osmanlioglu,ashokouf}@cs.drexel.edu
[2] Department of Computer Science, University of Toronto, Toronto, Canada
sven@cs.toronto.edu

Abstract. Motion segmentation is a well studied problem in computer vision. Most approaches assume a priori knowledge of the number of moving objects in the scene. In the absence of such information, motion segmentation is generally achieved through brute force search, e.g., searching over all possible priors or iterating over a search for the most prominent motion. In this paper, we propose an efficient method that achieves motion segmentation over a sequence of frames while estimating the number of moving segments; no prior assumption is made about the structure of scene. We utilize metric embedding to map a complex graph of image features and their relations into hierarchically well-separated tree, yielding a simplified topology over which the motions are segmented. Moreover, the method provides a hierarchical decomposition of motion for objects with moving parts.

Keywords: Non-rigid motion segmentation · Hierarchically well-separated trees · Metric embedding

1 Introduction

Motion segmentation aims to identify moving objects in a video sequence by clustering features or regions over consecutive frames. There exist a wide variety of methods for motion segmentation. Image differencing [4,18] is among the simplest methods available which consists of thresholding the intensity difference between consecutive frames. Another group of techniques used in segmentation is based on statistical models. Typically, the problem is formulated as a classification task in which each pixel is classified as either foreground or background. Maximum a posteriori (MAP) estimation [21], particle filters [20], and expectation maximization [22] are frameworks that are commonly exploited in statistical approaches. Wavelets [15], optical flow [25], layers [17], and factorization [9,11,23] form the basis of other common approaches to motion segmentation. One common drawback of many of these approaches is their reliance on a priori knowledge of the number of moving objects in the scene. In this paper, we overcome this drawback by approaching the motion segmentation problem from

© Springer International Publishing Switzerland 2015
A. Feragen et al. (Eds.): SIMBAD 2015, LNCS 9370, pp. 133–145, 2015.
DOI: 10.1007/978-3-319-24261-3_11

a graph theoretical perspective. From a complete graph over the set of image features, we use metric embedding techniques to yield a restricted tree topology, over which a quadratic optimization problem formulation yields an estimate of the number of motion clusters.

Due to its representational power, graphs are commonly used in many computer vision tasks. Features extracted from an image can be represented by an undirected complete graph with weighted edges. Since it is hard to solve problems over graphs in general, approximate solutions are a viable way to tackle such problems. *Metric embedding* is one of the fundamental techniques used to achieve this goal, and consists of mapping data from a source space to a "simpler" target space while preserving the distances. It is well known that approximate solutions to many NP-hard problems over graphs and general metric spaces can be achieved in polynomial time once the data is embedded into trees. However, such embeddings tend to introduce large distortion.

A common technique for overcoming such large distortion is the probabilistic approximation method of Karp [12]. Utilizing probabilistic embedding, Bartal [1] introduced the notion of *hierarchically well-separated trees* (HSTs), where edge weights on a path from the root to the leaves decrease by a constant factor in successive levels. Embedding graphs into HSTs is especially well-suited to segmentation problems in computer vision, since the internal nodes of the tree represent constellations of nodes of the original graph. Thus, HST structure captures the segment-level information at its internal nodes along with the individual features at its leaves. Following Bartal's seminal work, there have been several studies on HSTs which improved the upper bound of distortion and introduced deterministic embedding algorithms [2,3,16]. Finally, Fakcharoenphol et al. [8] devised a deterministic algorithm that achieved embedding of arbitrary metrics into HSTs with a tight distortion bound.

Given two consecutive frames of a video sequence along with a mapping between their features, our method first embeds the latter frame into an HST. Since internal nodes of the HST correspond to clusters of features in the image, our goal is to find a mapping between the features of the previous frame and the internal nodes of the HST. This goal is achieved by minimizing a quadratic cost function which maintains a balance between assigning similar features among frames and minimizing the number of segments identified in the latter frame. We also provide two extensions to our method. While our original formulation provides a single level of clustering for each feature, our first extension allows assigning a feature to more than one cluster. This translates into detection of non-rigid motion of objects such as motion of fingers in a moving hand. Our second extension is in applying the framework to an entire video sequence in an online fashion. We achieve this by keeping track of feature associations at each frame and calculate initial assignments of new frames by utilizing this information. In the rest of the paper, we explain the theoretical details of our method and provide its illustration over two consecutive frames of a video sequence as a proof of concept. We leave empirical evaluation of the method as a future work.

The rest of the paper is organized as follows: Sect. 2 gives an overview of notations and definitions. In Sect. 3, we state the optimization problem formulation, which is followed by its application to motion segmentation in Sect. 4. Finally, in Sect. 5, we draw conclusions and discuss future work.

2   Notations and Definitions

The term embedding refers to a mapping between two spaces. From a computational point of view, a major goal of embedding is to find approximate solutions to NP-hard problems. Another important use of embedding is to achieve performance gains in algorithms by decreasing the space or time complexity of a polynomial-time solvable problem. Given a set of points P, a mapping $d : P \times P \to R^+$ is called a distance function if $\forall\, p, q, r \in P$, the following four conditions are satisfied: $d(p, q) = 0$ iff $p = q$, $d(p, q) \geq 0$, $d(p, q) = d(q, p)$, and $d(p, q) + d(q, r) \geq d(p, r)$. The pair (P, d) is called a *metric space* or a *metric*. A finite metric space (P, d) can be represented as a weighted graph $G = (V, E)$ with shortest path as the distance measure, where points in P form the vertex set V and pairwise distances between points become the edge weights. However, the complexity of such graph-based problem formulations can be prohibitive, motivating approaches that reduce graph complexity. A commonly used approach for decreasing graph complexity is based on changing the structure of the graph by removing edges that change the distance metric of the graph, removing or adding vertices, or changing the weights of edges. This approach, however, introduces *distortion* on distances in the graph which is defined as the product of the maximum factors by which the distances in the graph are stretched and shrunk.

In general, it is hard to find an isometric embedding between two arbitrary metric spaces. Therefore, it is important to find an embedding in which the distances between vertices of the destination metric are as close as possible to their counterparts in the source metric space. In reducing the size of a graph by removing vertices and edges, we'd like the pruning process to culminate in a tree, since many problems can be solved much more efficiently on trees than on arbitrary graphs. Embedding of graphs into trees is a very challenging problem, even for the simple case of embedding an n-cycle into a tree. Karp [12] introduced the idea of *probabilistic embedding* for overcoming this difficulty, where given a metric d defined over a finite space P, the main idea is to find a set S of simpler metrics defined over P which dominates d and guarantees the expected distortion of any edge to be small.

Uniform metrics are among the simplest tessellation spaces where all distances are regularly distributed across cells. Such metrics are important from a computational point of view since one can easily apply a divide-and-conquer approach to problems under uniform metrics. Motivated by these observations, Bartal [1] defined the notion of *hierarchically well separated trees (HST)* for viewing finite metric spaces as a uniform metric. A k-HST is defined as a rooted weighted tree, where edge weights from a node to each of its children are the same and decrease by a factor of at least k along any root-to-leaf path. Assuming that the maximum distance between any pair of points (diameter) in the source space is Δ, the source space is separated into clusters (sub-metrics) of diameter $\frac{\Delta}{k}$. The resulting clusters are then linked to the root as child nodes with edges of weight $\frac{\Delta}{2}$. The relation between parent and child nodes continues recursively until the child nodes consist of single data elements.

Bartal has shown the lower bound for distortion of embedding into HSTs to be $\Omega(\log n)$. He also provided a randomized embedding algorithm that utilizes probabilistic partitioning with a distortion rate of $O(\log^2 n)$. In subsequent work, both Bartal [2] and Charikar et al. [3] introduced deterministic algorithms with smaller distortion $(O(\log n \log \log n))$. Konjevod et al. [16] were the first to improve the upper bound on distortion to $O(\log n)$ for the case of planar graphs. Fakcharoenphol et al. [8] closed the gap for arbitrary graphs by introducing a deterministic algorithm with a tight distortion rate $(\Theta(\log n))$. The deterministic nature of their algorithm made this result of great practical value.

A fundamental set of problems in computer science involves classifying a set of objects into clusters while minimizing a prescribed cost function. The main goal of the classification problem is to assign similar objects to the same cluster. Typical cost functions account for the cost of assigning an object to a cluster and the cost of assigning a pair of similar objects to two unrelated clusters (separation cost). The *multiway cut problem* of Dahlhaus et al. [5] is a simplified classification task that accounts only for the separation cost. Namely, for a given graph with nonnegative edge weights and a predefined set of terminal nodes, it builds an assignment of nonterminals to terminals that minimizes the sum of the edge weights between nodes assigned to distinct terminals:

Definition 1. *Given a graph* $G = (V, E)$ *with nonnegative edge weights* $w : E \rightarrow \mathbb{R}$ *and a subset* $T \subseteq V$ *of terminal nodes, find a mapping* $f : V \rightarrow T$ *that satisfies* $f(t) = t$ *for* $t \in T$, *and minimizes* $\sum_{uv \in E, f(u) \neq f(v)} w(u, v)$.

Karzanov [13] proposed a generalization of the multiway cut known as the *0-extension problem*. In his formulation, the cost function accounts for distance between terminals when measuring the cut weight of nonterminal edges. Specifically, each term $w(u, v)$ with $\{uv \in E, f(u) \neq f(v)\}$ of the cost function in Definition 1 will be replaced by $w(u, v)\delta(f(u), f(v))$, where $\delta(f(u), f(v))$ is the distance between terminals to which u and v are assigned.

Finally, Kleinberg and Tardos [14] presented the most general form of the classification task known as *metric labeling problem*. Given a set of objects P and a set of labels L with pairwise relationships defined among the elements of both sets, metric labeling assigns a label to each object by minimizing a cost function involving both separation and assignment costs. Separation cost penalizes assigning loosely related labels to closely related objects while assignment cost penalizes labeling an object with an unrelated label. The cost function $Q(f)$ can be stated as follows:

$$Q(f) = \sum_{p \in P} c(p, f(p)) + \sum_{e=(p,q) \in E} w_e d(f(p), f(q)).$$

where, $c(p, l)$ represents the cost of labeling an object $p \in P$ with a label $l \in L$ and $d(\cdot, \cdot)$ is a distance measure on the set L of labels. Although, there has been ample studies on solving classification problems using labeling methods, their work was the first study that provided a polynomial-time approximation algorithm with a nontrivial performance guarantee.

Metric labeling is closely related to one of the well-studied combinatorial optimization problems called *quadratic assignment*. Given n activities and n locations in a metric space, the goal of quadratic assignment is to place each activity at a different location by minimizing the cost. Similar to the metric labeling, there are two terms affecting the cost of assignments. Placing an activity i at a location l introduces an operating cost of $c(i, l)$. Moreover, popular activities should be located close to each other to minimize the overall cost which leads the cost function to penalize the separation of closely related activities. Assuming that a value w_{ij} measures the interaction between activities i and j, and a distance function $d(l_1, l_2)$ measures the distance between labels l_1 and l_2, the quadratic assignment problem seeks to minimize $\sum_i c(i, f(i)) + \sum_{i,j} w_{ij} d(f(i), f(j))$ over all bijections f.

3   Optimizing Number of Segments

Motivated by the quadratic assignment and metric labeling problems, we pose the following optimization problem:

Definition 2. *Given an object graph G_O and a label graph G_L both equipped with shortest path metric, and a similarity function defined between nodes of the two graphs, find a mapping f from nodes of G_O to clusters of nodes of G_L, in which similar nodes of the two graphs are matched and a minimum number of clusters of G_L is used in the mapping.*

This problem differs from the quadratic assignment problem in that the sizes of the two graphs can be different and the nodes of the first graph match to clusters of nodes in the second graph. The method that we propose to solve this problem involves HSTs which makes it closely related to Kleinberg and Tardos' approach on metric labeling. Our method differs from [14] in that we utilize HSTs to optimize the number of active labels whereas they use it in obtaining a linear programming formulation for the problem. In the next section, we will show how the solution to this problem can be applied to motion segmentation while overcoming the requirement of a priori knowledge of the number of clusters.

We tackle the problem in two steps which consist of: (1) embedding G_L into an HST; followed by (2) solving a quadratic optimization problem. We assume that a mapping of object nodes $p \in G_O$ to label nodes $a \in G_L$ is initially given. Our goal is to update this mapping by minimizing the number of so called *active* labels, *i.e.*, labels that have objects assigned to them.

Embedding G_L into the HST $\mathcal{H}$ results in a natural clustering of features of the label graph. The leaf nodes of $\mathcal{H}$ will correspond to the label nodes G_L, whereas internal nodes of $\mathcal{H}$ will represent clusters of labels in the G_L. The initial

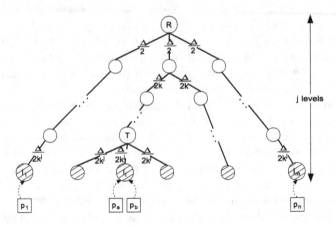

Fig. 1. Embedding of the object graph G_O into the HST representation $\mathcal{H}$ of the label graph G_L. Object nodes $p_i \in G_O$ that are assigned to labels $l_i \in G_L$ are shown connected to the leaves of the HST with $\mathcal{H}$ unweighted edges. T is an internal node that represents a cluster of labels, which is the root of the subtree emanating from it. R represents the root of H.

assignment between objects and labels can be visualized as assigning object nodes to the leaves of the resulting label tree, as shown in Fig. 1, where only the leaf level nodes are active. We utilize the hierarchical structure of $\mathcal{H}$ in order to update the mapping such that the object nodes get assigned to the internal nodes of $\mathcal{H}$ as labels instead of to its leaves. The following quadratic optimization problem provides an update mechanism to the initial mapping.

$$\min \quad \sum_{p \in G_O} \sum_{T \in \mathcal{H}} d(p,T) w_{p,T} x_T + \sum_{p,q \in G_O} \sum_{T,T' \in \mathcal{H}} d(T,T') w_{p,T} x_T w_{q,T'} x_{T'} \quad (1)$$

$$\text{s.t.} \quad \sum_{T \in \mathcal{H}} w_{p,T} x_T = 1, \ \forall p \in G_O \quad (2)$$

$$x_T \in \{0,1\}$$

where $w_{p,T} = 1$ if the leaf l_i that the object p is assigned to is a descendant of internal node $T \in \mathcal{H}$ and $w_{p,T} = 0$ otherwise, and $d(p,T)$ is the distance between l_i and T measured on HST $\mathcal{H}$. Note that value of $w_{p,T}$ is known a priori based on the initial assignment of objects to labels for all $p \in G_O$ and $T \in \mathcal{H}$. The first term in the above objective function will be minimized if all the objects in G_O are assigned to labels at the leaf level. The second term of the objective function will reduce the number of active labels by enabling nodes that are closer to each other in the tree. Constraint (2) ensures that only one of the labels on the path from $p_i \in G_O$ to the root R will become activated. In Fig. 2, as T and T' are chosen closer to the root R, the contribution of the second term to the cost will be reduced. Also note that the contribution of the second term will be zero for the two nodes p and q if one of their common ancestors becomes activated.

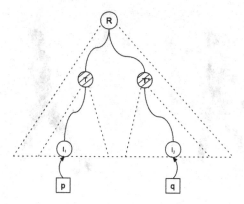

Fig. 2. Two objects being assigned to separate non-leaf labels.

We note that representing (1) as a positive semidefinite program will simplify the quadratic terms and help us prove the performance bound of the method after relaxation. Since $x_{T_i} \in \{0,1\}$, we have:

$$\min \sum_{p \in G_O} \sum_{T \in \mathcal{H}} d(p,T) w_{p,T} \cdot x_T = \min \sum_{p \in G_O} \sum_{T \in \mathcal{H}} d(p,T) w_{p,T} \cdot x_T^2.$$

Let $T_1, \cdots, T_c$ be the subtrees in $\mathcal{H}$ and $\mathcal{X}$ be a matrix such that $\mathcal{X} = [x_{T_i} x_{T_j}]_{i,j=1..c}$. Since $\mathcal{X} = x \cdot x^T$, where $x = [x_{T_1}, \cdots, x_{T_c}]$, $\mathcal{X}$ is clearly a PSD matrix. Thus, (1) can be reformulated as follows:

$$\min \quad \sum_{p \in G_O} \sum_{i=1..c} d(p,T_i) w_{p,T_i} \mathcal{X}_{i,i} + \sum_{p,q \in G_O} \sum_{i,j=1..c} d(T_i,T_j) w_{p,T_i} w_{q,T_j} \mathcal{X}_{i,j} \quad (3)$$

$$\text{s.t.} \quad \sum_{i=1..c} w_{p,T_i} \mathcal{X}_{i,i} = 1, \ \forall p \in G_O \quad (4)$$

$$\mathcal{X} \text{ is PSD}$$

$$\mathcal{X}_{i,j} \in \{0,1\}.$$

Since solving (3) is NP-hard, finding approximate results is desirable. One can obtain a fractional solution to (3) in polynomial time by relaxing the integrality constraint. Then, an approximation can be achieved by using a proper rounding technique [24]. We leave finding a proper rounding algorithm and making performance bound proofs as a future work.

4   Application to Motion Segmentation

Formulation (3) can be applied to the motion segmentation problem where graphs G_O and G_L correspond to features of two consecutive frames. Here the goal is to segment objects in a video sequence according to the relative movement of features across the frames. In this section, we illustrate the application

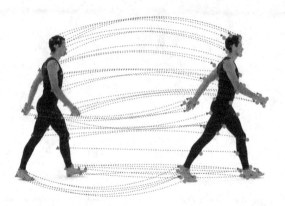

Fig. 3. Initial mapping between individual features of the two frames. Images taken from the video in [7].

of our method to motion segmentation as a proof of concept and then suggest improvements to the formulation.

Using the proposed method, we first obtain clusters of features by embedding $G_{\mathcal{L}}$ into the HST and then minimize the number of segments by solving the optimization problem based on the relative motion of the features. In general, motion segmentation methods fall short of segmenting sequences without a priori

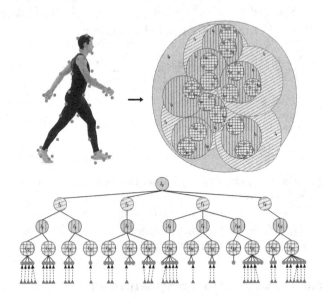

Fig. 4. Embedding features of the second frame into an HST. In the tree, features of the second frame are located at leaf level of the tree and represented as circles. The features of the first frame are represented as triangles and shown as mapping to corresponding features of second frame.

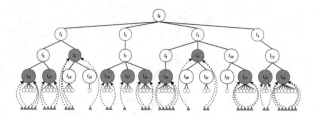

Fig. 5. Darkly shaded internal nodes of the HST are used as labels in the assignment. This implicitly enforces segmentation in the second frame, which is obtained based on the motion.

knowledge of the number of independently moving objects. Our formulation overcomes this problem by optimizing the number of segments.

We begin by establishing a mapping between the features of two consecutive frames by using a graph matching method such as [6,19] (see Fig. 3). Our method then embeds the feature graph of the second frame into an HST using the deterministic algorithm in [8]. As illustrated in Fig. 4, the embedding procedure recursively groups features into hierarchical clusters. In the resulting HST, actual features are located in the leaf level whereas internal nodes of the tree correspond to clusters of features of the original image. The initial mapping then can be visualized as an assignment of the features of the first frame into the leaves of the resulting HST. By solving the optimization problem (3), the initial mapping is updated such that features of the first frame are mapped to the internal nodes of the HST which represent segments of features in the second frame. Some of the segments will become active as a result of the optimization, shown in darker color in Fig. 5. Thus, features of the first frame enforce a clustering of the second frame based on the similarity between features and the choice of internal nodes of HST to become active. Figure 6 illustrates the result of the

Fig. 6. Image features are segmented into clusters representing independent motions; features with the same symbol belong to the same cluster.

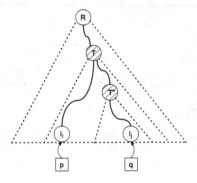

Fig. 7. An object having two active labels in its path to the root.

segmentation. In the rest of this section, we will propose further improvements to our method.

4.1 Adjusting Rigidity in Segmentation

Due to (4) being an equality, solving (3) will activate exactly one label in a path from each leaf to the root R, as shown in Fig. 2. By relaxing this constraint, we can obtain a partial hierarchical labeling where a node will be assigned to several labels that are hierarchically related to each other, demonstrated in Fig. 7. This can be achieved by replacing (2) with the following:

$$\sum_{T \in \mathcal{H}} w_{p,T} \cdot x_T \geq 1, \ \forall p \in \mathcal{O} \tag{5}$$

This relaxation can be used for relaxing the rigidity assumption in motion segmentation. For example, label T' might represent the features corresponding to the fingers of a hand, while label T represents the features of the entire hand, including the fingers, which move relative to each other.

4.2 Aggregating Motion Over Frames

So far we proposed a framework for establishing motion segmentation of two consecutive frames where we initially assumed in (1) that prior assignment information $w_{p,T}$ for all $p \in G_\mathcal{O}$ is given. Considering the application of the framework to a video sequence, we would be interested in utilizing the assignment information of the previous pair of frames in the calculation of the initial mappings of the succeeding frame pair. This will allow us to aggregate motion information over the video sequence in an online fashion as new frames appear. Assume without loss of generality that there exist k labels at a certain level of the tree, one can set the assignment probabilities as $w_{p,T} = 1/k$ for all internal nodes T at that level. This uniform association scheme is suitable for the features that appear for the first time in the sequence. For the features that appear in more than one frame, we propose a voting scheme over the image sequence which keeps track of associations between features and clusters. Specifically, if a feature p appears in close proximity of another feature q in several prior frames but it never appears close to feature r, then probability of assigning p and q to the same cluster will be higher than that of p and r at this level. Thus, newly appearing features will get assigned based only on feature similarities whereas assignment of reappearing features will be biased towards highly correlated recurring features.

5   Discussion and Future Work

In this paper, we presented a novel technique for motion segmentation which, unlike many existing techniques, does not require a priori knowledge of the number of moving objects. Our method overcomes this constraint by embedding image features into hierarchically well-separated trees and then solving a quadratic optimization problem over the tree. We demonstrate the use of our method over two consecutive frames of a walking athlete. We also provided two extensions to our initial formulation. First, we relax the constraint of assigning one label to each feature, enabling us to allow for nonrigidity in motion segmentation, such as detecting the motion of a hand versus the motions of fingers within a moving hand. Second, we propose using the footprints of a feature over previous frames to define an assignment probability for the features in the current frame. In future work, we will apply this strategy to a video sequence and compare the results with the state of the art.

Our method has a limitation arising from the way HST embedding is performed. The embedding algorithm of [8] clusters the features based on their spatial distribution. Thus, for example, in Fig. 6, the features located at the back of the walking athlete and the upper part of the arm are segmented together. However, we would expect the features at the arm to be clustered together with the features of the hand. One of the reasons for this artifact is the low density of the features that we used for demonstrating the method. As the number of features extracted in a frame increases, this misclassification will be less prominent.

Another direction for future improvement lies in the calculation of initial matchings for consecutive pairs of frames. Our method assumes that we are given an initial assignment of features between the former and the latter frames which is then updated to obtain the optimal number of active labels. As we noted earlier, this assumption is viable since existing methods can be efficiently utilized to obtain such a mapping. However, it would be interesting to update an existing initial mapping between the previous two frames to obtain an initial mapping for the next frame. This, in turn, translates to making dynamic updates in an existing matching as the underlying topology changes. Developing an algorithm along the lines of Goemans and Williamson's primal-dual method [10] for obtaining dynamic matching is a promising direction for future study. Proposed method provides an online segmentation in that it makes use of the motion information obtained so far in a video sequence to conclude about the clustering of features in a new frame. Investigating the possibility of an optimization formulation that calculates the segmentation over the entire video sequence is another promising direction for future study. We did not address how to handle the noise and occlusion of object in this study which requires further investigation.

References

1. Bartal, Y.: Probabilistic approximation of metric spaces and its algorithmic applications. In: Proceedings of the 37th Annual Symposium on Foundations of Computer Science, FOCS 1996, pp. 184–193. IEEE Computer Society, Washington, DC (1996)
2. Bartal, Y.: On approximating arbitrary metrices by tree metrics. In: Proceedings of the 30th Annual ACM Symposium on Theory of Computing, STOC 1998, pp. 161–168. ACM, New York (1998)
3. Charikar, M., Chekuri, C., Goel, A., Guha, S., Plotkin, S.: Approximating a finite metric by a small number of tree metrics. In: Proceedings of the 39th Annual Symposium on Foundations of Computer Science, FOCS 1998, pp. 379–388. IEEE Computer Society, Washington, DC (1998)
4. Colombari, A., Fusiello, A., Murino, V.: Segmentation and tracking of multiple video objects. Pattern Recogn. 40(4), 1307–1317 (2007)
5. Dahlhaus, E., Johnson, D.S., Papadimitriou, C.H., Seymour, P.D., Yannakakis, M.: The complexity of multiway cuts (extended abstract). In: Proceedings of the 24th Annual ACM Symposium on Theory of Computing, STOC 1992, pp. 241–251. ACM, New York (1992)
6. Demirci, M.F., Osmanlioglu, Y., Shokoufandeh, A., Dickinson, S.: Efficient many-to-many feature matching under the l1 norm. Comput. Vis. Image Underst. 115(7), 976–983 (2011)
7. Endlessreference. Animation reference - athletic male standard walk - realtime [Video file], 12 January 2015. https://www.youtube.com/watch?v=GBkJY86tZRE
8. Fakcharoenphol, J., Rao, S., Talwar, K.: A tight bound on approximating arbitrary metrics by tree metrics. In: Proceedings of the 35th Annual ACM Symposium on Theory of Computing, STOC 2003, pp. 448–455. ACM, New York (2003)
9. Flores-Mangas, F., Jepson, A.D.: Fast rigid motion segmentation via incrementally-complex local models. In: 2013 IEEE Conference on Computer Vision and Pattern Recognition (CVPR), pp. 2259–2266. IEEE (2013)
10. Goemans, M.X., Williamson, D.P.: The primal-dual method for approximation algorithms and its application to network design problems. In: Hochbaum, D.S. (ed.) Approximation Algorithms for NP-hard Problems, pp. 144–191. PWS Publishing Co., Boston (1997)
11. Julià, C., Sappa, A.D., Lumbreras, F., Serrat, J., López, A.: Motion segmentation from feature trajectories with missing data. In: Martí, J., Benedí, J.M., Mendonça, A.M., Serrat, J. (eds.) IbPRIA 2007. LNCS, vol. 4477, pp. 483–490. Springer, Heidelberg (2007)
12. Karp, R.M.: A 2k-competitive algorithm for the circle. Manuscript, 5 August 1989
13. Karzanov, A.V.: Minimum 0-extensions of graph metrics. Eur. J. Comb. 19(1), 71–101 (1998)
14. Kleinberg, J., Tardos, É.: Approximation algorithms for classification problems with pairwise relationships: metric labeling and Markov random fields. J. ACM 49(5), 616–639 (2002)

15. Kong, M., Leduc, J.P., Ghosh, B.K., Wickerhauser, V.M.: Spatio-temporal continuous wavelet transforms for motion-based segmentation in real image sequences. In: Proceedings of the 1998 International Conference on Image Processing, ICIP 1998, vol. 2, pp. 662–666. IEEE (1998)

16. Konjevod, G., Ravi, R., Salman, F.S.: On approximating planar metrics by tree metrics. Inf. Process. Lett. **80**(4), 213–219 (2001)

17. Kumar, M.P., Torr, P.H., Zisserman, A.: Learning layered motion segmentations of video. Int. J. Comput. Vis. **76**(3), 301–319 (2008)

18. Li, R., Songyu, Y., Yang, X.: Efficient spatio-temporal segmentation for extracting moving objects in video sequences. IEEE Trans. Consum. Electron. **53**(3), 1161–1167 (2007)

19. Osmanlıoğlu, Y., Shokoufandeh, A.: Multi-layer tree matching using HSTs. In: Liu, C.-L., Luo, B., Kropatsch, W.G., Cheng, J. (eds.) GbRPR 2015. LNCS, vol. 9069, pp. 198–207. Springer, Heidelberg (2015)

20. Rathi, Y., Vaswani, N., Tannenbaum, A., Yezzi, A.: Tracking deforming objects using particle filtering for geometric active contours. IEEE Trans. Pattern Anal. Mach. Intell. **29**(8), 1470–1475 (2007)

21. Shen, H., Zhang, L., Huang, B., Li, P.: A map approach for joint motion estimation, segmentation, and super resolution. IEEE Trans. Image Process. **16**(2), 479–490 (2007)

22. Stolkin, R., Greig, A., Hodgetts, M., Gilby, J.: An EM/E-MRF algorithm for adaptive model based tracking in extremely poor visibility. Image Vis. Comput. **26**(4), 480–495 (2008)

23. Tomasi, C., Kanade, T.: Shape and motion from image streams under orthography: a factorization method. Int. J. Comput. Vis. **9**(2), 137–154 (1992)

24. Vazirani, V.V.: Approximation Algorithms. Springer, Heidelberg (2003)

25. Zhang, J., Shi, F., Wang, J., Liu, Y.: 3D motion segmentation from straight-line optical flow. In: Sebe, N., Liu, Y., Zhuang, Y., Huang, T.S. (eds.) MCAM 2007. LNCS, vol. 4577, pp. 85–94. Springer, Heidelberg (2007)

Transitive Assignment Kernels
for Structural Classification

Michele Schiavinato[✉], Andrea Gasparetto, and Andrea Torsello

Università Ca' Foscari Venezia, Venice, Italy
mschiavi@dais.unive.it,
{andrea.gasparetto,andrea.torsello}@unive.it

Abstract. Kernel methods provide a convenient way to apply a wide range of learning techniques to complex and structured data by shifting the representational problem from one of finding an embedding of the data to that of defining a positive semi-definite kernel. One problem with the most widely used kernels is that they neglect the locational information within the structures, resulting in less discrimination. Correspondence-based kernels, on the other hand, are in general more discriminating, at the cost of sacrificing positive-definiteness due to their inability to guarantee transitivity of the correspondences between multiple graphs. In this paper we adopt a general framework for the projection of (relaxed) correspondences onto the space of transitive correspondences, thus transforming any given matching algorithm onto a transitive multi-graph matching approach. The resulting transitive correspondences can then be used to provide a kernel that both maintains locational information and is guaranteed to be positive-definite. Experimental evaluation validates the effectiveness of the kernel for several structural classification tasks.

1 Introduction

Graph-based representations have proven invaluable in several application domains due to their ability to characterize complex ensembles in terms of parts and binary relations. Concrete examples include the use of graphs to represent shapes [1], metabolic networks [2], protein structure [3], and road maps [4]. However, the expressive power of graphs comes at the cost of a reduced pattern analysis toolset available to the practitioner. In fact, our ability to analyse data abstracted in terms of graphs is severely limited by the restrictions posed by standard feature-based paradigm dominating pattern recognition techniques, which require data to be representable in a vectorial form.

There are two reasons why graphs are not easily reduced to a vectorial form. First, unlike the components of a vector, there is no canonical ordering for the nodes in a graph, requiring correspondences to be established as a prerequisite for analysis. Second, the variation in the graphs of a particular class may manifest itself as subtle changes in structure. Hence, even if the nodes or the edges of a graph could be encoded in a vectorial manner, the vectors would be of variable length, thus residing in different spaces.

A. Feragen et al. (Eds.): SIMBAD 2015, LNCS 9370, pp. 146–159, 2015.
DOI: 10.1007/978-3-319-24261-3_12

The first 30 years of research in structural pattern recognition have been mostly concerned with the solution of the graph matching problem as the fundamental means of assessing structural similarity [5]. With the correspondences at hand, similarity-based recognition and classification techniques can be used. Alternatively, graphs can be embedded in a low-dimensional pattern space using either multidimensional scaling or non-linear manifold leaning techniques.

Another alternative is to extract feature vectors from the graphs providing a pattern-space representation by extracting structural or topological features. For example, spectral features extracted from the singular value decomposition of the graph Laplacian have been proven effective [6–9]. For an overall survey about the current state-of-the-art in the graph matching problem, refers to the work by Livi and Lizzi [10].

1.1 Graph Kernels

The famous kernel trick [11] has shifted the problem from the vectorial representation of data, which now becomes implicit, to a similarity representation. This has allowed standard learning techniques to be applied to data for which no easy vectorial representation exists. Once we define a positive semi-definite kernel $k : X \times X \to \mathbb{R}$ on a set X, there exists a map $\phi : X \to \mathcal{H}$ into a Hilbert space $\mathcal{H}$, such that $k(x, y) = \phi(x)^\top \phi(y)$ for all $x, y \in X$. Also, given the kernel value between $\phi(x)$ and $\phi(y)$ one can easily compute the distance between them by noting that $||\phi(x) - \phi(y)||^2 = \phi(x)^\top \phi(x) + \phi(y)^\top \phi(y) - 2\phi(x)^\top \phi(y)$. Thus, any algorithm that can be formulated in terms of dot products between the input vectors can be applied to the implicitly mapped data points through the direct substitution of the kernel for the dot product. For this reason, in recent years the structural pattern recognition field has witnessed an increasing interest in graph kernels. However, due to the rich expressiveness of graphs, this task has also proven to be difficult, with the problem of defining *complete* kernels, *i.e.*, ones where the implicit map ϕ is injective, sharing the same computational complexity of the graph isomorphism problem [12].

One of the most influential works on structural kernels is the definition of the class of R-convolution kernel proposed by Haussler [13]. Here graph kernels are computed by comparing the similarity of the basic elements for a given decomposition of the two graphs. Depending on the decomposition chosen, we obtain different kernels. Most R-convolution kernels simply count the number of isomorphic substructures in the two graphs. For example, Kashima et al. [14] compute the kernel by decomposing the graph into random walks, while Borgwardt et al. [15] have proposed a kernel based on shortest paths. Here, the similarity is determined by counting the numbers of pairs of shortest paths of the same length in a pair of graphs. Shervashidze et al. [16] have developed a subtree kernel on subtrees of limited size, where the number of subtrees common between two graphs is computed efficiently using the Weisfeiler-Lehman graph invariant. Recently, Kriege et al. [17] proposed that a kernel based on the number of isomorphisms between pairs of subgraphs, while Neumann et al. [18]

have introduced the concept of propagation kernels to handle partially labelled graphs through the use of continuous-valued vertex attributes.

1.2 Assignment Kernels

One drawback of these kernels is that they neglect the locational information for the substructures in a graph. In other words, the similarity does not depend on the relationships between substructures. As a consequence, these kernels cannot establish reliable structural correspondences. This limits the precision of the resulting similarity measure. Ong et al. [19] introduce several kernel methods about indefinite kernel for general structures, while Geibel et al. [20,21] gives a solution to deal with not positive semidefinited kernel based on Schur-Hadamard Inner Product applied on graphs. Further, Schietgat et al. [22] propose a graph metric which is based on the maximum common subgraph, while in [23] the authors exploit indefinite maximum common subgraph kernels using the potential of support vector machine for indefinite matrices, extending the work proposed by Hochreiter and Obermayer [24]. Another interesting solution described by Fröhlich et al. [25] presents alternative optimal assignment kernels. Here each pair of structures is aligned before comparison. Another example of alignment-based kernels are the edit-distance-based kernels introduced by Neuhaus and Bunke [26]. Here the alignments obtained from graph-edit distance are used to guide random walks on the structures being compared.

Unfortunately, the introduction of the alignment step results in a kernel that is not positive definite in general [27]. The problem results from the fact that alignments are not in general transitive. In other words, if σ is the vertex-alignment between graph A and graph B, and π is the alignment between graph B and graph C, in general we cannot guarantee that the optimal alignment between graph A and graph C is $\pi \circ \sigma$. Lacking positive definiteness the optimal assignment kernels cannot be guaranteed to represent an implicit embedding into a Hilbert space. However, they have proven to be very effective in classifying structures.

1.3 Multi-graph Matching

The problem of estimating a transitive set of correspondences between structures, known as the multi-graph matching problem, has received much less attention by the research community than pairwise matching. One of the earliest work, due to Williams et al. [28], imposes the transitive vertex-matching constraint in a softened Bayesian manner, inducing inference triangles by forming fuzzy compositions of pairwise matching functions. Sole-Ribalta and Serratosa [29] extended the Graduated Assignment algorithm [30] to the multi-graph scenario by raising the assignment matrices associated to pair of graphs to assignment hypercube, or tensors, between all the graphs. For computational efficiency, the hypercube is constructed via sequential local pair matching. More recently, Yan et al. [31,32] proposed a new framework explicitly extending the Integer

Quadratic Programming (IQP) formulation of pairwise matching to the multi-graph matching scenario. The resulting IQP is then solved through alternating optimization approach. Pachauri et al. [33], on the other hand, synchronize a given set of assignments through a spectral relaxation.

1.4   Contribution

In this paper we want to investigate the use of multi-graph matching techniques in the context of graph kernels. By forcing the correspondences between the structures under study to satisfy transitivity, we obtain an alignment kernel that, not only is positive definite, but also makes use of more reliable locational information obtained through the enforcement of global consistency constraints. In fact, when the alignments are transitive, there is a common simultaneous alignment of all the graphs. Under this alignment, the kernel is simply the sum over all the vertex/edge kernels, which is positive definite since it is the sum of separate positive definite kernels.

Here we adopt an approach similar to Pachauri et al. [33] in avoiding the definition of a specific multi-graph matching algorithm. Rather, we project a set of (possibly relaxed) assignments to the set of transitive correspondences. Transformation synchronization techniques such as this have been proven effective in several fields due to their effectiveness, their ability to leverage the state of the art in pairwise transformation estimation, and their computational efficiency [34,35]. The proposed synchronization technique shares some similarities with [33], but we adopt a different relaxation scheme that does not result in a generalized low rank Rayleigh problem, but can however be solved with a projected power method, avoiding the requirement for an eigendecomposition of the matching tensor.

2   Projection on the Transitive Alignment Space

Let $G_1, G_2, \ldots, G_N$ be graphs and let P_{ij} for $i, j = 1, \ldots, N$ be a matrix matching vertices in G_i to vertices in G_j obtained with any pairwise matching algorithm. Here we assume that $(P_{ij})_{vw}$ expresses a likelihood that node v in G_i is matched to node w in G_j, but is not required to represent a permutation, and can be in a relaxed space such as the space of doubly stochastic matrices. Our goal is to find a set of permutation matrices $\overline{P}_{ij} \in \Sigma_n$ (with Σ_n the permutation space and $i, j = 1, \ldots, N$) as similar as possible, in the least square sense, to P_{ij}, which satisfy the transitivity constraint. Namely,

$$\forall i, j, k = 1, \ldots, N \qquad \overline{P}_{ij}\overline{P}_{jk} = \overline{P}_{ik}. \tag{1}$$

In order to do this first we force the graphs all to the same size n by padding them with dummy disconnected nodes to the maximum size of all the graphs of the set (see Fig. 1).

Once the graphs are all of the same size, we can enforce transitivity through the introduction of an unknown reference canonical ordering and the alignment

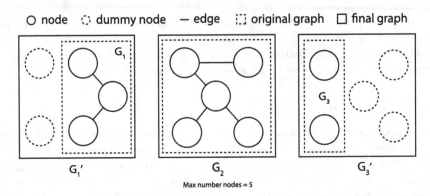

Fig. 1. Graphical example about the refinement task of our datasets. In the figure, the set is composed of three graphs G_1, G_2 and G_3. The maximum number of nodes is 5 (the second graph), hence we add two disconnected nodes in G_1 and three in G_3 in order to obtain respectively the extended graphs G_1' and G_2'. The final dataset with the same number of nodes $n = 5$ is composed by the graphs set G_1', G_2 and G_3'.

matrices $Q_i \in \Sigma_n$ $i = 1, \ldots, N$ that map vertices in G_i to the reference order. With these matrices to hand we set $\overline{P}_{ij} = Q_i Q_j^T$. Note that there is no lack in representation power, as the transitivity constraint guarantees the existence of such canonical ordering. In fact, let for example $Q_i = \overline{P}_{i1}$. For transitivity, we have

$$\overline{P}_{ij} = \overline{P}_{i1}\overline{P}_{1j} = \overline{P}_{i1}\overline{P}_{j1}^T = Q_i Q_j^T. \tag{2}$$

Furthermore, such canonical ordering is not unique, since for any permutation matrix $P \in \Sigma_n$, we have

$$\overline{P}_{ij} = Q_i Q_j^T = (Q_i P)(P^T Q_j^T). \tag{3}$$

With the canonical ordering representation the projection on the transitive space of permutations cast as the following minimization process

$$\underset{Q \in (\Sigma_n)^N}{\mathrm{argmin}} \sum_{i,j=1}^{N} ||P_{ij} - Q_i Q_j^T||_2^2 =$$

$$\underset{Q \in (\Sigma_n)^N}{\mathrm{argmin}} \sum_{i,j=1}^{N} \left(||P_{ij}||_2^2 + ||Q_i Q_j^T||_2^2 - 2\,\mathrm{Tr}(Q_j Q_i^T P_{ij}) \right) =$$

$$\underset{Q \in (\Sigma_n)^N}{\mathrm{argmin}}\ 2N^2 n - 2 \sum_{i,j=1}^{N} \mathrm{Tr}(Q_i^T P_{ij} Q_j) =$$

$$\underset{Q \in (\Sigma_n)^N}{\mathrm{argmin}}\ 2N^2 n - 2 \sum_{i,j=1}^{N} \mathrm{vec}(Q_i)^T \left(I \otimes P_{ij} \right) \mathrm{vec}(Q_j), \tag{4}$$

where $|| \cdot ||_2$ is the Frobenius matrix norm while Tr is the linear trace operator.

This is equivalent to the following Integer Quadratic Problem

$$\underset{\mathbf{Q}\in(\Sigma_n)^N}{\text{argmax}} \underbrace{\begin{pmatrix} \text{vec}(Q_1) \\ \text{vec}(Q_2) \\ \vdots \\ \text{vec}(Q_N) \end{pmatrix}}_{\text{vec}(\mathbf{Q})^T}^T \underbrace{\begin{pmatrix} I \otimes P_{11} & I \otimes P_{12} & \dots & I \otimes P_{1N} \\ I \otimes P_{21} & I \otimes P_{22} & \dots & I \otimes P_{2N} \\ \vdots & \vdots & \ddots & \vdots \\ I \otimes P_{N1} & I \otimes P_{N2} & \dots & I \otimes P_{NN} \end{pmatrix}}_{\Pi} \underbrace{\begin{pmatrix} \text{vec}(Q_1) \\ \text{vec}(Q_2) \\ \vdots \\ \text{vec}(Q_N) \end{pmatrix}}_{\text{vec}(\mathbf{Q})}. \quad (5)$$

where $\otimes$ represents the Kronecker product while I is the identity matrix. Note that if the pairwise matches are symmetric, $i.e.$, $P_{ij} = P_{ji}^T$, then Π is symmetric as well. However, as in all quadratic problem, Π (and thus P_{ij}) can be made symmetric without affecting the result.

Our proposal is to relax this to the problem

$$\text{maximize } \mathbf{x}^T \Pi \mathbf{x}$$
$$\text{s.t.} \quad \mathbf{x} \in (S_n)^N \quad (6)$$

where S_n is the unit sphere in $\mathbb{R}^n$, and then project the solution to $(\Sigma_n)^N$ in order to obtain the alignment matrices S_i (which differs from the Q_I seen before since we are working on a relaxed space) and, consequently, the transitive permutation matrices $\overline{P}_{ij} = S_i S_j^T$.

We solve 6 efficiently through a power iteration projected to $(S_n)^N$ by noting that the gradient of the quadratic form can be computed in terms of multiplications and additions of the matching and alignment matrices:

$$\Pi \mathbf{x} = \begin{pmatrix} I \otimes P_{11} & I \otimes P_{12} & \dots & I \otimes P_{1N} \\ I \otimes P_{21} & I \otimes P_{22} & \dots & I \otimes P_{2N} \\ \vdots & \vdots & \ddots & \vdots \\ I \otimes P_{N1} & I \otimes P_{N2} & \dots & I \otimes P_{NN} \end{pmatrix} \begin{pmatrix} \mathbf{x}_1 \\ \mathbf{x}_2 \\ \vdots \\ \mathbf{x}_N \end{pmatrix}$$

$$= \begin{pmatrix} \sum_{i=1}^N P_{1i}X_i \\ \sum_{i=1}^N P_{2i}X_i \\ \vdots \\ \sum_{i=1}^N P_{Ni}X_i \end{pmatrix}, \quad (7)$$

where $\mathbf{x}^T = (\mathbf{x}_1^T, \dots, \mathbf{x}_N^T)^T$ expresses the N spherical components of $\mathbf{x}$, and X_i is the matrix representing the current relaxation of Q_i, for which we have $\mathbf{x}_i = \text{vec}(X_i)$.

Hence, we can maximize 6 by iterating the recurrence

$$X_i^{(t+1)} = \frac{\sum_{j=1}^N P_{ij}X_j^{(t)}}{||\sum_{j=1}^N P_{ij}X_j^{(t)}||_2} \quad (8)$$

Once the matrices X_i are at hand, we obtain the closest (in the least square sense) permutations Q_i by solving N maximum bipartite assignment problems.

3 Transitive Assignment Kernel

With transitive matches to hand, we follow Fröhlich et al. [25] in the definition of an assignment kernel between graphs $G_i = (V_i, E_i)$ and $G_j = (V_j, E_j)$: we define two sets of kernels, one $K_v : V_i \times V_j \to \mathbb{R}$ for the vertices, and one $K_e : V_i^2 \times V_j^2 \to \mathbb{R}$ for the edges and fuse them with the transitive correspondence $\pi_{ij} : V_i \to V_j$ encoded in $\overline{P}_{ij}$, to obtain the *Transitive Assignment Kernel*:

$$\mathrm{TAK}(G_i, G_j) = \sum_{v \in V_i} K_v\big(v, \pi_{ij}(v)\big) + \sum_{v \in V_i} \sum_{w \in V_i} K_e\big((v, w), (\pi_{ij}(v), \pi_{ij}(w))\big) \quad (9)$$

Here, both kernels are assumed to be positive semidefinite and symmetric. In our experiments we used the dot product between Heat Kernel Signatures [36] (HKS) for the vertex kernel K_v. More precisely, given an undirected graph G of n nodes, let $A = (a_{ij})$ the $n \times n$ adjacency matrix (where a_{ij} is the weight of the edge between the nodes i and j in G) and D the degree matrix, we compute the related $n \times n$ Laplacian matrix L as

$$L = D - A$$

Let ϕ_i the i-th eigenvector of L (with $i = 1, \ldots, n$) and $\Lambda = (\lambda_1, \lambda_2, \ldots, \lambda_n)^T$ the eigenvalues of the Laplacian. Finally, let m be a set of time values $\{t_1, t_2, \ldots, t_m\}$. We define the HKS feature vector $f = (f_1, f_2, \ldots, f_m)^T$ as

$$f_j = \sum_{k=1}^{n} \exp(-t_j \lambda_k) \phi_k^2$$

Once computed, the feature vectors are collected on a $n \times m$ matrix F as columns

$$F = (f_1, f_2, \cdots, f_m)$$

Given two graph G^i and G^j (with the same number of nodes n), our HKS kernel is defined as the sum of the dot product between the respective feature matrices $k = F_i \cdot F_j = (k_1, k_2, \ldots, k_n)^T$. Hence, the kernel matrix is defined as

$$K_v(G^i, G^j) = \sum_{w=1}^{n} k_w$$

On the other hand, the edge kernel K_e was chosen to be a discrete enforcement of the topological structure:

$$K_e\big((u, v), (a, b)\big) = \begin{cases} 1 & \text{if } \big((u, w) \in E_i \wedge (a, b) \in E_j\big) \vee \big((u, w) \notin E_i \wedge (a, b) \notin E_j\big) \\ 0 & \text{otherwise.} \end{cases}$$

$$(10)$$

The positive semidefiniteness of the proposed kernel can be proved through the closure properties of positive definite functions. The closure under sum states that, given a non-empty set X and two positive semidefinite symmetric kernels $K_A, K_B : X \times X \to \mathbb{R}$, it holds

$$K = K_A + K_B : X \times X \to \mathbb{R} \tag{11}$$

Then, K is a positive semidefinite symmetric kernel. In other words, in order to construct a new positive semidefinite kernel as the sum of existing ones (K_v and K_e in our instance), first the kernels need to be positive semidefinite. Second, they all must be defined in the same space. The kernels employed in 9 are positive semidefinite by hypothesis. Furthermore, since the projection on the transitive alignment space introduces a reference canonical order (and such canonical ordering is guaranteed by the transitivity constraints, see Sect. 2), the space of the kernels is the same. In fact, the kernels defined as the sum of all K_vs (K_A) and the sum of all K_es (K_B) are clearly positive semidefinite since all K_vs and all K_es belong to the same respective spaces. Hence, the kernel defined in 9 is positive semidefinite. Note that without the transitive alignment and its induced canonical ordering, the assumption that all K_vs and K_es belong to the same respective spaces would be wrong.

4   Experimental Evaluation

We evaluate the performance of the proposed method in terms of classification accuracy and we compare it with a number of well-known kernels, namely the Weisfeiler-Lehman kernel [37] (where the number of iterations parameter was set to $h = 3$ and we used the degree of each node as the node attribute), the graphlet kernel [38], the shortest-path kernel [39], the random walk kernel [14] and an experimental kernel based on the Heat Kernel Signature [36] method. In particular, we employ the Heat Kernel Signature to compute the feature descriptors with respect to $k = 100$ time parameters t uniformly distributed within the range $[1, 10]$ and we build the kernel as described in Sect. 3.

Furthermore, we compare the performance of the proposed method with respect to the state-of-the-art of graph matching methods, namely the Spectral Matching (SM) [40] and Reweighted Random Walks Matching (RRWM) [41]. In order to do so, we address the classification task using several popular datasets with and without the permutations computed by the graph matching methods.

Given a pair of graphs (G^p, G^q) with the same number of nodes n, we compute the $n^2 \times n^2$ affinity matrix $M_{pq} = (m_{ia,jb})$ as

$$m_{ia,jb} = \exp\left(-\frac{(a_{ij}^p - a_{ab}^q)^2}{\sigma^2} \right)$$

where σ^2 is a scale factor which is experimentally set to 0.15. This affinity matrix is employed as the input of one of the graph matching technique (GM) introduced above (SM and RRWM), obtaining the $n \times n$ weight matrix $W_{pq} = \mathrm{GM}(M_{pq})$. Note that the number of nodes of the graphs G^p and G^q are not required to be same, since if they are different, we will just add some disconnected dummy nodes in order to make the number of the nodes equal, as explained in Sect. 2. Finally, we use the real matrix W_{pq} as the input for the Hungarian algorithm, which is a well-known method that performs a combinatorial optimization finding a maximum weight matching in a weighted bipartite graph. This results in a discretized version of the weight matrix, which is, in practice, a permutation matrix. Hence, we define the permutation matrix P_{pq} as

$$P_{pq} = \text{Hungarian}(W_{pq})$$

We run our experiments on the following datasets:

MUTAG dataset [42] was constructed based on data from review of literatures about mutagenicities in *Salmonella Typhimurium* based on 200 aromatic and heteroaromatic nitro compounds. As a result, 188 congeners were extracted together with their structure-activity relationship (SAR) data.

PPI dataset, which consists of protein-protein interaction (PPIs) networks related to histidine kinase [43] (40 PPIs from *Acidovorax avenae* and 46 PPIs from *Acidobacteria*).

PTC (The Predictive Toxicology Challenge) dataset, which records the carcinogenicity of several hundred chemical compounds for male rats (MR), female rats (FR), male mice (MM) and female mice (FM) [44] (here we use the 344 graphs in the MR class).

COIL dataset, which consists of 5 objects from [45], each with 72 views obtained from equally spaced viewing directions, where for each view a graph was built by triangulating the extracted Harris corner points.

Reeb dataset, which consists of a set of adjacency matrices associated to the computation of reeb graphs of 3D shapes [46].

ENZYMES dataset [47] is based on graphs representing protein tertiary structures consisting of 600 enzymes from the BRENDA enzyme database, which are correctly assigned to one of the 6 EC top-level classes.

SHOCK dataset consists of graphs from the Shock 2D shape database. Each graph of the 150 graphs divided into 10 classes is a skeletal-based representation of the differential structure of the boundary of a 2D shape.

For efficiency purposes, the experiments do not involve the whole datasets. In particular, we select a certain number of classes and a certain number of graphs for each class. The selection of these subsets is performed randomly on the original datasets. Table 1 shows the number of classes and the number of graphs of each dataset that has been used to compute the results. In order to get an homogeneous number of nodes within the graphs of the same dataset, we add to each graph $n_{MAX} - n_i$ dummy nodes (*i.e.* not connected nodes), where n_{MAX} is the maximum number of nodes among the graphs of a certain dataset, while n_i is the number of nodes of the i-th graph.

We used a binary C-SVM to test the efficacy of the kernels. We performed 10-fold cross validation, where for each sample we independently tune the value of C, the SVM regularizer constant, by considering the training data from that sample. The process was averaged over 100 random partitions of the data, and the results are reported in terms of average accuracy $\pm$ standard error. In particular, at

Table 1. Details of the datasets.

Dataset name	Classes	Graphs per class	Total Graphs	Graph nodes
MUTAG	2	≈94	188	28
PPI	2	20	40	161
PTC	2	30	60	70
COIL	3	20	60	112
Reeb	3	20	60	86
ENZYMES	3	20	60	26
SHOCK	10	15	150	33

each 10-fold cross validation iteration, the dataset is randomly permuted and subdivided in 10 folds. Every fold is used as a crossvalidation fold, while the remaining are use to train the SVM. The process is repeated 100 times. Finally, we define the standard error as

$$\hat{\sigma}_X = \sqrt{n} \cdot \sqrt{\frac{\sum_{i=1}^{n}(x - \bar{x})^2}{n}} = \sqrt{\sum_{i=1}^{n}(x - \bar{x})^2}$$

where $\bar{x}$ is the mean accuracy obtained in a crossvalidation iteration with n samples $X = \{x_1, x_2, \ldots, x_n\}$.

Table 2 shows the average classification accuracy (± standard error) of the different kernels on the selected datasets. The first part of the table shows the accuracy computed using the datasets after the pruning operation mentioned before. The second part of the table (after the double line) shows the classification accuracy achieved after the application of the permutations yielded by the compared graph matching methods. More precisely, given $\mathbf{P}_{ij}$ the permutation matrix which defines the correspondences of the graph i with respect to graph j, we compute the value of the kernel between the permuted graph i and the graph j. In particular, HKS-SM shows the classification accuracy obtained permuting the graphs using the Spectral Matching results, while HKS-TSM shows the results obtained using the proposed method which has been initialized using Spectral Matching. The results show that the proposed method is competitive and outperform the other graph matching algorithms in almost all the datasets. COIL and PTC datasets are an exception, since HKS-RRWM performs slightly better with respect to our proposal. Note that the first part of the table should be treated by the reader just as a reference of the accuracies that the current state-of-the-art kernel methods achieve. Indeed, these kernels work independently from the alignment of the graphs to be classified. The main goal of the experimental results is the comparison between the proposed alignment method with respect to the compared ones, namely Spectral Matching and Reweighted Random Walks Matching. In particular, we want to show the performance achieved by the current state-of-the-art in graph matching methods with respect to the transitive approach we are presenting.

Table 2. Classification accuracy (± standard error) on unattributed graph datasets. Respectively, HKS is the Heat Kernel Signature [36], WL is the Weisfeiler-Lehman kernel [37], GR denotes the graphlet kernel computed using all graphlets of size 3 [38], SP is the shortest-path kernel [39], and RW is the random walk kernel [14]. The second part of the table collects the accuracy of HKS kernel employing the permutations from Spectral Matching (SM) [40] and Reweighted Random Walks Matching (RRWM) [41] with respect to the transitive versions produced by our method (denoted by the prefix T). For each kernel and dataset, the best performing kernel is highlighted in italic, while the bold highlights the maximum just considering data in the second part of the table for each pair of graph matchings (non transitive w.r.t. transitive).

Kernel	MUTAG	PPI	PTC	COIL	Reeb	ENZYMES	SHOCK
HKS	80.5 ± 0.2	63.6 ± 0.7	50.2 ± 0.5	*87.8 ± 0.8*	46.6 ± 0.6	56.9 ± 0.6	*46.8 ± 0.3*
WL	78.3 ± 0.2	*70.4 ± 0.8*	*67.1 ± 0.6*	70.6 ± 0.7	*68.7 ± 0.4*	55.4 ± 0.6	35.0 ± 0.2
SP	*83.3 ± 0.2*	58.5 ± 0.7	50.5 ± 0.6	86.7 ± 0.6	68.1 ± 0.4	52.2 ± 0.5	39.0 ± 0.3
RW	80.1 ± 0.2	48.5 ± 0.8	41.6 ± 0.6	65.2 ± 0.7	49.8 ± 0.6	13.6 ± 0.3	1.7 ± 0.1
GR	81.5 ± 0.2	30.3 ± 0.5	51.6 ± 0.6	87.1 ± 0.5	22.7 ± 0.6	47.0 ± 0.6	26.1 ± 0.3
HKS-SM	69.0 ± 0.3	60.9 ± 0.8	49.4 ± 0.6	84.8 ± 1.0	45.7 ± 0.6	49.1 ± 0.6	39.4 ± 0.4
HKS-TSM	**80.7 ± 0.2**	64.2 ± 0.8	**50.1 ± 0.6**	87.0 ± 0.9	46.2 ± 0.5	*57.2 ± 0.7*	**46.7 ± 0.3**
HKS-RRWM	79.8 ± 0.2	60.4 ± 0.9	**52.1 ± 0.5**	**87.3 ± 0.9**	44.5 ± 0.6	44.9 ± 0.6	25.7 ± 0.2
HKS-TRRWM	**80.5 ± 0.2**	**64.3 ± 0.8**	50.9 ± 0.5	86.1 ± 0.9	**44.8 ± 0.6**	45.5 ± 0.6	46.4 ± 0.3

5   Conclusion

In this paper we investigated the use of multi-graph matching techniques in the context of graph kernels. By forcing the correspondences between the structures under study to satisfy transitivity, we obtain an alignment kernel that, not only is positive definite, but also makes use of more reliable locational information obtained through the enforcement of global consistency constraints. We proposed a general framework for the projection of (relaxed) correspondences onto the space of transitive correspondences, thus transforming any given matching algorithm to a transitive multi-graph matching approach. The resulting transitive correspondences where used to provide an alignment-based kernel that was able to both maintain locational information and guarantee positive-definiteness. Experimental evaluation shows that the projection onto the transitive space almost invariably increases the classification performance of the alignment kernel, often taking it to a performance level that is at least statistically equivalent to the best performing well-tuned graph kernels present in the literature.

References

1. Siddiqi, K., Shokoufandeh, A., Dickinson, S., Zucker, S.: Shock graphs and shape matching. Int. J. Comput. Vis. **35**, 13–32 (1999)
2. Jeong, H., Tombor, B., Albert, R., Oltvai, Z., Barabási, A.: The large-scale organization of metabolic networks. Nature **407**, 651–654 (2000)
3. Ito, T., Chiba, T., Ozawa, R., Yoshida, M., Hattori, M., Sakaki, Y.: A comprehensive two-hybrid analysis to explore the yeast protein interactome. Proc. Natl. Acad. Sci. **98**, 4569 (2001)

4. Kalapala, V., Sanwalani, V., Moore, C.: The structure of the united states road network. Preprint, University of New Mexico (2003)
5. Conte, D., Foggia, P., Sansone, C., Vento, M.: Thirty years of graph matching in pattern recognition. IJPRAI **18**, 265–298 (2004)
6. Luo, B., Wilson, R.C., Hancock, E.R.: Spectral embedding of graphs. Pattern Recogn. **36**, 2213–2230 (2003)
7. Wilson, R.C., Hancock, E.R., Luo, B.: Pattern vectors from algebraic graph theory. IEEE Trans. Pattern Anal. Mach. Intell. **27**, 1112–1124 (2005)
8. Gasparetto, A., Minello, G., Torsello, A.: A non-parametric spectral model for graph classification. In: Proceedings of the International Conference on Pattern Recognition Applications and Methods, pp. 312–319 (2015)
9. Torsello, A., Gasparetto, A., Rossi, L., Bai, L., Hancock, E.R.: Transitive state alignment for the quantum Jensen-Shannon kernel. In: Fränti, P., Brown, G., Loog, M., Escolano, F., Pelillo, M. (eds.) S+SSPR 2014. LNCS, vol. 8621, pp. 22–31. Springer, Heidelberg (2014)
10. Livi, L., Rizzi, A.: The graph matching problem. Pattern Anal. Appl. **16**, 253–283 (2013)
11. Scholkopf, B., Smola, A.J.: Learning with Kernels: Support Vector Machines, Regularization, Optimization, and Beyond. MIT Press, Cambridge (2001)
12. Gärtner, T., Flach, P.A., Wrobel, S.: On graph kernels: hardness results and efficient alternatives. In: Schölkopf, B., Warmuth, M.K. (eds.) COLT/Kernel 2003. LNCS (LNAI), vol. 2777, pp. 129–143. Springer, Heidelberg (2003)
13. Haussler, D.: Convolution kernels on discrete structures. Technical Report UCS-CRL-99-10, University of California at Santa Cruz, Santa Cruz, CA, USA (1999)
14. Kashima, H., Tsuda, K., Inokuchi, A.: Marginalized kernels between labeled graphs. In: ICML, pp. 321–328 (2003)
15. Borgwardt, K.M., Kriegel, H.P.: Shortest-path kernels on graphs. In: Proceedings of the Fifth IEEE International Conference on Data Mining (ICDM 2005), Washington, DC, USA, pp. 74–81. IEEE Computer Society (2005)
16. Shervashidze, N., Schweitzer, P., van Leeuwen, E.J., Mehlhorn, K., Borgwardt, K.M.: Weisfeiler-lehman graph kernels. J. Mach. Learn. Res. **12**, 2539–2561 (2011)
17. Kriege, N., Mutzel, P.: Subgraph matching kernels for attributed graphs. In: ICML. icml.cc/Omnipress (2012)
18. Neumann, M., Patricia, N., Garnett, R., Kersting, K.: Efficient graph kernels by randomization. In: Flach, P.A., De Bie, T., Cristianini, N. (eds.) ECML PKDD 2012, Part I. LNCS, vol. 7523, pp. 378–393. Springer, Heidelberg (2012)
19. Ong, C.S., Canu, S., Smola, A.J.: Learning with non-positive kernels. In: Proceedings of the 21st International Conference on Machine Learning (ICML), pp. 639–646 (2004)
20. Jain, B.J., Geibel, Wysotzki, F.: SVM learning with the SH inner product. In: 12th European Symposium on Artificial Neural Networks, Bruges, Belgium
21. Jain, B.J., Geibel, P., Wysotzki, F.: SVM learning with the Schur-Hadamard inner product for graphs. Neurocomputing **64**, 93–105 (2005)
22. Schietgat, L., Ramon, J., Bruynooghe, M., Blockeel, H.: An efficiently computable graph-based metric for the classification of small molecules. In: Boulicaut, J.-F., Berthold, M.R., Horváth, T. (eds.) DS 2008. LNCS (LNAI), vol. 5255, pp. 197–209. Springer, Heidelberg (2008)
23. Mohr, J., Jain, B.J., Sutter, A., ter Laak, A., Steger-Hartmann, T., Heinrich, N., Obermayer, K.: A maximum common subgraph kernel method for predicting the chromosome aberration test. J. Chem. Inf. Model. **50**, 1821–1838 (2010)

24. Hochreiter, S., Obermayer, K.: Support vector machines for dyadic data. Neural Comput. **18**, 1472–1510 (2006)
25. Fröhlich, H., Wegner, J.K., Sieker, F., Zell, A.: Optimal assignment kernels for attributed molecular graphs. In: de Raedt, L., Wrobel, S. (eds.) Proceedings of the 22nd International Conference on Machine Learning (ICML 2005), pp. 225–232. ACM Press, Bonn (2005)
26. Neuhaus, M., Bunke, H.: Edit distance-based kernel functions for structural pattern classification. Pattern Recogn. **39**, 1852–1863 (2006)
27. Vert, J.P.: The optimal assignment kernel is not positive definite. CoRR abs/0801.4061 (2008)
28. Williams, M.L., Wilson, R.C., Hancock, E.R.: Multiple graph matching with bayesian inference. Pattern Recogn. Lett. **18**, 080 (1997)
29. Solé-Ribalta, A., Serratosa, F.: Models and algorithms for computing the common labelling of a set of attributed graphs. Comput. Vis. Image Underst. **115**, 929–945 (2011)
30. Gold, S., Rangarajan, A.: A graduated assignment algorithm for graph matching. IEEE Trans. Pattern Anal. Mach. Intell. **18**, 377–388 (1996)
31. Yan, J., Tian, Y., Zha, H., Yang, X., Zhang, Y., Chu, S.M.: Joint optimization for consistent multiple graph matching. In: Proceedings of the 2013 IEEE International Conference on Computer Vision, ICCV 2013, Washington, DC, USA, pp. 1649–1656. IEEE Computer Society (2013)
32. Yan, J., Wang, J., Zha, H., Yang, X., Chu, S.: Consistency-driven alternating optimization for multigraph matching: a unified approach. IEEE Trans. Image Process. **24**, 994–1009 (2015)
33. Pachauri, D., Kondor, R., Singh, V.: Solving the multi-way matching problem by permutation synchronization. In: Burges, C.J.C., Bottou, L., Ghahramani, Z., Weinberger, K.Q. (eds.) NIPS, pp. 1860–1868 (2013)
34. Torsello, A., Rodolà, E., Albarelli, A.: Multiview registration via graph diffusion of dual quaternions. In: The 24th IEEE Conference on Computer Vision and Pattern Recognition, CVPR 2011, Colorado Springs, CO, USA, 20–25 June 2011, pp. 2441–2448. IEEE Computer Society (2011)
35. Hartley, R.I., Trumpf, J., Dai, Y., Li, H.: Rotation averaging. Int. J. Comput. Vis. **103**, 267–305 (2013)
36. Sun, J., Ovsjanikov, M., Guibas, L.: A concise and provably informative multi-scale signature based on heat diffusion. In: Proceedings of the Symposium on Geometry Processing, SGP 2009, Aire-la-Ville, Switzerland, Switzerland, pp. 1383–1392. Eurographics Association (2009)
37. Shervashidze, N., Schweitzer, P., van Leeuwen, E.J., Mehlhorn, K., Borgwardt, K.M.: Weisfeiler-Lehman graph kernels. J. Mach. Learn. Res. **12**, 2539–2561 (2011)
38. Shervashidze, N., Vishwanathan, S., Petri, T., Mehlhorn, K., Borgwardt, K.: Efficient graphlet kernels for large graph comparison. In: Proceedings of the International Workshop on Artificial Intelligence and Statistics (2009)
39. Borgwardt, K.M., peter Kriegel, H.: Shortest-path kernels on graphs. In: Proceedings of the 2005 International Conference on Data Mining, pp. 74–81 (2005)
40. Leordeanu, M., Hebert, M.: A spectral technique for correspondence problems using pairwise constraints. In: Tenth IEEE International Conference on Computer Vision, 2005, ICCV 2005, vol. 2, pp. 1482–1489 (2005)
41. Cho, M., Lee, J., Lee, K.M.: Reweighted random walks for graph matching. In: Daniilidis, K., Maragos, P., Paragios, N. (eds.) ECCV 2010, Part V. LNCS, vol. 6315, pp. 492–505. Springer, Heidelberg (2010)

42. Debnath, A.K., de Com-padre, R.L.L., Debnath, G., Schusterman, A.J., Hansch, C.: Structure-activity relationship of mutagenic aromatic and heteroaromatic nitro compounds. correlation with molecular orbital energies and hydrophobicity. Med. Chem. **34**, 786–797 (1991)

43. Jensen, L.J., Kuhn, M., Stark, M., Chaffron, S., Creevey, C., Muller, J., Doerks, T., Julien, P., Roth, A., Simonovic, M., et al.: String 8a global view on proteins and their functional interactions in 630 organisms. Nucleic Acids Res. **37**, D412–D416 (2009)

44. Li, G., Semerci, M., Yener, B., Zaki, M.J.: Effective graph classification based on topological and label attributes. Stat. Anal. Data Min. **5**, 265–283 (2012)

45. Nene, S.A., Nayar, S.K., Murase, H.: Columbia object image library (COIL-20). Technical report, Department of Computer Science, Columbia University, New York (1996)

46. Biasotti, S., Marini, S., Mortara, M., Patané, G., Spagnuolo, M., Falcidieno, B.: 3D shape matching through topological structures. In: Nyström, I., Sanniti di Baja, G., Svensson, S. (eds.) DGCI 2003. LNCS, vol. 2886, pp. 194–203. Springer, Heidelberg (2003)

47. Schomburg, I., Chang, A., Ebeling, C., Gremse, M., Heldt, C., Huhn, G., Schomburg, D.: Brenda, the enzyme database: updates and major new developments. Nucleic Acids Res. **32**, D431–D433 (2004)

Large Scale Indefinite Kernel Fisher Discriminant

Frank-Michael Schleif[1]($\boxtimes$), Andrej Gisbrecht[2], and Peter Tino[1]

[1] School of Computer Science, University of Birmingham, Birmingham B15 2TT, UK
{schleify,pxt}@cs.bham.ac.uk
[2] CITEC Centre of Excellence, Bielefeld University, 33615 Bielefeld, Germany
agisbrec@techfak.uni-bielefeld.de

Abstract. Indefinite similarity measures can be frequently found in bioinformatics by means of alignment scores. Lacking an underlying vector space, the data are given as pairwise similarities only. Indefinite Kernel Fisher Discriminant (iKFD) is a very effective classifier for this type of data but has cubic complexity and does not scale to larger problems. Here we propose an extension of iKFD such that linear runtime and memory complexity is achieved for low rank indefinite kernels. Evaluation at several larger similarity data from various domains shows that the proposed method provides similar generalization capabilities while being substantially faster for large scale data.

1 Introduction

Domain specific proximity measures, like alignment scores in bioinformatics [19], the modified Hausdorff-distance for structural pattern recognition [7], shape retrieval measures like the inner distance [12] and many other ones generate non-metric or indefinite similarities or dissimilarities. Classical learning algorithms like kernel machines assume Euclidean metric properties in the underlying data space and may not be applicable for this type of data.

Only few machine learning methods have been proposed for non-metric proximity data, like the indefinite kernel Fisher discriminant (iKFD) [11,15], the probabilistic classification vector machine (PCVM) [3] or the indefinite Support Vector Machine (iSVM) [1,10]. In contrast to the iKFD the PCVM is a *sparse* probabilistic kernel classifier pruning unused basis functions during training, applicable to arbitrary positive definite *and* indefinite kernel matrices. A recent review about learning with indefinite proximities can be found in [18].

While being very efficient these methods do not scale to larger datasets with in general cubic complexity. In [9,16] the authors proposed a few Nyström based [20] approximation techniques to improve the scalability of the PCVM for low rank matrices. The suggested techniques use the Nyström approximation in a non-trivial way to provide *exact* eigenvalue estimations also for *indefinite* kernel matrices. This approach is very generic and can be applied in different algorithms. In this contribution we show this for an approximation of the indefinite kernel Fisher discriminant. The obtained Ny-iKFD approach is linear in runtime

© Springer International Publishing Switzerland 2015
A. Feragen et al. (Eds.): SIMBAD 2015, LNCS 9370, pp. 160–170, 2015.
DOI: 10.1007/978-3-319-24261-3_13

and memory consumption for low rank matrices. The formulation is exact if the rank of the matrix equals the number of independent landmarks points.

First we review iKFD and PCVM as well as some approximation concepts proposed by the authors in [16]. Subsequently we reformulate iKFD based on the introduced concepts and show the efficiency in comparison to PCVM and Ny-PCVM for various indefinite proximity benchmark data sets.

2   Indefinite Fisher and Kernel Quadratic Discriminant

In [11,15] the indefinite kernel Fisher discriminant analysis (iKFD) and indefinite kernel quadratic discriminant analysis (iKQD) was proposed focusing on binary classification problems, recently extended by a weighting scheme in [21][1].

The initial idea is to embed the training data into a Krein space and to apply a modified kernel Fisher discriminant analysis or kernel quadratic discriminant analysis for indefinite kernels. Consider binary classification and a data set of input-target training pairs $D = \{\mathbf{x}_i, y_i\}_{i=1}^{N}$, where $y_i \in \{-1, +1\}$. Given the indefinite kernel matrix K and the embedded data in a pseudo-Euclidean space (pE), the linear Fisher Discriminant function $f(x) = \langle w, \Phi(\mathbf{x}) \rangle_{pE} + b$ is based on a weight vector $\mathbf{w}$ such that the between-class scatter is maximized while the within-class scatter is minimized along w. $\Phi(\mathbf{x})$ is a vector of basis function evaluations for data item $\mathbf{x}$ and b is a bias term. This direction is obtained by maximizing the Fisher criterion in the pseudo Euclidean space

$$J(\mathbf{w}) = \frac{\langle \mathbf{w}, \Sigma_{pE}^{b} \mathbf{w} \rangle_{pE}}{\langle \mathbf{w}, \Sigma_{pE}^{w} \mathbf{w} \rangle_{pE}}$$

where $\Sigma_{pE}^{b} = \Sigma_b J$ is the pseudo Euclidean between scatter matrix, with $J = diag(1_p, -1_q)$ where $1_p \in \mathbb{R}^p$ denotes the p-dimensional vector of all ones. The number of positive eigenvalues is denoted by p and for the negative eigenvalues by q. The within scatter matrix in the pseudo-Euclidean space is given as $\Sigma_{pE}^{w} = \Sigma_w J$. The used *Euclidean* between and within scatter matrices can be expressed as:

$$\Sigma_b = (\mu_+ - \mu_-)(\mu_+ - \mu_-)^{\top} \tag{1}$$

$$\Sigma_w = \sum_{i \in I_+} (\phi(\mathbf{x}_i) - \mu_+)(\phi(\mathbf{x}_i) - \mu_+)^{\top} + \sum_{i \in I_-} (\phi(\mathbf{x}_i) - \mu_-)(\phi(\mathbf{x}_i) - \mu_-)^{\top} \tag{2}$$

where the set of indices of each class are $I_+ := \{i : y_i = +1\}$ and $I_- := \{i : y_i = 1\}$. In [11] it is shown that the Fisher Discriminant in the pE space $\in \mathbb{R}^{(p,q)}$ is identical to the Fisher Discriminant in the associated Euclidean space $\mathbb{R}^{p+q}$. To avoid the explicit embedding into the pE space a kernelization is considered such that the weight vector $w \in \mathbb{R}^{p,q}$ is expressed as a linear combination of the training data $\phi(\mathbf{x}_i)$, hence $w = \sum_{i=1}^{N} \alpha_i \phi(\mathbf{x}_i)$. Transferred to the Fisher criterion this allows to use the kernel trick. A similar strategy can be used for KQD as well as the indefinite kernel PCA.

---

[1] For multiclass problems a classical 1 vs rest wrapper is used within this paper.

3   Probabilistic Classification Vector Learning

PCVM uses a kernel regression model $\sum_{i=1}^{N} w_i \phi_i(\mathbf{x}) + b$ with a link function, with w_i being again the weights of the basis functions $\phi_i(\mathbf{x})$ and b as a bias term. The Expectation Maximization (EM) implementation of PCVM [4] uses the probit link function, i.e. $\Psi(x) = \int_{-\infty}^{x} \mathcal{N}(t|0,1)dt$, where $\Psi(x)$ is the cumulative distribution of the normal distribution $\mathcal{N}(0,1)$. We get: $l(\mathbf{x}; \mathbf{w}, b) = \Psi\left(\sum_{i=1}^{N} w_i \phi_i(\mathbf{x}) + b\right) = \Psi\left(\Phi(\mathbf{x})\mathbf{w} + b\right)$.

In the PCVM formulation [3], a truncated Gaussian prior N_t with support on $[0, \infty)$ and mode at 0 is introduced for each weight w_i and a zero-mean Gaussian prior is adopted for the bias b. The priors are assumed to be mutually independent. $p(\mathbf{w}|\alpha) = \prod_{i=1}^{N} p(w_i|\alpha_i) = \prod_{i=1}^{N} N_t(w_i|0, \alpha_i^{-1})$, $\quad p(b|\beta) = \mathcal{N}(b|0, \beta^{-1})$, $\delta(\cdot) = \mathbf{1}_{x>0}(x)$.

$$p(w_i|\alpha_i) = \begin{cases} 2\mathcal{N}(w_i|0, \alpha_i^{-1}) & \text{if } y_i w_i > 0 \\ 0 & \text{otherwise} \end{cases} = 2\mathcal{N}(w_i|0, \alpha_i^{-1}) \cdot \delta(y_i w_i).$$

We follow the standard probabilistic formulation and assume that $z(\mathbf{x}) = \Phi(\mathbf{x})\mathbf{w} + b$ is corrupted by an additive random noise ϵ, where $\epsilon \sim \mathcal{N}(0,1)$. According to the probit link model, we have:

$$h(\mathbf{x}) = \Phi(\mathbf{x})\mathbf{w} + b + \epsilon \geq 0, y = 1, \quad h(\mathbf{x}) = \Phi(\mathbf{x})\mathbf{w} + b + \epsilon < 0, y = -1 \quad (3)$$

and obtain: $p(y = 1|\mathbf{x}, \mathbf{w}, b) = p(\Phi(\mathbf{x})\mathbf{w} + b + \epsilon \geq 0) = \Psi(\Phi(\mathbf{x})\mathbf{w} + b)$. $h(\mathbf{x})$ is a latent variable because ϵ is an unobservable variable. We collect evaluations of $h(\mathbf{x})$ at training points in a vector $\mathbf{H}(\mathbf{x}) = (h(\mathbf{x_1}), \ldots, h(\mathbf{x_N}))^{\top}$. In the expectation step the expected value $\bar{\mathbf{H}}$ of $\mathbf{H}$ with respect to the posterior distribution over the latent variables is calculated (given old values $\mathbf{w}^{\text{old}}, b^{\text{old}}$). In the maximization step the parameters are updated through

$$\mathbf{w}^{\text{new}} = M(M\Phi^{\top}(\mathbf{x})\Phi(\mathbf{x})M + I_N)^{-1} M(\Phi^{\top}(\mathbf{x})\bar{\mathbf{H}} - b\Phi^{\top}(\mathbf{x})\mathbf{I}) \quad (4)$$

$$\mathbf{b}^{\text{new}} = t(1 + tNt)^{-1}t(\mathbf{I}^{\top}\bar{\mathbf{H}} - \mathbf{I}^{\top}\Phi(\mathbf{x})\mathbf{w}) \quad (5)$$

where I_N is a N-dimensional identity matrix and $\mathbf{I}$ a all-ones vector, the diagonal elements in the diagonal matrix M are:

$$m_i = (\bar{\alpha}_i)^{-1/2} = \begin{cases} \sqrt{2}w_i & \text{if } y_i w_i \geq 0 \\ 0 & \text{else} \end{cases} \quad (6)$$

and the scalar $t = \sqrt{2}|b|$. For further details see [3].

4   Nyström Approximation

The Nyström approximation for kernel methods (details in [20]) gives:

$$\tilde{K} = K_{N,m} K_{m,m}^{-1} K_{m,N}. \quad (7)$$

Thereby m (columns/rows) of the original kernel matrix have been selected as so called landmarks and $K_{m,m}^{-1}$ denotes the Moore-Penrose pseudoinverse of this landmark matrix. The matrix $K_{N,m}$ refers to the rectangular submatrix of K containing all rows of K but only with the columns corresponding the respective landmark indices. The matrix $K_{m,N}$ is the transposed matrix of $K_{N,m}$. Strategies how to chose the landmarks have been recently been addressed in [22]. In our experiments we simply chose a reasonable large number of landmarks randomly selected from the data. The approximation is exact, if $K_{m,m}$ has the same rank as K. In [16] the authors have shown how the PCVM can be modified such that a linear complexity method is obtained. Beside using the standard Nyström approximation to approximate a kernel matrix as shown in Eq. (7) especially a linear time eigenvalue correction for (potentially indefinite) low rank matrices was proposed. This low rank eigenvalue decomposition is used in PCVM to approximate the Hessian matrix in the EM parameter optimization steps. While we will not review the specific steps for PCVM we review subsequently the necessary components which we can apply to iKFD.

4.1 Pseudo Inverse, SVD and EVD of a Nyström Approximated Matrix

In the Ny-PCVM approach we need the pseudo inverse of a Nyström approximated matrix while for the Ny-iKFD a Nyström approximated eigenvalue decomposition (EVD) is needed.

A Nyström approximated pseudo inverse can be calculated by a modified singular value decomposition (SVD) with a rank limited by $r^* = \min\{r, m\}$ where r is the rank of the pseudo inverse and m the number of landmark points. The output is given by the rank reduced left and right singular vectors and the reciprocal of the singular values. The singular value decomposition based on a Nyström approximated similarity matrix $\tilde{K} = K_{Nm}K_{m,m}^{-1}K_{Nm}^{\top}$ with m landmarks, calculates the left singular vectors of $\tilde{K}$ as the eigenvectors of $\tilde{K}\tilde{K}^{\top}$ and the right singular vectors of $\tilde{K}$ as the eigenvectors of $\tilde{K}^{\top}\tilde{K}^2$. The non-zero singular values of $\tilde{K}$ are then found as the square roots of the non-zero eigenvalues of both $\tilde{K}^{\top}\tilde{K}$ or $\tilde{K}\tilde{K}^{\top}$. Accordingly one only has to calculate a new Nyström approximation of the matrix $\tilde{K}\tilde{K}^{\top}$ using e.g. the same landmark points as for the input matrix $\tilde{K}$. Subsequently an eigenvalue decomposition (EVD) is calculated on the approximated matrix $\zeta = \tilde{K}\tilde{K}^{\top}$. For a matrix approximated by Eq. (7) it is possible to compute its exact eigenvalue estimators in linear time.

To compute the eigenvectors and eigenvalues of an *indefinite* matrix we first compute the squared form of the Nyström approximated kernel matrix. Let K be a psd similarity matrix, for which we can write its decomposition as

$$\tilde{K} = K_{N,m}K_{m,m}^{-1}K_{m,N} = K_{N,m}U\Lambda^{-1}U^{\top}K_{N,m}^{\top} = BB^{\top},$$

where we defined $B = K_{N,m}U\Lambda^{-1/2}$ with U and Λ being the eigenvectors and eigenvalues of $K_{m,m}$, respectively.

---

[2] For symmetric matrices we have $\tilde{K}\tilde{K}^{\top} = \tilde{K}^{\top}\tilde{K}$.

Further it follows for the *squared* $\tilde{K}$:

$$\tilde{K}^2 = BB^\top BB^\top = BVAV^\top B^\top,$$

where V and A are the eigenvectors and eigenvalues of $B^\top B$, respectively. Apparently the square operation does not change the eigenvectors of K but only the eigenvalues. The corresponding eigenequation can be written as $B^\top Bv = av$. Multiplying with B from left we get: $\underbrace{BB^\top}_{\tilde{K}}\underbrace{(Bv)}_{u} = a\underbrace{(Bv)}_{u}$. It is clear that A must be the matrix with the eigenvalues of $\tilde{K}$. The matrix Bv is the matrix of the corresponding eigenvectors, which are orthogonal but not necessary orthonormal. The normalization can be computed from the decomposition:

$$\tilde{K} = B\underbrace{VV^\top}_{diag(1)}B^\top = BVA^{-1/2}AA^{-1/2}V^\top B^\top = CAC^\top,$$

where we defined $C = BVA^{-1/2}$ as the matrix of orthonormal eigenvectors of K. The eigenvalues of $\tilde{K}$ can be obtained using $A = C^\top \tilde{K}C$. Using this derivation we can obtain exact eigenvalues and eigenvectors of an indefinite low rank kernel matrix K, given rank$(K) = m$ and the landmarks points are independent.[3]

5 Nyström Based Indefinite Kernel Fisher Discriminant

Given a Nyström approximated kernel matrix a few adaptations have to be made to obtain a valid iKFD formulation solely based on the Nyström approximated kernel, without any full matrix operations.

First we need to calculate the classwise means μ_+ and μ_- based on the row/column sums of the approximated input kernel matrix. This can be done by rather simple matrix operations on the two low rank matrices of the Nyström approximation of K. For better notation let us define the matrices K_{Nm} as Ψ and K_{mm} as Υ then for each row k of the matrix K we get the row/column sum as:

$$\sum_i [\tilde{K}]_{k,i} = \sum_{l=1}^{m}\left(\sum_{j=1}^{N}\Psi_{j,\cdot}\Upsilon^{-1}\right)\Psi_{l,k}^\top \tag{8}$$

This can obviously also be done in a single matrix operation for all rows in a batch, with linear complexity only. Based on these mean estimates we can calculate Eq. (1). In a next step we need to calculate a squared approximated kernel matrix for the positive and the negative class with removed means

---

[3] An implementation of this linear time eigen-decomposition for low rank indefinite matrices is available at: http://www.techfak.uni-bielefeld.de/~fschleif/eigenvalue_corrections_demos.tgz.

μ_+ or μ_- respectively. For the positive class with n_+ entries, we can define a new Nyström approximated (squared) matrix with subtracted mean as:

$$\hat{K}_{N,m}^+ = K_{N,m} \cdot K_{m,m}^{-1} \cdot (K_{I_+,m}^\top \cdot K_{I_+,m}) \cdot K_{m,m}^{-1} \cdot K_{m,m}^\top - \mu_+ \cdot \mu_+^\top \cdot n_+ \quad (9)$$

An equivalent term can be derived for the negative class providing $\hat{K}_{N,m}^-$. It should be noted that no obtained matrix in Eq. (9) has more than $N \times m$ entries. Finally $\hat{K}_{N,m}^+$ and $\hat{K}_{N,m}^-$ are combined to approximate the within class matrix as shown in Eq. (2). From the derivation in [11] we know, that only the eigenvector of the Nyström approximated kernel matrix based on $\hat{K}_{N,m} = \hat{K}_{N,m}^+ + \hat{K}_{N,m}^-$ are needed. Using a Nyström based eigen-decomposition (explained before) on $\hat{K}_{N,m}$ we obtain:

$$\alpha = C \cdot A^{-1} \cdot (C' \cdot (\mu_+ - \mu_-))$$

where C contains the eigenvectors and A the eigenvalues of $\hat{K}_{N,m}$. Instead of A^{-1} one can use the pseudo-inverse. The bias term b is obtained as $b = -\alpha^\top(\mu_+ + \mu_-)/2$.

6 Complexity Analysis

The original iKFD update rules have costs of $\mathcal{O}(N^3)$ and memory storage $\mathcal{O}(N^2)$, where N is the number of points. The Ny-iKFD may involve the extra Nyström approximation of the kernel matrix to obtain $K_{N,m}$ and $K_{m,m}^{-1}$, if not already given. If we have m landmarks, $m \ll N$, this gives costs of $\mathcal{O}(mN)$ for the first matrix and $\mathcal{O}(m^3)$ for the second, due to the matrix inversion. Further both matrices are multiplied within the optimization so we get $\mathcal{O}(m^2N)$. Similarly, the matrix inversion of the original iKFD with $\mathcal{O}(N^3)$ is reduced to $\mathcal{O}(m^2N)+\mathcal{O}(m^3)$ due to the Nyström approximation of the pseudo-inverse. If we assume $m \ll N$ the overall runtime and memory complexity of Ny-iKFD is linear in N. For the Ny-PCVM we obtain a similar analysis as shown in [16] but with extra costs to calculate the Nyström approximated SVD. Additionally, Ny-PCVM uses an iterative optimization scheme to optimize and sparsify w with constant costs C_I and C_I as the number of iterations. Accordingly Ny-iKFD and Ny-PCVM have both linear memory and runtime complexity $\mathcal{O}(N)$, but Ny-PCVM maybe slower than Ny-iKFD due to extra overhead costs.

7 Experiments

We compare iKFD, Ny-iKFD, Ny-PCVM and PCVM on various larger indefinite proximity data. In contrast to many standard kernel approaches, for iKFD and PCVM, the indefinite kernel matrices need not to be corrected by costly eigenvalue correction [5,17].[4]

---

[4] In [18] various correction methods have been studied on the same data indicating that eigenvalue corrections may be helpful if indefiniteness can be attributed to noise.

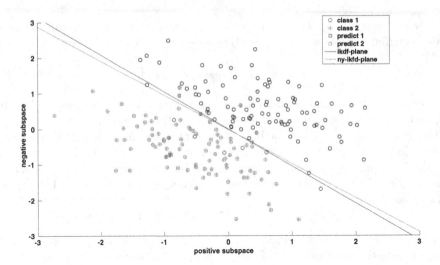

Fig. 1. Visualization of the indefinite Fisher kernel for two Gaussians in a two-dimensional pseudo-Euclidean space $\mathbb{R}^{(1,1)}$. The predicted labels are with respect to the iKFD classification.

Further the iKFD and PCVM provides direct access to probabilistic classification decisions. First we show a small simulated experiment for two Gaussians which exist in an intrinsically two dimensional pseudo-Euclidean space $\mathbb{R}^{(1,1)}$. The plot in Fig. 1 shows a typical result for the obtained decision planes using the iKFD or Ny-iKFD. The Gaussians are slightly overlapping and both approaches achieve a good separation with 93.50 % and 88.50 % prediction accuracy, respectively.

Subsequently we consider a few public available datasets for some real life experiments. The data are *Zongker* (2000pts, 10 classes) and *Proteom* (2604pts, 53 classes) from [8]; *Chromo* (4200pt, 21 classes) from [14] and the SwissProt database *Swiss* (82525pts, 46 classes) from [2], (version 10/2010, reduced to prosite labeled classes with at least 1000 entries and 1000 randomly chosen landmarks). Further we used the *Sonatas* data (1068pts, 5 classes) taken from [13]. All data are processed as indefinite kernels with 100 landmarks if not stated otherwise[5]. For all experiments we report mean and standard errors as obtained by a 10 fold crossvalidation. For PCVM we fixed the upper number of optimization cycles to 500. The probabilistic outputs can be directly used to allow for a reject region but can also be used to provide alternative classification decisions e.g. in a ranking framework

In Tables 1 and 2 we show the results for different non-metric proximity datasets using Ny-PCVM, PCVM and iKFD or Ny-iKFD. Considering Table 1 we see that iKFD and PCVM are similarly effective with slightly better results

---

[5] An increase of the number of landmarks leads to a better kernel reconstruction in the Frobenius norm until the full rank of the matrix is reached. Landmarks have not been changed between methods but only for each dataset.

Table 1. Accuracies - indefinite kernels. iKFD* is provided for a better judgment of the two approximation levels of the Ny-iKFD method and refers to a classical iKFD model but with a Nyström approximated and subsequently reconstructed kernel. iKFD and PCVM use the original indefinite kernel without approximations. Ny-iKFD and Ny-PCVM use the Nyström approximation within the implementation as discussed before and the same Nyström approximated kernel.

	iKFD	iKFD*	Ny-iKFD	PCVM	Ny-PCVM
Sonatas	90.17 ± 2.14	83.52 ± 4.77	83.71 ± 3.32	91.20 ± 2.69	86.15 ± 3.91
Zongker	96.60 ± 1.97	91.85 ± 2.27	90.45 ± 2.36	93.60 ± 2.00	90.45 ± 1.78
Proteom	99.58 ± 0.38	93.39 ± 0.68	82.13 ± 20.40	99.58 ± 0.28	93.32 ± 1.49
Chromo	97.24 ± 0.94	94.98 ± 1.07	95.12 ± 0.76	93.29 ± 1.51	92.40 ± 0.61
Swiss	–	–	75.11 ± 1.3	–	67.63 ± 6.6

Table 2. Runtimes - indefinite kernels

	iKFD	Ny-iKFD	PCVM	Ny-PCVM
Sonatas	5.04 ± 0.22	1.85 ± 0.06	60.07 ± 2.54	7.01 ± 0.24
Zongker	51.61 ± 1.43	5.53 ± 0.16	184.07 ± 14.97	16.91 ± 0.24
Proteom	559.25 ± 15.29	42.08 ± 1.92	352.08 ± 18.05	111.22 ± 1.88
Chromo	763.24 ± 31.54	27.91 ± 1.77	694.43 ± 15.61	54.36 ± 0.77
Swiss	–	178.79 ± 10.63	–	123.29 ± 2.72

Table 3. Model complexity - indefinite kernels (threshold $1e^{-4}$)

	iKFD	Ny-iKFD	PCVM	Ny-PCVM
Sonatas	100.00 ± 0	99.98 ± 0.04	11.24 ± 0.56	3.61 ± 0.49
Zongker	100.00 ± 0	100.00 ± 0	14.42 ± 3.65	2.71 ± 0.28
Proteom	100.00 ± 0	100.00 ± 0	5.23 ± 0.36	4.91 ± 0.30
Chromo	100.00 ± 0	100.00 ± 0	7.49 ± 0.51	3.62 ± 0.11
Swiss	–	94.60 ± 0.74	–	0.79 ± 0.12

for iKFD. The Nyström approximation of the kernel matrix only, often leads to a in general small decrease of the accuracy, as can be seen by comparing the iKFD and iKFD* results. In Ny-iKFD and Ny-PCVM we also use the Nyström approximation in the algorithm itself, to approximate e.g. the calculation of a large inverse matrix. The effect of this approximation can be best judged for iKFD by comparing iKFD* and Ny-iKFD. In general the additional approximation step, in the algorithm itself, does not substantially decrease the prediction accuracy[6]. In our experiments we found only for the proteom dataset a

---

[6] Also the runtime and model complexity are similar and therefore not reported in the following.

substantial decrease using Ny-iKFD (but not for Ny-PCVM). The proteom data are very imbalanced with sometimes very small classes hence the calculation of an approximated inverse may become numerically in-stable. Considering the overall results in Table 1 the approximations used in the algorithms Ny-iKFD and Ny-PCVM appear to be effective. The runtime analysis in Table 2 clearly shows that the classical iKFD is very complex. As expected, the integration of the Nyström approximation leads to substantial speed-ups. Larger datasets like the Swiss data with $\gg$ 10.000 entries could not be analyzed by iKFD or PCVM before.

The PCVM is focusing on a sparse parameter vector w in contrast to the iKFD. For the iKFD most training points are also used in the model ($\geq$ 94 %) whereas for Ny-PCVM often less than 5 % are kept in general as shown in Table 3. In practice it is often costly to calculate the non-metric proximity measures like sequence alignments and accordingly sparse models are very desirable. Considering the runtime again Ny-PCVM and Ny-iKFD are in general faster than the original algorithms, typically by at least a magnitude. the PCVM and Ny-PCVM are also very fast in the test case or out-of sample extension due to the inherent model sparsity.

8   Conclusions

We presented an alternative formulation of the iKFD employing the Nyström approximation. We found that Ny-iKFD is competitive in the prediction accuracy with the original iKFD and alternative approaches, while taking substantially less memory and runtime but being less sparse then Ny-PCVM. The Ny-iKFD provides now an effective way to obtain a *probabilistic* classification model for medium to large psd *and* non-psd datasets, in *batch mode* with *linear* runtime and memory complexity. Using the presented approach we believe that iKFD is now applicable for realistic problems and may get a larger impact then before. In future work it could be interesting to incorporate sparsity concepts into iKFD and Ny-iKFD similar as shown for classical KFD in [6].

Implementation: The Nyström approximation for iKFD is provided at http://www.techfak.uni-bielefeld.de/~fschleif/source/ny_ikfd.tgz and the PCVM/Ny-PCVM code can be found at https://mloss.org/software/view/610/.

Acknowledgment. A Marie Curie Intra-European Fellowship (IEF): FP7-PEOPLE-2012-IEF (FP7-327791-ProMoS) and support from the Cluster of Excellence 277 Cognitive Interaction Technology funded by the German Excellence Initiative is gratefully acknowledged. PT was supported by the EPSRC grant EP/L000296/1, "Personalized Health Care through Learning in the Model Space". We would like to thank R. Duin, Delft University for various support with distools and prtools and Huanhuan Chen,University of Science and Technology of China, for providing support with the Probabilistic Classification Vector Machine.

References

1. Alabdulmohsin, I.M., Gao, X., Zhang, X.: Support vector machines with indefinite kernels. In: Phung, D., Li, H. (eds.) Proceedings of the Sixth Asian Conference on Machine Learning, ACML 2014. JMLR Proceedings, Nha Trang City, Vietnam, 26–28 November 2014, vol. 39 (2014). JMLR.org
2. Boeckmann, B., Bairoch, A., Apweiler, R., Blatter, M.-C., Estreicher, A., Gasteiger, E., Martin, M., Michoud, K., O'Donovan, C., Phan, I., Pilbout, S., Schneider, M.: The SWISS-PROT protein knowledgebase and its supplement TrEMBL in 2003. Nucleic Acids Res. **31**, 365–370 (2003)
3. Chen, H., Tino, P., Yao, X.: Probabilistic classification vector machines. IEEE Trans. Neural Netw. **20**(6), 901–914 (2009)
4. Chen, H., Tino, P., Yao, X.: Efficient probabilistic classification vector machine with incremental basis function selection. IEEE TNN-LS **25**(2), 356–369 (2014)
5. Chen, Y., Garcia, E.K., Gupta, M.R., Rahimi, A., Cazzanti, L.: Similarity-based classification: concepts and algorithms. JMLR **10**, 747–776 (2009)
6. Diethe, T., Hussain, Z., Hardoon, D.R., Shawe-Taylor, J.: Matching pursuit kernel fisher discriminant analysis. In: Dyk, D.A.V., Welling, M. (eds.) Proceedings of the Twelfth International Conference on Artificial Intelligence and Statistics, AISTATS 2009. JMLR Proceedings, 16–18 April 2009, Clearwater Beach, Florida, USA, vol. 5, pp. 121–128 (2009). JMLR.org
7. Dubuisson, M., Jain, A.: A modified hausdorff distance for object matching. In: Proceedings of the 12th IAPR International Conference on Pattern Recognition, 1994. Vol. 1 - Conference A: Computer Vision amp; Image Processing., vol. 1, pp. 566–568, October 1994
8. Duin, R.P.: prtools, March 2012
9. Gisbrecht, A., Schleif, F.-M.: Metric and non-metric proximity transformations at linear costs. Neurocomputing (2015, to appear)
10. Haasdonk, B.: Feature space interpretation of svms with indefinite kernels. IEEE Trans. Pattern Anal. Mach. Intell. **27**(4), 482–492 (2005)
11. Haasdonk, B., Pekalska, E.: Indefinite kernel fisher discriminant. In: 19th International Conference on Pattern Recognition (ICPR 2008), 8–11 December 2008, Tampa, Florida, USA, pp. 1–4. IEEE Computer Society (2008)
12. Ling, H., Jacobs, D.W.: Shape classification using the inner-distance. IEEE Trans. Pattern Anal. Mach. Intell. **29**(2), 286–299 (2007)
13. Mokbel, B., Hasenfuss, A., Hammer, B.: Graph-based representation of symbolic musical data. In: Torsello, A., Escolano, F., Brun, L. (eds.) GbRPR 2009. LNCS, vol. 5534, pp. 42–51. Springer, Heidelberg (2009)
14. Neuhaus, M., Bunke, H.: Edit distance based kernel functions for structural pattern classification. Pattern Recogn. **39**(10), 1852–1863 (2006)
15. Pekalska, E., Haasdonk, B.: Kernel discriminant analysis for positive definite and indefinite kernels. IEEE Trans. Pattern Anal. Mach. Intell. **31**(6), 1017–1031 (2009)
16. Schleif, F.-M., Gisbrecht, A., Tino, P.: Probabilistic classification vector machine at large scale. In: Proceedings of ESANN 2015, pp. 555–560 (2015)
17. Schleif, F.-M., Gisbrecht, A.: Data analysis of (non-)metric proximities at linear costs. In: Hancock, E., Pelillo, M. (eds.) SIMBAD 2013. LNCS, vol. 7953, pp. 59–74. Springer, Heidelberg (2013)
18. Schleif, F.-M., Tino, P.: Indefinite proximity learning - a review. Neural Computation (2015, to appear)

19. Smith, T.F., Waterman, M.S.: Identification of common molecular subsequences. J. Mol. Biol. **147**(1), 195–197 (1981)
20. Williams, C.K.I., Seeger, M.: Using the nyström method to speed up kernel machines. In: NIPS 2000, pp. 682–688 (2000)
21. Yang, J., Fan, L.: A novel indefinite kernel dimensionality reduction algorithm: weighted generalized indefinite kernel discriminant analysis. Neural Process. Lett. **40**(3), 301–313 (2014). doi:10.1007/s11063-013-9330-9
22. Zhang, K., Kwok, J.T.: Clustered nyström method for large scale manifold learning and dimension reduction. IEEE Trans. Neural Netw. **21**(10), 1576–1587 (2010)

Similarity-Based User Identification Across Social Networks

Katerina Zamani[1,2]([⊠]), Georgios Paliouras[2], and Dimitrios Vogiatzis[2,3]

[1] Department of Informatics and Telecommunications,
National and Kapodistrian University of Athens, Athens, Greece
kat.zamani@gmail.com
[2] Institute of Informatics and Telecommunications,
National Centre for Scientific Research, "Demokritos", Aghia Paraskevi, Greece
paliourg@iit.demokritos.gr
[3] The American College of Greece, Athens, Greece
dimitrv@iit.demokritos.gr

Abstract. In this paper we study the identifiability of users across social networks, with a trainable combination of different similarity metrics. This application is becoming particularly interesting as the number and variety of social networks increase and the presence of individuals in multiple networks is becoming commonplace. Motivated by the need to verify information that appears in social networks, as addressed by the research project REVEAL, the presence of individuals in different networks provides an interesting opportunity: we can use information from one network to verify information that appears in another. In order to achieve this, we need to identify users across networks. We approach this problem by a combination of similarity measures that take into account the users' affiliation, location, professional interests and past experience, as stated in the different networks. We experimented with a variety of combination approaches, ranging from simple averaging to trained hybrid models. Our experiments show that, under certain conditions, identification is possible with sufficiently high accuracy to support the goal of verification.

Keywords: User identification · Similarity learning · Entity resolution

1 Introduction

Social network services have become part of our everyday life. It is now commonplace that people have accounts in multiple social networks, sharing their thoughts, promoting their work and probably influencing a part of the population via them. A variety of functionalities are provided by these services, such as video and photo uploading, posting, messaging, republishing etc., differing according to the platform and its aim.

Motivated by the need to verify the validity and trustworthiness of information that appears on social networks, the presence of individuals in different

A. Feragen et al. (Eds.): SIMBAD 2015, LNCS 9370, pp. 171–185, 2015.
DOI: 10.1007/978-3-319-24261-3_14

networks can be proved particularly useful. Public information from one network can be used to validate the source of information in another network. To achieve this goal, there is a need for user identification across social networks.

In this paper, we try to identify users across two popular networks: LinkedIn and Twitter. Our approach relies on novel similarity measures, that mainly take into consideration professional information about the users. To achieve a satisfactory combination of the proposed similarity metrics, we experiment with various supervised classification techniques, such as decision trees, naive bayes, knn and a hybrid classifier that merges naive bayes and decision tables efficiently. In addition, an attempt is made to deal with the imbalanced data problem and estimate the value of missing fields. Experiments based on a real world scenario and show the high accuracy in user identification between these networks. Thus, the main contribution of our work is to prove that the proposed approach of combining different similarity metrics is a viable solution to the identification of users, which in turn can be used to verify the validity of public information in social network.

The remainder of the paper is organized as follows. In the next section, we give a brief summary of the REVEAL project and describe the main characteristics of the problem that we address. In Sect. 3, we present the proposed similarity metrics and describe the classification techniques that we have used to combine these metrics. In Sect. 4, we first describe our dataset and then we analyze our experimental results. Closely related work is presented in Sect. 5. Finally in Sect. 6, we summary the main conclusions and propose possible extensions of our work.

2   Problem Description

The trustworthiness of information in social networks, according to the REVEAL project[1], can be assessed on the basis of three pillars: Contributor, Content and Context, themselves supported by various modalities that are organised in two levels. The first-level modalities, such as reputation, presence, influence etc., are calculated directly from social media data, while the modalities of the second level, such as trustworthiness, misbehavior etc., rely on the results of the first level [17]. Our study contributes to the presence modality of REVEAL, as user identification provides information about individuals in different platforms. Our research relies on Reveal's Journalism scenario, where verification and validation of information providers are necessary.

In this study, we focus on individuals that are interested in promoting their professional activities in social media. We assume that these individuals often provide their real name in different social networks and therefore, the problem that we need to solve is primarily that of name disambiguation. Specifically, our approach compares users that have similar names, based on public information provided by the users, as returned by search engine of the respective network. In other words, starting with the account of a user in one social network SN_1

---

[1] http://revealproject.eu/.

we want to identify the account of a user with a similar name in another social network SN_2, that most likely belongs to the same user.

In our study we try to identify users across two popular social networks: Twitter and LinkedIn. We experiment on those networks because they are both used mainly, though not exclusively, for professional purposes. Focusing on the journalism scenario of REVEAL, we form our target group with well-known professionals.

Within a social network, each user is represented by a set of attributes that forms their user profile. We derive a subset of these attributes based on the public accounts of users in the respective network. The LinkedIn profile of a user includes the following attributes: screen name, summary, location, specialization, current/past jobs with the respective affiliations, education, as well as projects and publications. On the other hand, the Twitter profile of a user contains: screen name, short biography, location and the user mentions, that the user specifies in her tweets. Although the process starts with a name search, screen name can be considered as a feature because the results of the search engine do not always fit exactly to the query. Figure 1 presents a simple example of how the user's attributes are aligned in the two networks, in order to be used in the similarity metrics. Some attributes can be aligned in a straightforward manner, e.g. Name, Location and Description, while others require the combination of various fields in the original user profile, e.g. Achievements and Affiliation-Education.

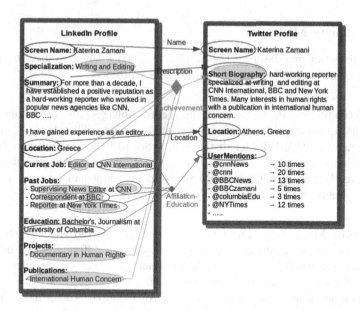

Fig. 1. Example profiles and the alignment of their attributes, as used in the similarity metrics.

3   Approach

3.1   Description of Profiles

As explained in the previous section, the basic idea of our approach is to pair accounts that result from name search and identify those that belong to the same user. Therefore, the task that we are dealing with is translated to a classification of account pairs into two classes: "match" and "mis-match".

Specifically, in order to identify users we create a similarity vector for each pair of users' profiles. The representation of our similarity vector is based on the definition proposed by [12]. Suppose that we have two user profiles from different social networks:

$$u_1 \in SN_1 \quad and \quad u_2 \in SN_2. \tag{1}$$

The similarity vector of the two profiles is defined as:

$$V(u_1, u_2) = < score_1, score_2, \cdots, score_n >. \tag{2}$$

where $score_k$ corresponds to the score, returned by the kth similarity metric. In order to facilitate the comparison, the similarity scores are normalized in the range [0.0, 1.0].

In the following subsections, we first present the similarity measures that we use and then the methods we tested for classifying similarity vectors.

3.2   Similarity Measures

In this subsection we describe the similarity metrics that we use, in order to construct the similarity vectors for pairs of user profiles.

Name Measures. Previous work in record linkage [10] recommend Jaro-Winkler as an appropriate similarity for short strings. Therefore, in our approach we use the Jaro-Winkler distance in order to find the similarity between the screen names of users – first and last name that a user provides during her registration. Due to name ambiguity problem mentioned in Sect. 2, additional information is needed for user identification.

Description Measures. The basic idea is inspired from the fact that users often provide common phrases in their description in different social networks. This measure estimates the similarity between the short biographies or summaries that users provide in different social networks, in order to describe themselves, their work and their specialization. An example is shown in Fig. 1. In order to measure similarity according to this short description, we pre-processed corresponding fields of the two profiles. We removed the punctuation, lowercased and tokenized the description, thereby creating two different token lists. Taking into consideration the example in Fig. 1, the two token lists are as follows:

A_1 = [for, more, than, a, decade, i, have, established, a, positive, reputation, as, a, hard, working, reporter, who, worked, in, popular, news, agencies, like, cnn, bbc, i, have, gained, experience, as, an, editor].

A_2 = [hard, working, reporter, specialized, at, writing, and, editing, at, cnn, international, bbc, and, new, york, times, many, interests, in, human, rights, with, a, publication, in, international, human, concern].

The similarity of the two token lists is computed as the ratio of their common words, to the total number of all words in both description fields.

Location Measures. A recent study associates location with the user's posts, based on attached geo-tags [3]. Although it is a promising approach, it is not directly applicable to all social networks, e.g. LinkedIn doesn't provide geo-tagging. For this reason our comparison utilizes the textual representation of the location field in a geospatial semantic way. We convert the locations provided in the different social networks to bounding boxes, with the use of the geonames ontology [14]. The similarity score of the two locations is defined as follows:

1. The ratio of bounding box areas if one bounding box is within the other.
2. The Euclidean distance between the centers of the bounding boxes when the locations belong to the same country.
3. 0.0 otherwise.

Specifically, the above enumeration can be defined by the following equation:

$$LocSim(l_1, l_2) = \begin{cases} Bbox(l_1)/Bbox(l_2) & \text{if } Bbox(l_1) \subseteq Bbox(l_2) \\ Bbox(l_2)/Bbox(l_1) & \text{if } Bbox(l_2) \subseteq Bbox(l_1) \\ 1/(1 + \|l_1 - l_2\|_2) & \text{if } l_1, l_2 \text{ in SC} \\ 0.0 & \text{otherwise} \end{cases} \quad (3)$$

where $Bbox$ represents the bounding box of the respective location and SC refers to the same country. The similarity score in all situations is normalized in the range [0.0 , 1.0].

For example lets assume that we have $SN_{location1}$ = "New York", that appears in one social network and $SN_{location2}$ = "Manhattan", that appears in the other. Since Manhattan is a borough of New York City, its bounding box – imagine it as a quadrilateral that covers the Manhattan area – will be included into the bounding box of New York city. Thus, the similarity of the two locations is measured as the ratio between the covering area of Manhattan's bounding and the area of New York City's bounding box. In the example of Fig. 1, the similarity of the two locations will be 1.0 since the bounding boxes, which are returned from the ontology, coincide.

Now suppose that we retrieve two locations that belong to the same country but their bounding boxes are not subsumed – $SN_{location3}$ = "Athens" and $SN_{location4}$ = "Sparta". In this case, their similarity is computed by the Euclidean distance of the coordinates of the centers of two bounding boxes, as shown in Fig. 2.

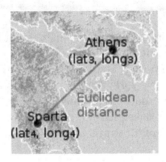

Fig. 2. Compute location similarity by the Euclidean distance.

Affiliation-Education Measure. This measure attempts to match the current/past affiliation and educational experience of the users, as stated in the social network profiles. In order to measure the similarity score we create two token sets, one for each corresponding network. Figure 1 shows the profile fields that participate in this score. In LinkedIn's set we use the affiliation of current and past experiences and the educational schools, while in Twitter's set we use the userMentions (@ symbol in Twitter) that appear in the user's tweets. We assume that the user is likely to mention her affiliation and school names in her micro-blogging posts to promote her work. While neither of the two token sets include duplicates, the token set obtained from Twitter contains additionally the frequency of each userMention. An additional practical problem with userMentions is that they appear in an abbreviated form. So, there is a need for a textual comparison measure that is suitable for substring matching. Based on the related survey [6], the Smith-Waterman distance measure seems adequate, because it combines edit and affine gap distances. In particular we used the implementation of the measure from the simmetrics library [15]. We measure the similarity between each pair of tokens in the two token sets and keep only those similarity scores that exceed a predefined threshold t. Then we weigh the resulting scores according to the frequency of a userMention in Twitter profile. Therefore, the overall similarity score is calculated as shown in the following equation:

$$\sum_{i=1}^{n}(score_i \times freq_i) \, / \sum_{i=1}^{n} freq_i \qquad (4)$$

where $score_i$ is the Smith-Waterman similarity score of a pair of tokens that is above the threshold t and $freq_i$ is the frequency of appearance of the specific userMention in the user's tweets. The weight indicates a significance estimate of the corresponding userMention.

Some similarity scores, that exceed the threshold, may correspond to the same token of one of the sets. This is acceptable because many userMentions or jobs often refer to different variants of the same entity. For instance in Fig. 1, "@BBCNews" and "BBCzamani" refer to the same entity. So, the affiliation "BBC" in LinkedIn will combine the two similarity scores if they are above the threshold.

Achievements Measure. It is common that users highlight their professional achievements and their job specialization in the short biography field of their profile. The main idea is based on the observation where the words that a user often provides in description field in Twitter, belong to the same family with the ones that she provides for her job, publication etc. in LinkedIn. We attempt to capture this by using SoftTFIDF metric, which takes into consideration "similar" and not only identical tokens [6]. We compose a textual summary of the most significant professional achievements of a user, as she provides in LinkedIn: we combine current and past job experiences and the corresponding affiliations, professional specialization, projects and publications that she has participated in. The similarity between this "profession summary" and the short biography in Twitter is computed with the use of SoftTFIDF as implemented in the second-String library [9,16]. SoftTFIDF converts the two texts into two bags-of-tokens and calculates the overall similarity score, by computing the TFIDF distance between each pair of tokens. SoftTFIDF method prunes the tokens where their similarity score, computed by Jaro-Winkler metric, is below 0.9.

3.3 Classification

As mentioned above, the various similarity measures are used to built similarity-vectors. These vectors are then classified in order to achieve the required user identification. Below we describe the different classification approaches that we tested.

Baseline Classification Results. As a baseline we calculate the average of the scores in the similarity vectors:

$$AvgScore(V) = \sum_{i=1}^{n}(score_i)/n \tag{5}$$

where $score_i$ corresponds to the respective score in the similarity vector.

As an example, lets assume the following 3 user profiles:

$$u_1 \in SN_1 \quad and \quad u_2, u_3 \in SN_2. \tag{6}$$

We pair the resulting profiles and two different similarity vectors are created. Suppose that the similarity vectors of the five scores are as follows:
$V_1(u_1, u_2) = <1.0, 0.345, 0.456, 0.678, 0.879 >$
$V_2(u_1, u_3) = <1.0, 0.432, 1.0, 0.789, 0.654 >$

The simple combination computes the following average scores:
$AvgScore(V_1) = 3.358 / 5 = 0.6716$
$AvgScore(V_2) = 3.875 / 5 = 0.775.$

The higher the score, the more likely it is that the corresponding profiles belong to the same user.

Binary Classifiers. A different way to classify similarity vectors is by training binary classifiers. We use binary classifiers because we formulate the problem as a two-class one – match and mis-match.

For each profile set, we declare as "match" the profile that is assigned maximum probability by the classifier, depending on the classes' distribution of the respective binary classifier.

The classifiers that we tested are presented below in brief:

- **Decision Tree:** this method creates a decision tree model, by analyzing a training set of instances, i.e. similarity vectors with the correct classification. Each internal node of the tree represents a test on one of the five similarity scores, that most effectively splits the respective set into subsets of more homogeneity. The measure of the purity of each node is its entropy – lower entropy denotes higher homogeneity/purity. Each leaf node of the tree holds a class label, corresponding to the majority class in the training instances. During the test phase, the classifier decides whether a pair is a match or not by traversing the decision model tree from root to the leaf. In our study, we experiment with the C4.5 decision tree and use pruning to avoid overfitting.
- **Naive Bayes:** this classifier uses Bayes theorem to calculate the probability of a class given a test instance, assuming that all features of the vector, i.e. the five scores, are independent. As we use continuous features we calculate probabilities by fitting a Gaussian distribution. In the training phase, the classifier estimates two probability distributions, one for each class. During testing, the classifier decides the label of a specific pair, depending on its probability of belonging to each of the two classes. The computation of these probabilities is based on the respective distributions that were estimated in the training phase.
- **KNN:** this classifier chooses the label of a test, based on the majority class among its k nearest training instances. In our study, we set the value of k to 5. Moreover, the nearest neighbors are determined by the Euclidean distance of the pair to the training instances.
- **DTNB:** this is a hybrid approach that involves Naive Bayes and Decision Tables classifiers. Decision Tables have their origins to classification rules, as each row of the table represents a rule and is associated with a class label [4]. Initially in DTNB, all features are modeled in Decision Tables. Afterwards with the use of forward selection, the classifier adds in a stepwise manner the feature that improves classification in the validation set the most. Then DTNB selects features with Naive Bayes while it uses the Decision Tables for the rest. The label of a pair results from the combination of class probability estimations of both classifiers (Decision Table and Naive Bayes)

4   Experimental Results

4.1   Data Collection

The collection of the data was based on name search, as denoted in Sect. 2. We started with a list of "target users" in mind, e.g. "Katerina Zamani", the

Table 1. Profiles in the datasets

	LinkedIn	Twitter
Number of profiles	2766	3373
Number of profile sets	262	262

first author of this paper. Each target-user had a different name. Given the name of a particular target-user, we gathered the first 25 profile-results from each network, using the network's search engine. Thus, we created two sets of profiles (one for each network), each set containing the results of the search for a particular name. The aim of our study was to identify within each such set only the profile of the target-user, given the user's profile in the other network, e.g. given Zamani's profile in Twitter, we wanted to identify the profile of the same person in LinkedIn, among the set of profiles that the search for "Katerina Zamani" has returned. We did this matching both ways, i.e. from Twitter to LinkedIn and vice versa, but only for a single target-user with that name. This set-up is motivated by our goal of verifying the validity of profiles of professional individuals in social networks. We also assumed that each target-user has a single account in each network. Therefore, in each set we identified one profile as the correct match, while all others were considered mismatches.

In Table 1 the total number of profiles in each of the two networks that we used is provided. We separate the data into two datasets—one for each network. Each data set contains 262 profiles sets and each set includes at most 25 profiles.

4.2   Experimental Setup

Starting with a profile from a social network (SN_1) and a set of profiles from a different one (SN_2), our aim is to find the profile that most likely matches the one from (SN_1). In order to select the most likely match, we compare each profile in each set from one social network with each profile of the corresponding set from the second network. Each comparison produces a similarity vector, as described in Sect. 3.2, which is classified as a match or not. In our experiments we use two different datasets corresponding to the "direction" of the identification, i.e. starting with a profile from LinkedIn we compare it against the profiles of the corresponding set in the Twitter dataset and vice versa. Henceforth, we refer to the former task as *Twitter identification* and the latter as *LinkedIn identification*.

Missing Values. It is common that users do not complete every fill in all fields of their profile. This influences the performance of our approach because many profile fields that we use, are not available. Table 2 presents the number of missing fields for each similarity metric.

As shown in Table 2, the name of the user is never missing as it is a compulsory field during the user's registration. However, the location field in Twitter

Table 2. Number of missing values

SN/metric	Name metric	Description metric	Location metric	Affiliation-Education metric	Achievements metric
LinkedIn	0	1866	0	462	221
Twitter	0	1431	1582	735	1431

is only available for 53 % of the users in our dataset. The availability of description/summary fields varies from 33 % for LinkedIn to 58 % for Twitter, while the userMention attribute in tweets is used by 78 % of the users. Regarding the Affiliation-Education and Achievements metrics, LinkedIn provides more complete information than Twitter. This is due to the use of many fundamental and professional fields, such as affiliation, professional experience etc., that many users usually provide in their LinkedIn account.

Imbalanced Data. The nature of the identification problem across social networks results in considerable imbalance between the two classes (match vs. mismatch). In our study, only 9.5 % of the LinkedIn profiles and 7.8 % of the Twitter profiles comprise the minority (match) class. This imbalance can cause problems during training for some classifiers. In order to handle this issue, we suggest a procedure during the testing phase of classification.

4.3   Results for Separate Measures

In this section we evaluate separately each similarity measure that we used. Taking into consideration the large amount of missing values and how this could influence the accuracy of classification, we examined the following solutions:

- **Set a default score:** We set 0.5 as a default similarity score, when the score cannot be calculated. It was worth recalling that all scores are normalised in the range $[0.0, 1.0]$.
- **Set the average score:** We set the missing similarity score to the average value of the similarity scores, that can be computed from the available fields. This average score is different for each metric and it depends on the measured similarity scores of the respective measure.
- **Set the median score:** The basic idea of this approach is similar to previous one, but instead of the average, we use the median value of the computed similarity scores.

In particular, we compute the recall of each similarity score separately. Note that precision is the same as recall here, since all methods are required to return exactly 262 matches. Specifically, we select as the most likely matching set the one with the maximum similarity score. Tables 3 and 4 provide the results for the two datasets (*LinkedIn identification* and *Twitter identification*), and for the different strategies to deal with missing values.

Table 3. Recall for LinkedIn identification for different measures and different strategies for missing values. Results are presented as percentages to facilitate readability.

Strategy for missing values	Name measure	Description measure	Location measure	Affiliation-Education measure	Achievements measure
Default	68.70 %	60.31 %	67.94 %	80.15 %	83.59 %
Average	68.70 %	64.12 %	69.08 %	79.77 %	87.02 %
Median	68.70 %	63.74 %	68.70 %	79.77 %	87.02 %

Table 4. Recall for Twitter identification for different measures and different strategies for missing values. Results are presented as percentages to facilitate readability.

Strategy for missing values	Name measure	Description measure	Location measure	Affiliation-Education measure	Achievements measure
Default	90.84 %	80.92 %	75.57 %	75.19 %	74.81 %
Average	90.84 %	85.50 %	82.44 %	75.19 %	79.77 %
Median	90.84 %	85.50 %	79.78 %	74.43 %	79.77 %

As we expected, the success scores in name metric are the same in all approaches because name fields are always available in social networks. However, the score in *Twitter's identification* case is much higher, due to the different nature of network's search engines. On one hand the sequence of results, that is returned from a search query in Twitter, depends on the popularity of each account, while on the other hand LinkedIn's search engine categorize different its resulting user accounts. In addition, the high success scores of the two last metrics in *LinkedIn's identification* case, indicate the importance of the professional fields in the identification. Regarding the two tables we conclude that the average score approach predominates in missing values problem, so we choose this for the rest of our experiments.

4.4 Baseline Classification Results

In this subsection we assess the results of the simple average combination of the similarity measures as described in Sect. 3.3. For each profile set, we define as "match" the pair with the maximum average score. As in the previous subsection we use recall to measure performance.

In the *LinkedIn identification* task, the simple combination recognizes correctly 227 pairs out of 262, arriving at a recall of 86.64 %. In the *Twitter identification* task the respective recall is 88.55 %. Although the results are promising for a simple combination, are somewhat lower than the best individual scores, i.e. the Achievement measure for LinkedIn (see Table 3) and the Name measure for Twitter (see Table 4).

Table 5. LinkedIn identification results for various classifiers

LinkedIn's identification	Decision Tree	Naive Bayes	KNN (k = 5)	DTNB
Precision	89.58 %	90.35 %	92.66 %	94.98 %
Recall	88.96 %	89.69 %	91.99 %	94.27 %
F-measure	89.27 %	90.02 %	92.33 %	94.62 %

Table 6. Twitter identification results for various classifiers

Twitter's identification	Decision Tree	Naive Bayes	KNN (k = 5)	DTNB
Precision	86.49 %	86.10 %	90.73 %	90.73 %
Recall	86.49 %	86.10 %	90.73 %	90.73 %
F-measure	86.49 %	86.10 %	90.73 %	90.73 %

4.5   Results of the Trained Classifiers

At this subsection we refer to our classification strategy and we present the results from the different classifiers we use. To estimate the performance of our classifiers we utilize the k-fold cross validation technique. Due to the structure of our datasets, we split our sets to 7-folds in order to test the 14 % of the database each time. Our analysis is based on Information Retrieval, so we evaluate the performance of our approach with the use of well-known measures, such as precision, recall, F-measure and ROC curve, which plots the true positive rate as a function of false positive rate. The results we present, are the average estimation of the resulting measures at every step of cross validation.

Due to imbalanced data problem, we specify as "match" the pair with the maximum probability. This probability, which is derived from the distribution of the positive class during training, denotes the likelihood membership of the instance in that class [13]. The two tables above show the results in *LinkedIn's identification* and *Twitter's identification* of every classifier.

As we can notice from Tables 5 and 6, our approach performs well for detecting matches and especially with the use of DTNB classifier. Even the low proportion of ground-truth data, the results for precision and recall in match class are satisfactory, so we achieve a high score in accuracy.

In the Figs. 3 and 4 we can see the ROC curves of the classification results in the *LinkedIn's identification* (first graph) and *Twitter's identification* (second graph) cases. We can notice that the DTNB classifier performs better, because its ROC curve is closer to upper left corner than the others.

5   Related Work

A variety of recent studies focus on the problem of user identification across the web. To the best of our knowledge this is the first study that is motivated by

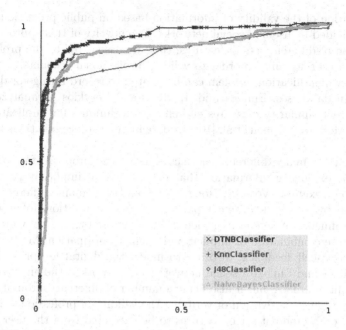

Fig. 3. ROC curves of the classifiers for the *LinkedIn identification* task. y-axis represents true positive rate (TPR) while x-axis the false positive rate (FPR).

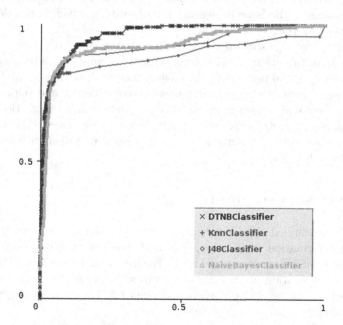

Fig. 4. ROC curves of the classifiers for the *Twitter identification* task. y-axis represents true positive rate (TPR) while x-axis the false positive rate (FPR).

the verification of the validity of information based on public professional information provided by users in social networks. The novelty of this approach is the combination of different sets of features, that are associated to the professional aspects of a user account, in order to validate professional accounts.

The user identification problem can be related to record linkage or duplicate detection in databases. Elmagarmid, Ipeirotis and Verykios [6] analyze extensively different similarity measures and efficient techniques for duplicate record detection. Moreover, Cohen et al. [10] evaluate many distance functions for name matching.

Additionally, many different approaches have been proposed for correlating accounts by exploiting information that is explicitly or implicitly provided by the users. For example Vosecky, Hong, and Shen [12] combine different explicit profile fields by setting definite comparison vectors. In addition, Iofciu et al. [2] study the influence of tags in user identification across tagging network services relying on the combination of implicit and explicit information. Malhotra et al. [11] utilize explicit feedback, in order to model the digital footprints of users in the Twitter and LinkedIn social networks. Their work is the one that comes closest to our approach, but it also bears a number of differences from it. Firstly, due to our original motivation of verifying the validity of professional accounts, we focused on a different set of features to be extracted from the user profiles. Also, Malhotra et al. [11] handle differently the problem of imbalanced data. Namely they use random sub-sampling to balance the training data, thus training their model with the same number of match and mis-match examples. Finally, our work addresses the issue of missing feature values, which is not dealt with in Malhotra et al. [11].

The authors of [3] focus on the use of implicit features of a user's activity, such as location, timestamps and writing style. That approach is only applicable to activity-based social networks. The most recent work of Goga et al. [1] is also the one closer to our work, correlates users across different and popular social networks in large scale. Their study is based on public feature extraction and the proposed similarity metrics deal with explicit information. Due to the large scale of data, they present a classification strategy in order to deal with availability of fields and imbalance.

6   Conclusion and Future Work

In our work, we studied user identification in two popular social networks in order to support information verification. We used different similarity measures for different pieces of information provided by the user, and we combined them using supervised classification upon similarity vectors. As shown by our experiments, on the specific data set, using a hybrid classifier (DTNB) we can achieve a very high user identification performance.

A possible future extension of the presented work, would be the handling of class imbalance with a more sophisticated approach, either by using ensemble filtering (e.g. SMOTE [8]), or by setting higher weights to the matches during training [1]. Moreover, we could enrich location information provided by the users with estimations of locations as mentioned by the user in tweets or job descriptions, as [7] suggests. Finally it would be interesting to study the potential contribution of our approach to the difficult problem of identifying fake or compromised account in social networks [5].

Acknowledgments. This work was partially supported by the research project REVEAL (REVEALing hidden concepts in Social Media), which is funded by the European Commission, under the FP7 programme (contract number 610928).

References

1. Goga, O., Perito, D., Lei, H., Teixeira, R., Sommer, R.: Large-scale correlation of accounts across social networks. Technical report (2013)
2. Iofciu, T., Fankhauser, P., Abel, F., Bischoff, K.: Identifying users across social tagging systems. In: Adamic, L.A., Baeza-Yates, R.A., Counts, S. (eds.) ICWS. The AAAI Press (2011)
3. Goga, O., Lei, H., Parthasarathi, S., Friedland, G., Sommer, R., Teixeira, R.: On exploiting innocuous user activity for correlating accounts across social network sites. Technical report, ICSI Technical Reports University of Berkeley (2012)
4. Hall, M., Frank, E.: Combining Naive Bayes and decision tables. In: FLAIRS Conference, vol. 2118, pp. 318–319 (2008)
5. Egele, M., et al.: COMPA: detecting compromised accounts in social networks. In: NDSS (2013)
6. Elmagarmid, A.K., Ipeirotis, P.G., Verykios, V.S.: Duplicate record detection: a survey. IEEE Trans. Knowl. Data Eng. **19**, 1–16 (2007)
7. Chen, Y., Zhao, J., Hu, X., Zhang, X., Li, Z., Chua, T.S.: From interest to function: location estimation in social media. In: AAAI (2013)
8. Chawla, N.V., Bowyer, K.W., Hall, L.O., Kegelmeyer, W.P.: SMOTE: synthetic minority over-sampling technique. J. Artif. Intell. Res. **16**, 321–357 (2002)
9. Moreau, E., Yvon, F., Capp, O.: Robust similarity measures for named entities matching. In: Proceedings of the 22nd International Conference on Computational Linguistics, vol. 1, pp. 593–600. Association for Computational Linguistics (2008)
10. Cohen, W., Ravikumar, P., Fienberg, S.: A comparison of string metrics for matching names and records. In: KDD Workshop on Data Cleaning and Object Consolidation, vol. 3, pp. 73–78 (2003)
11. Malhotra, A., Totti, L., Meira, Jr., W., Kumaraguru, P., Almeida, V.: Studying user footprints in different online social networks. In: Proceedings of the 2012 International Conference on Advances in Social Networks Analysis and Mining, ASONAM, pp. 1065–1070. IEEE Computer Society (2012)
12. Vosecky, J., Hong, D., Shen, V.Y.: User identification across multiple social networks. In: First International Conference on Networked Digital Technologies, NDT 2009, pp. 360–365. IEEE (2009)
13. Machine Learning Group at the University of Waikato. http://www.cs.waikato.ac.nz/ml/index.html
14. GeoNames Ontology. http://www.geonames.org/
15. Simmetrics Library. https://github.com/Simmetrics/simmetrics
16. SecondString Library. https://github.com/TeamCohen/secondstring
17. Reveal Project: Social Media Verification. http://revealproject.eu/

Dominant-Set Clustering Using Multiple Affinity Matrices

Eyasu Zemene[1]([✉]), Samuel Rota Bulò[2], and Marcello Pelillo[1]

[1] Ca' Foscari University, Venice, Italy
eyasu201011@gmail.com
[2] FBK-irst, Trento, Italy

Abstract. Pairwise (or graph-based) clustering algorithms typically assume the existence of a single affinity matrix, which describes the similarity between the objects to be clustered. In many practical applications, however, several similarity relations might be envisaged and the problem arises as to how properly select or combine them. In this paper we offer a solution to this problem for the case of dominant sets, a well-known formalization of the notion of a cluster, which generalizes the notion of maximal clique to edge-weighted graphs and has intriguing connections to evolutionary game theory. Specifically, it has been shown that dominant sets can be bijectively related to Evolutionary Stable Strategies (ESS) - a classic notion of equilibrium in the evolutionary game theory field - of a so-called "clustering game". The clustering game is a non-cooperative game between two-players, where the objects to cluster form the set of strategies, while the affinity matrix provides the players' payoffs. The proposed approach generalizes dominant sets to multiple affinities by extending the clustering game, which has a single payoff, to a multi-payoff game. Accordingly, dominant sets in the multi-affinity setting become equivalent to ESSs of a corresponding multi-payoff clustering game, which can be found by means of so-called Biased Replicator Dynamics. Experiments conducted over standard benchmark datasets consistently show that the proposed combination scheme allows one to substantially improve the performance of dominant-set clustering over its single-affinity counterpart.

1 Introduction

Since their introduction [15,16], dominant sets have proven to be an effective tool for graph-based clustering and have found applications in a variety of different domains, such as bioinformatics [6], computer vision [15,24], image processing [2,26], group detection [11,25], security and video surveillance [1,8], etc. Although they were originally rooted in optimization and graph theory (being a generalization of the notion of maximal clique to edge-weighted graphs), recent work has shown intriguing connections with non-cooperative game theory and this perspective has opened the door to elegant generalizations to directed graphs [23] and hypergraphs [18]. The basic idea behind this connection is considering the clustering problem as a non-cooperative "clustering game" between two

© Springer International Publishing Switzerland 2015
A. Feragen et al. (Eds.): SIMBAD 2015, LNCS 9370, pp. 186–198, 2015.
DOI: 10.1007/978-3-319-24261-3_15

players. Players simultaneously select an object to cluster and receive a payoff proportional to the similarity of the selected objects. Since clusters are sets of objects that are highly similar, the competition induced by the game forces the players to coordinate by selecting objects from the same cluster. Indeed, by doing so, both players are able to maximize their expected payoff. In this setting, cluster hypotheses are modelled in terms of mixed strategies, i.e.probability distribution over the set of objects, and the notion of a dominant set turns out to be equivalent to a classic equilibrium concept known as *Evolutionary Stable Strategy* (ESS), which satisfies both the internal coherency and external incoherency conditions pertaining to a cluster [23]. From an algorithmic perspective, ESSs, and hence dominant sets, are sought by means of Replicatory Dynamics, i.e.evolutionary dynamics under which ESSs turn out to be asymptotically stable points.

In virtually all practical applications there might be several ways of determining a similarity relation between objects and then the problem arises as to how select or combine them in a principled way. For example, in figure-ground separation problems the similarity of edge elements (edgels) can be measured using co-circularity, smoothness, proximity, and contrast [10]. Another example is image segmentation, where the similarity between two pixels can be measured by using e.g.proximity, color, texture etc.

The problem of combining multiple sources of information has received considerable attention within the pattern recognition and machine learning communities, which resulted in a whole arsenal of *ensemble methods* (see [29] for an up-to-date introduction to the topic). In the supervised learning literature, for example, we find multi-kernel algorithms (see, e.g.[7] and references therein). Another related method is consensus clustering [22]. The goal of consensus clustering is to combine different clustering results (a.k.a.clustering ensemble) obtained from different algorithms into a single partition. If we constructed the ensemble by running the base clustering algorithms on the different similarities, the consensus solution would integrate the information from multiple sources.

Motivated by the game-theoretic interpretation of dominant sets [17,18,23], in this paper we propose a principled solution to the problem of integrating multiple affinity matrices or, in other words, the problem of clustering weighted multi-graphs, i.e.graphs that are permitted to have multiple edges between vertices [9]. Contrary to the consensus clustering idea, instead of combining the results obtained by using different affinity matrices, we focus instead on the problem of properly combining the matrices themselves. From our game-theoretic perspective this problem can be seen in the context of multi-payoff (or multi-criteria) games, a topic that has been the subject of intensive studies by game theorists since the late 1950's [3,4,19,28]. Under this setting, payoffs are no longer scalar quantities but take the form of vectors whose components represent different commodities. Clearly, the main difficulty that arises here is that the players' payoff spaces now can be given only a partial ordering. Although in "classical" game theory several solution concepts have been proposed during the years, the game theory community has typically given little attention to the evolutionary setting. Recently, a solution to this problem has been put forward by the authors of [21], who extended both the equilibrium concept of ESS and the replicator dynamics to multi-payoff games [13]. Another recent attempt towards this direction, though more theoretical in nature, can be found in [12]. In this work, we exploit the results in [13,21] to provide a principled solution to the problem of integrating multiple payoff functions within the dominant set framework. The idea is to extend the clustering game to a multi-payoff setting, in such a way that dominant sets become equivalent to evolutionary stable strategies of the resulting multi-payoff clustering game. ESSs of multi-payoff games can then be sought by means of so-called Biased Replicator Dynamics, $i.e.$replicator dynamics that integrate k affinity matrices $A_1, \ldots, A_k$ into a single payoff matrix

$$A_\lambda = \sum_{i=1}^{k} \lambda_i A_i, \tag{1}$$

where the λ_i's ($i = 1 \ldots k$) represent appropriate non-negative trade-off weights associated to the different matrices, subject to the constraint $\sum_i \lambda_i = 1$. We demonstrate the potential of our approach using both synthetic and real-world datasets from the UCI machine learning repository archive.ics.uci.edu/ml/datasets.html. In addition we show the viability of our approach for image segmentation.

2   Dominant Sets as Equilibria of Evolutionary Games

A *dominant set* is a graph-theoretic notion of cluster introduced by Pavan and Pelillo [15,16] that generalizes maximal cliques to edge-weighted graphs. In [23], dominant sets have been linked to game theory, by showing that they can be characterized in terms of a classic equilibrium concept known as evolutionary stable strategy of a particular non-cooperative game that can be constructed given a clustering problem instance (*a.k.a.*, *clustering game*).

The clustering game can be summarized as follows. Given a set of elements $\mathcal{O} = \{1 \ldots n\}$ and an $n \times n$ (possibly asymmetric) affinity matrix $A = (a_{ij})$, which quantifies the pairwise similarities between the objects in $\mathcal{O}$, we envisage a situation whereby two players play a game that consists of simultaneously selecting an element from $\mathcal{O}$. After showing their choice the players get a reward, which is proportional to the similarity of the chosen elements. In game-theoretic jargon the elements of set $\mathcal{O}$ are the "pure strategies" available to both players and the affinity matrix A represents the "payoff" function (specifically, a_{ij} represents the payoff received by an individual playing strategy i against an opponent playing strategy j).

A central notion in game theory is that of a *mixed strategy*, which is simply a probability distribution $x = (x_1, \ldots, x_n)^T$ over the set of pure strategies $\mathcal{O}$. From the clustering perspective, mixed strategies can be regarded as a cluster hypothesis, where x_i represents the probability of having the ith object in the cluster. Mixed strategies clearly belong to the $(n-1)$-dimensional standard simplex:

$$\Delta = \left\{ x \in \mathbb{R}^n : \sum_{i=1}^{n} x_i = 1 \text{ and } x_i \geq 0, \ i = 1, \ldots, n \right\}.$$

Given a mixed strategy $x \in \Delta$, we define its *support* as $\sigma(x) = \{i \in \mathcal{O} : x_i > 0\}$.

The expected payoff received by an individual playing mixed strategy y against an opponent playing mixed strategy x is given by $y^\top A x$. The set of *best replies* against a mixed strategy x is defined as

$$\beta(x) = \{y \in \Delta : y^\top A x = \max_z z^\top A x\}.$$

A mixed strategy $x \in \Delta$ is said to be a *Nash equilibrium* if it is a best reply to itself, namely if $x \in \beta(x)$ or, in other words, if

$$x^\top A x \geq y^\top A x \qquad \text{for all } y \in \Delta. \tag{2}$$

Intuitively, at a Nash equilibrium no player has an incentive to unilaterally deviate from it.

An *Evolutionary Stable Strategy* (ESS) is an equilibrium concept developed within evolutionary game theory. An ESS is a mixed strategy x being a Nash equilibrium satisfying an additional stability condition given below:

$$y \in \beta(x) \setminus \{x\} \implies x^\top A y > y^\top A y.$$

Intuitively, ESS's are strategies such that any small deviation from them will lead to an inferior payoff (see [27] for an excellent introduction to evolutionary game theory).

An *ESS-cluster* is the support of an ESS equilibrium of a clustering game. In [18,23] a combinatorial characterization of ESSs is given, which establishes the link to dominant sets and makes them plausible candidates for the notion of a cluster. Indeed, it can be shown that ESS-clusters do incorporate the two basic properties, which characterize a cluster, *i.e.*

- *internal coherency*: elements belonging to the cluster should have high mutual similarities;
- *external incoherency*: the overall cluster internal coherency decreases by introducing external elements.

The internal coherency follows from the Nash condition. Indeed, if x is an ESS, then Eq. (2) implies that $(Ax)_i = x^\top A x$ for all $i \in \sigma(x)$, *i.e.* every element of the cluster ($i \in \sigma(x)$) has the same average similarity with respect to the cluster. On the other hand, the external incoherency (*a.k.a.* cluster maximality) follows from the ESS stability condition, which implies that no ESS-cluster can contain another ESS-cluster.

The problem of clustering becomes the problem of finding ESS-clusters of a clustering game. One of the distinguishing features of this approach is its generality as it allows one to deal in a unified framework with a variety of scenarios, including cases with asymmetric, negative, or high-order affinities. Moreover, when the affinity matrix A is symmetric (that is, $A = A^\top$), the notion of an ESS-cluster coincides with the original notion of dominant set introduced by Pavan and Pelillo, which amounts to finding a (local) maximizer of $x^\top A x$ over the standard simplex Δ [23].

Algorithmically, to find an ESS-cluster one can use the classical *replicator dynamics* [27], a class of dynamical systems, which mimic a Darwinian selection process over the set of pure strategies. The discrete-time version of these dynamics is given by the following update rule:

$$x_i(t+1) = x_i(t)\frac{(Ax(t))_i}{x(t)^\top Ax(t)} \qquad (3)$$

for all $i \in \mathcal{O}$. The process starts from a point $x(0)$ usually close to the barycenter of the simplex Δ, and it is iterated until convergence (typically when distance between two successive states is smaller than a given threshold). It is clear that the whole dynamical process is driven by the payoff function, which, in our case, is defined precisely to favor the evolution of highly coherent objects. Accordingly, the support $\sigma(x)$ of the converged state x does represent a cluster, the non-null components of which providing a measure of the degree of membership of its elements.

The support of an ESS corresponds to the indices of the elements in the same group. To extract all the ESS-clusters we implemented a simple peel-off strategy: when an ESS-cluster is computed the corresponding elements are removed from the original and the replicator dynamics is executed again on the remaining elements.

3   Pareto Nash Equilibra in Multi-payoff Games

Pareto reply and Pareto Nash equilibrium are notions from multi-payoff games, which are equivalent to Nash best reply and Nash equilibrium of single payoff game. In single objective games, moving away from the equilibrium strategies results in no gain for a player. Similarly, in multi-payoff games moving away from the equilibrium eventually results in a payoff decrease in at least one payoff function for any of the players.

Consider a symmetric multi-payoff game with k payoff matrices $A_1, \ldots, A_k$. The vector payoff that a player obtains by adopting strategy $y \in \Delta$ against an opponent playing $x \in \Delta$ is given by:

$$u(y, x) = (u^1, u^2, \ldots u^k)(y, x) = (y^\top A_1 x, y^\top A_2 x \ldots y^\top A_k x).$$

The set of *Pareto best replies* $\beta^P(x)$ to a strategy $x \in \Delta$ is given by those strategies for which no other strategy exists performing comparably well against x on all the payoff functions and better on at least one:

$$\beta^P(x) = \{y \in \Delta \mid (\nexists z \in \Delta)(u(z, x) > u(y, x))\},$$

where $a > b$ holds if $(\forall i)(a_i \geq b_i)$ and $a \neq b$. A strategy $x \in \Delta$ is a *Pareto Nash equilibrium* if it is a Pareto best reply to itself, *i.e.* $x \in \beta^P(x)$.

In [20], the set of Pareto best replies is characterized using notions from MCLP and, specifically, in terms of the so-called *weighted sum scalarization* program. Given $x \in \Delta$, the weighted sum scalarization program corresponding to $\beta^P(x)$ is a linear program, which is defined for a trade-off weight-vector $\lambda > 0 \in \mathbb{R}^k$ as

$$L_{\text{wss}}(x, \lambda) = \underset{y \in \Delta}{\text{argmax}} \, y^\top A_\lambda x.$$

The set of Pareto best replies to x is the collection of all solutions in $L_{\text{wss}}(x, \lambda)$ for all $\lambda > 0$, *i.e.*

$$\beta^P(x) = \bigcup_{\lambda > 0} L_{\text{wss}}(x, \lambda).$$

Interestingly, there exists a finite set of weight-vectors $\Lambda(x) = \{\lambda_1, \ldots, \lambda_m\}$, with $\lambda_i > 0 \in \mathbb{R}^k$, that allows to construct the set of Pareto best replies to x, *i.e.* $\beta^P(x) = \bigcup_{i=1}^m L_{\text{wss}}(x, \lambda_i)$. Moreover, this finite set of weight-vectors can be efficiently computed by solving the following MCLP:

$$\underset{y \in \Delta}{\overset{P}{\max}} \, U y, \tag{4}$$

where the superscript P stands for Pareto maximization, and U is a $k \times n$ matrix, the ith row being $x^\top A_i$. In particular we employ the multi-criteria simplex method. We refer the reader to Chap. 7 of [5] and to the original paper [21] for further details.

Given the re-interpretation of the Pareto best replies in terms of solution to the weighted sum scalarization problem, it becomes evident that for any $\lambda > 0$, all Nash equilibria of a two-person symmetric game with payoff matrix A_λ are also Pareto Nash equilibria of the multi-payoff game. Indeed, for any fixed $\lambda > 0$ and any Nash equilibrium $x \in \Delta$ of A_λ we have that

$$x^\top A_\lambda x = \underset{y \in \Delta}{\max} \, y^\top A_\lambda x.$$

Hence, $x \in L_{\text{wss}}(x)$, which implies $x \in \beta^P(x)$, *i.e.* x is a Pareto Nash equilibrium.

4   Dominant Sets with Multiple Affinities

In the previous section we have characterized Nash equilibria in multi-payoff games and in Sect. 2 we have introduced dominant sets in the single-objective case as ESS of two-person symmetric games. Hence, the natural extension of the notion of dominant set in the presence of multiple affinities is via a generalization of the notion of ESS equilibrium to multi-payoff games.

There exist several definitions of ESS for multi-payoff games [12,21], but in this work we adhere to the so-called Biased-ESS proposed in [21]. A strategy $x \in \Delta$ is a *Biased-ESS* (BESS) if there exists $\lambda > 0$ such that

- $u(x,x) \geq_\lambda u(y,x)$ for all $y \in \Delta$;
- $u(x,x) =_\lambda u(y,x) \implies u(x,y) >_\lambda u(y,y)$,

where, for a relation $R \in \{=, \geq, >, \leq, <\}$, $(a\ R_\lambda b) \iff (\lambda^\top a\ R\ \lambda^\top b)$. Each Biased-ESS is a Pareto Nash equilibrium because it is a Nash equilibrium of A_λ (see previous section). Biased-ESS can be extracted for any $\lambda > 0$ by employing biased Replicator Dynamics [21], ie standard replicator dynamics in (3) run on the payoff matrix A_λ. Given a Biased-ESS $x \in \Delta$ we obtain the corresponding dominant set by taking its support $\sigma(x)$.

As it turns out, enumerating all dominant sets corresponding to Biased-ESSs of multi-payoff games is a poser, because every $\lambda > 0$ might potentially lead to one or more Biased-ESSs. Many of them will of course agree in their support, for there are uncountably many λs versus a finite set of possible dominant sets (not more than $2^{|\mathcal{O}|} - 1$), but in general characterizing the set of dominant sets will remain an intractable problem. For this reason we rely on some heuristic that allow us to efficiently extract some of the Biased-ESSs in multi-payoff games. The corresponding set of dominant sets will then be used to construct a single affinity matrix, from which we compute the ultimate dominant set clustering result.

4.1 Heuristics for Selecting Multi-objective Dominant Sets

We compute the finite set of weight-vectors $\Lambda(x)$ that characterizes the set of Pareto best replies to the barycenter of the simplex, $i.e.x_i = 1/n$ for all $i \in \{1, \ldots, n\}$. This computation is performed by running a MCLP simplex solver for the multi-criteria optimization problem in (4). As a result, we typically obtain several hundreds of weight-vectors, depending on the affinity matrices. In order to reduce the number of weight-vectors, we cluster them by using dominant sets clustering (see, Sect. 2) with affinity $A_{ij} = \mathbb{k}_{i \neq j} \exp(-\|\lambda_i - \lambda_j\|^2)$, where $\mathbb{k}_P = 1$ if P is true, 0 otherwise. For each dominant set, we retain as a cluster representative the element having highest entry in the corresponding ESS equilibrium. The set of representatives after this procedure consists of few tens of elements. For each representative weight-vector λ, we compute the corresponding Biased-ESSs by running the biased replicatory dynamics under a peeling-off strategy. The set of supports of all the computed Biased-ESSs, $i.e.$the corresponding dominant-sets, is the output of the heuristic.

We tried also another heuristic, which is computationally more demanding. We first collected the set $\mathcal{X}$ of single-payoff ESS equilibria from each affinity matrix using the replicator dynamics under peeling-off strategy. For each collected equilibrium $x \in \mathcal{X}$, we computed the set of weight-vectors $\Lambda(x)$ by solving the corresponding MCLP. For each weight-vector in $\lambda \in \bigcup_{x \in \mathcal{X}} \Lambda(x)$, we extracted the corresponding set of biased-ESS equilibria using the biased replicator dynamics under peeling-off strategy. The supports of those equilibria were finally returned by the heuristic. However, experimentally it turned out that this second approach yields results, which are comparable to the ones achieved by the simpler heuristic. Therefore, in the experiments we rely on the first one.

4.2   Combination into a Single Affinity Matrix and Final Clustering

Given a set of m multi-objective dominant sets obtained with the heuristic proposed in the previous section, the final affinity matrix is built using a cluster embedding technique. For each data point $i \in \mathcal{O}$, we construct a m-dimensional binary vector $\boldsymbol{v}^i \in \{0,1\}^m$, where $v_k^i = 1$ if i belongs to the kth dominant set. We then build an affinity matrix $\hat{A}_{ij} = \mathbb{K}_{i \neq j} \exp(\beta \|\boldsymbol{v}^i - \boldsymbol{v}^j\|^2)$, where $\beta > 0$ is a free, scale parameter, and we obtain the final result by running the single-objective dominant set clustering algorithm on $\hat{A}$.

5   Experimental Results

In this section we present two types of experiments. In both cases we evaluated the clustering result based on the number of correct predictions our framework made from all predictions, which is just the classification accuracy. The first one addresses the problem of data clustering on both synthetic and real-world datasets, while the second one addresses the problem of image segmentation. Our approach was tested against the single-payoff dominant set clustering and against an affinity combination approach based on consensus clustering.

5.1   Data Clustering

We perform experiments on data clustering using affinities constructed from the Gaussian kernel and the polynomial kernel, under different parametrizations. In the specific, if $\boldsymbol{f}_i$ is the ith data point, we consider affinities of the type $A_{ij}^\sigma = exp(\|\boldsymbol{f}_i - \boldsymbol{f}_j\|^2/2\sigma^2)$ constructed in terms of the Gaussian kernel, where σ is sampled from $(0,1)$. We considered also the following two dataset-dependent value of the scaling parameter: $\sigma_M = \max_{i \neq j} \|\boldsymbol{f}_i - \boldsymbol{f}_j\|$. Finally, we considered an affinity constructed using the polynomial kernel, *i.e.* $A_{ij}^p = (1 + \boldsymbol{f}_i^\top \boldsymbol{f}_j)$.

The datasets that we have used are summarized in the first three rows of Table 1. The first is a toy datasets that we generated, while the other are taken from the well-known UCI Machine Learning repository. The toy dataset has 250 points in 3-dimensional space, with two Gaussian-distributed clusters of points. Each cluster has 100 points, while 50 points are uniformly-distributed clutter points.

To give an idea of the positive effect of the combination of multiple affinities, we report in Fig. 2, how the accuracy changes as the number of affinity matrices that are combined increases. Affinity matrices were randomly sampled (without replacement) from a set of 20 available matrices and clustered with the proposed multi-objective dominant set algorithm. We reported the average accuracies of 20 trials obtained on Toy-1 and the Iris data set. The bars represent the variance which, as can be seen from the figure, decreases with increasing similarities. We can also notice that there is a clear benefit from the combination method that we propose, which is more evident on the real-world dataset Iris.

We tested our algorithm on all the datasets using eight affinities (A^σ with 6 randomly sampled $\sigma \in (0,1)$, A^{σ_M} and A^p). In Table 1 we report the accuracies

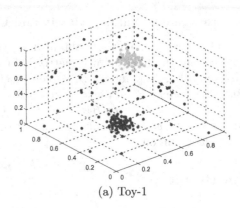

(a) Toy-1

Fig. 1. Exemplary dataset generated synthetically. Red points correspond to clutter (best viewed in color) (Color figure online).

Table 1. Accuracies of single-objective dominant sets on the 8 affinities S_i, $i = 1..8$, and the multi-objective dominant sets S_C. On the Classes row, '2+1' means 2 classes plus additional background clutter noise (see, e.g. Fig. 1)

	Toy	*Iris*	*Ionos.*	*Seeds*	*Haber.*	*Wine*	*Hayes*	*Blood*	*Spect.*
Instances	250	150	351	210	306	178	132	748	267
Features	3	4	33	7	3	13	5	10	8
Classes	2+1	3	2	3	2	3	3	2	2
S_1	0.963	0.913	0.652	0.552	0.667	0.652	0.405	0.701	0.689
S_2	0.959	0.893	0.672	0.895	0.667	0.719	0.423	0.701	0.772
S_3	0.962	0.880	0.672	0.890	0.673	0.702	0.415	0.707	0.742
S_4	0.960	0.893	0.681	0.886	0.686	0.702	0.409	0.707	0.697
S_5	0.971	0.860	0.678	0.900	0.693	0.674	0.402	0.723	0.704
S_6	0.964	0.833	0.681	0.890	0.696	0.556	0.411	0.723	0.697
S_7	0.958	0.333	0.641	0.333	**0.735**	0.404	0.386	0.762	**0.794**
S_8	0.965	0.920	0.541	0.895	0.533	0.517	0.417	0.701	0.558
S_C	**0.997**	**0.947**	**0.710**	**0.914**	0.727	**0.736**	**0.439**	**0.775**	**0.794**

obtained by single-objective dominant sets clustering on each of the 8 affinities (S_i, $i = 1, \ldots, 8$), as well as the results obtained by our multi-objective dominant set (S_C). As we can see, the quantitative results confirm that the proposed multi-objective clustering method based on dominant sets is consistently able to improve the results that one would obtain by employing the single similarities, on all tested real-world and synthetic datasets.

We compared the result of our algorithm also against a consensus clustering [22] method, by using an ensemble of clusterings constructed with the information coming from all the available affinities. Specifically, we adopt the single-objective dominant set clustering run on the different affinities to create the

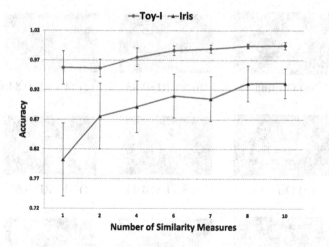

Fig. 2. Accuracy for different numbers of similarity measures

clustering ensemble. The different clusterings are then combined into a single affinity matrix according to the Evidence Accumulation paradigm, *i.e.* we built a matrix A known as *co-association matrix*, where A_{ij} is (for distinct i and j) the fraction of times object i and object j were clustered together among all clusterings in the ensemble, while $A_{ij} = 0$ if $i = j$. To get the final clustering result, we run the single-objective dominant set clustering on the co-association matrix raised to a power γ between 0 and 1, *i.e.* $A = A^{\gamma}$, where $\gamma = 1$ recovers the standard co-association matrix. The results reported in Fig. 3 show the score that we obtain under the best gamma. As we can see, the proposed multi-objective clustering approach is consistently better than the consensus clustering approach, even though by a small margin.

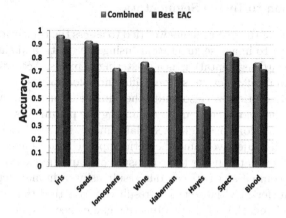

Fig. 3. Comparison Against Consensus Clustering

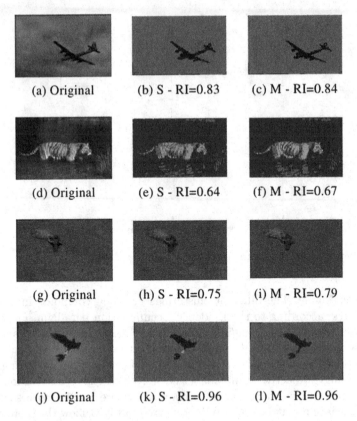

(a) Original   (b) S - RI=0.83   (c) M - RI=0.84

(d) Original   (e) S - RI=0.64   (f) M - RI=0.67

(g) Original   (h) S - RI=0.75   (i) M - RI=0.79

(j) Original   (k) S - RI=0.96   (l) M - RI=0.96

Fig. 4. Segmentation results and their corresponding Rand Index. The multi-objective version (M) is compared against the best result a single affinity measure (S).

5.2   Application to Image Segmentation

With the last part of the experiments we tried to assess the robustness of the approach with respect to image segmentations using the multi- and single-objective approach. We regard segmentation as a clustering of pixels. According, we define different pixel-similarity measures from different color spaces: RGB, grayscale, HSV and Lab. In-addition, we also built other similarity measures using different combinations of the color spaces and by changing the parameters σ. The qualitative experiments are done over few exemplary images from the Berkeley dataset [14] using the multi-objective game-theoretic approach and single-objective one. Both results are evaluated using their measure of Rand-Index which enables us for a numerical comparison between our result using a human segmented natural images from Berkeley dataset. The result confirms that the multi-similarity approach outperforms that of single objective game-theoretic one.

6   Conclusions

In this paper we have a proposed an approach to combine multiple affinity matrices within the dominant-set clustering framework. The proposed idea is motivated by the game-theoretic interpretation of dominant sets and has its roots in multi-criteria (evolutionary) game theory. Basically, the problem of extracting dominant sets in the presence of multiple affinities is cast into the problem of finding and combining Biased-ESS equilibria in the corresponding multi-payoff game. Due to the intractability of a complete enumeration of equilibria, we introduced an heuristic to extract some of them, which are then combined into a single affinity for the final clustering (Fig. 4).

Results on several synthetic as well as standard benchmark datasets have consistently demonstrated the effectiveness of the proposed approach. As a matter of future work, we plan to apply the proposed approach to different real-world scenarios involving multiple-cues, and devise more principled way of characterizing the set of dominant sets under multiple afifnities.

References

1. Alata, E., Dacier, M., Deswarte, Y., Kaaâniche, M., Kortchinsky, K., Nicomette, V., Pham, V.H., Pouget, F.: Collection and analysis of attack data based on honeypots deployed on the internet. In: Gollmann, D., Massacci, F., Yautsiukhin, A. (eds.) Quality of Protection. Advances in Information Security, vol. 23, pp. 79–91. Springer, USA (2006)
2. Albarelli, A., Bulò, S.R., Torsello, A., Pelillo, M.: Matching as a non-cooperative game. In: ICCV 2009, pp. 1319–1326 (2009)
3. Blackwell, D.: An analog of the minimax theorem for vector payoffs. Pac. J. Math. 6(11), 1–8 (1956)
4. Contini, B.M.: A decision model under uncertainty with multiple objectives. In: Mensch, A. (ed.) Theory of Games: Techniques and Applications. Elsevier, New York (1966)
5. Ehrgott, M.: Multicriteria Optimization, 2nd edn. Springer, Heidelberg (2005)
6. Frommlet, F.: Tag snp selection based on clustering according to dominant sets found using replicator dynamics. Adv. Data Anal. Classif. 4(1), 65–83 (2010)
7. Gönen, M., Alpaydin, E.: Multiple kernel learning algorithms. J. Mach. Learn. Res. 12, 2211–2268 (2011)
8. Hamid, R., Johnson, A.Y., Batta, S., Bobick, A.F., Isbell, C.L., Coleman, G.: Detection and explanation of anomalous activities: representing activities as bags of event n-grams. In: CVPR (1), pp. 1031–1038 (2005)
9. Harary, F.: Graph Theory. Addison Wesley, Reading (1969)
10. Hérault, L., Horaud, R.: Figure-ground discrimination: a combinatorial optimization approach. IEEE Trans. Pattern Anal. Mach. Intell. 15(9), 899–914 (1993)
11. Hung, H., Kröse, B.J.A.: Detecting f-formations as dominant sets. In: Proceedings of the 13th International Conference on Multimodal Interfaces, ICMI 2011, November 14–18 2011, Alicante, Spain, pp. 231–238 (2011). http://doi.acm.org/10.1145/2070481.2070525
12. Kawamura, T., Kanazawa, T., Ushio, T.: Evolutionarily and neutrally stable strategies in multicriteria games. IEICE Trans. Fundam. Electr. Commun. Comput. Sci. E96–A(4), 814–820 (2013)

13. Lozovanu, D., Solomon, D., Zelikovsky, A.: Multiobjective games and determining Pareto-Nash equilibria. Bul. Acad. Stiinte Rep. Moldova Mat. **3**(49), 115–122 (2005)

14. Martin, D., Fowlkes, C., Tal, D., Malik, J.: A database of human segmented natural images and its application to evaluating segmentation algorithms and measuring ecological statistics. In: Proceedings of the 8th International Conference Computer Vision, vol. 2, pp. 416–423, July 2001

15. Pavan, M., Pelillo, M.: A new graph-theoretic approach to clustering and segmentation. In: Proceedings of the IEEE Conference Computer Vision and Pattern Recognition (CVPR), pp. 145–152 (2003)

16. Pavan, M., Pelillo, M.: Dominant sets and pairwise clustering. IEEE Trans. Pattern Anal. Mach. Intell. **29**(1), 167–172 (2007)

17. Pelillo, M.: What is a cluster? Perspectives from game theory. In: Proceedings of the NIPS Workshop on Clustering Theory (2009)

18. Rota Bulò, S., Pelillo, M.: A game-theoretic approach to hypergraph clustering. IEEE Trans. Pattern Anal. Mach. Intell. **35**(6), 1312–1327 (2013)

19. Shapley, L.S.: Equilibrium points in games with vector payoffs. Naval Res. Logistics Q. **1**, 57–61 (1959)

20. Somasundaram, K., Baras, J.S.: Pareto nash replies for multiobjective games. In: Technical report, Institute for Systems Research (2008)

21. Somasundaram, K., Baras, J.S.: Achieving symmetric Pareto Nash equilibria using biased replicator dynamics. In: Proceedings of the 48th IEEE Conference Decision and Control, pp. 7000–7005 (2009)

22. Topchy, A.P., Law, M.H.C., Jain, A.K., Fred, A.L.N.: Analysis of consensus partition in cluster ensemble. In: Proceedings of the 4th IEEE International Conference on Data Mining (ICDM 2004), November 1–4 2004, Brighton, UK, pp. 225–232 (2004). http://dx.doi.org/10.1109/ICDM.2004.10100

23. Torsello, A., Rota Bulò, S., Pelillo, M.: Grouping with asymmetric affinities: a game-theoretic perspective. In: Proceedings of the IEEE Conference Computer Vision and Pattern Recognition (CVPR), pp. 292–299 (2006)

24. Torsello, A., Pelillo, M.: Hierarchical pairwise segmentation using dominant sets and anisotropic diffusion kernels. In: Cremers, D., Boykov, Y., Blake, A., Schmidt, F.R. (eds.) EMMCVPR 2009. LNCS, vol. 5681, pp. 182–192. Springer, Heidelberg (2009)

25. Vascon, S., Mequanint, E.Z., Cristani, M., Hung, H., Pelillo, M., Murino, V.: A game-theoretic probabilistic approach for detecting conversational groups. In: Cremers, D., Reid, I., Saito, H., Yang, M.-H. (eds.) ACCV 2014. LNCS, vol. 9007, pp. 658–675. Springer, Heidelberg (2015)

26. Wang, M., Ye, Z.L., Wang, Y., Wang, S.X.: Dominant sets clustering for image retrieval. Signal Process. **88**, 2843–2849 (2008)

27. Weibull, J.W.: Evolutionary Game Theory. MIT Press, Cambridge (2005)

28. Zeleny, M.: Games with multiple payoffs. Int. J. Game Theor. **4**(4), 179–191 (1975)

29. Zhou, Z.H.: Ensemble Methods: Foundations and Algorithms. Chapman & Hall, Boca Raton (2012)

Discovery of Salient Low-Dimensional Dynamical Structure in Neuronal Population Activity Using Hopfield Networks

Felix Effenberger[1]([⊠]) and Christopher Hillar[2]

[1] Max-Planck-Institute for Mathematics in the Sciences,
Inselstr. 22, 04103 Leipzig, Germany
`felix.effenberger@mis.mpg.de`
[2] Redwood Center for Theoretical Neuroscience,
Berkeley, CA 94720, USA
`chillar@berkeley.edu`

Abstract. We present here a novel method for the classical task of finding and extracting recurring spatiotemporal patterns in recorded spiking activity of neuronal populations. In contrast to previously proposed methods it does not seek to classify exactly recurring patterns, but rather approximate versions possibly differing by a certain number of missed, shifted or excess spikes. We achieve this by fitting large Hopfield networks to windowed, binned spiking activity in an unsupervised way using minimum probability flow parameter estimation and then collect Hopfield memories over the raw data. This procedure results in a drastic reduction of pattern counts and can be exploited to identify prominently recurring spatiotemporal patterns. Modeling furthermore the sequence of occurring Hopfield memories over the original data as a Markov process, we are able to extract low-dimensional representations of neural population activity on longer time scales. We demonstrate the approach on a data set obtained in rat barrel cortex and show that it is able to extract a remarkably low-dimensional, yet accurate representation of population activity observed during the experiment.

Keywords: Neuronal population activity · Parallel spike train analysis · Spatiotemporal patterns · Hopfield network · Ising model

1 Introduction

Finding recurring spatiotemporal patterns (STP) in recorded spiking activity of neuronal populations is a classical problem in the data analysis of parallel spike trains, and quite a number of approaches to detect and classify recurring spatiotemporal patterns of neural population activity have been proposed [3,6]. Yet, most published methods so far either focus solely on synchrony detection [15,16,18] or assume a more or less noiseless scenario, seeking to classify exactly recurring STP in neuronal activity (apart from allowing some jitter in spike timing), see e.g. [5].

© Springer International Publishing Switzerland 2015
A. Feragen et al. (Eds.): SIMBAD 2015, LNCS 9370, pp. 199–208, 2015.
DOI: 10.1007/978-3-319-24261-3_16

Given the usually high variability of population responses to stimuli, the re-occurrence of such exactly repeating STP becomes more and more unlikely with increasing population size though. Despite this variability, there is strong experimental evidence that neural populations code information about stimuli in some form of STP, see e.g. [1,2]. Thus, a much more plausible situation is that some underlying STP appears in several "corrupted" variants, both expressing jitter in spike times and differing in a few missing or excess spikes. To find and classify recurring STP in parallel spike trains, we fit Hopfield networks (HN) to windowed, binned spiking activity of a population of cells using minimum probability flow [19] (MPF), a novel probabilistic learning rule for HN with many desirable properties [8,10]. We then use Hopfield network dynamics to classify the raw data and identify recurring STP. The presented method is robust to the aforementioned variability in the signal and able to extract the underlying recurring patterns, even for seldom occurring STP and large population sizes.

Modeling furthermore the sequence of occurring Hopfield memories as a Markov process, we are able to extract low-dimensional representations of neural population activity. We demonstrate the approach on a data set obtained from rat barrel cortex [14] and show that it is able to extract a remarkably low-dimensional, yet accurate representation of the average population response to whisker stimulation.

The paper is organized as follows. In Sect. 2 we give a short overview of the theoretical background, namely Hopfield networks and minimum probability flow parameter estimation. We then present our method in Sect. 3, followed by a demonstration of the method in Sect. 4. We conclude in Sect. 5.

2   Background

Hopfield networks [11] are a well-known model of memory and collective processing in networks of abstract McCulloch-Pitts [13] neurons.

The possible *states* of a HN are the same as those of a non-ferromagnetic Ising model, a classical model in statistical physics [12]. This discrete probability distribution has as states all binary vectors of length n, with the probability of a particular state $\mathbf{x} = (x_1, \ldots, x_n) \in \{0,1\}^n$ being

$$p_\mathbf{x} = \frac{1}{Z} \exp\left(\sum_{i<j} J_{ij} x_i x_j - \sum_i \theta_i x_i \right) = \frac{1}{Z} \exp\left(-E_\mathbf{x}\right), \qquad (1)$$

in which $J \in \mathbb{R}^{n \times n}$ is a real symmetric matrix with zero diagonal (the *coupling matrix*), the vector $\theta \in \mathbb{R}^n$ is a bias or *threshold* term, and $Z = \sum_\mathbf{x} \exp(-E_\mathbf{x})$ is the *partition function* (which normalizes $\mathbf{p} = (p_\mathbf{x})_{\mathbf{x} \in \{0,1\}^n}$ to sum to 1). Typically, the expression inside the exponential of (1) is viewed as the negative of a quadratic energy function,

$$E_\mathbf{x} = -\frac{1}{2}\mathbf{x}^\top J \mathbf{x} + \theta^\top \mathbf{x}. \qquad (2)$$

Thus, states **x** with low energy (2) appear most often under sampling from (1). It follows from basic theory (e.g. [4]) that the distribution defined by (1) is the maximum entropy distribution on binary vectors given its first and second order statistics (mean and covariance).

A HN is a recurrent network of binary nodes (representing spiking neurons) with deterministic dynamics. Formally, a HN on n nodes $\{1, \ldots, n\}$ consists of a symmetric coupling matrix $J \in \mathbb{R}^{n \times n}$ and a threshold vector $\theta \in \mathbb{R}^n$.

An *asynchronous dynamics update* of state **x** in a HN consists of iteratively replacing each x_i in **x** with a new value

$$x_i = \begin{cases} 1 & \text{if } \sum_{j \neq i} J_{ij} x_j > \theta_i, \\ 0 & \text{otherwise.} \end{cases} \tag{3}$$

The update given by Eq. (3) is inspired by computations exhibited in neurons [13] and a model neuron with such an update rule is often called a *McCulloch-Pitts neuron*. A fundamental property of HNs is that an asynchronous dynamics update given by Eq. (3) does not increase the energy given by Eq. (2). Thus, after a finite number of updates, each initial state **x** converges to a *fixed-point* **x*** (also called *stable-point* or *memory*) of the dynamics. Intuitively, we may interpret the dynamics as an inference technique, producing the most probable nearby memory given a noisy version. See Fig. 1 for an example of a small HN and its energy landscape.

A basic problem is to construct Hopfield networks with a given set $\mathcal{D}$ of binary patterns as memories (i.e. local minima of $E_\mathbf{x}$). Such networks are useful

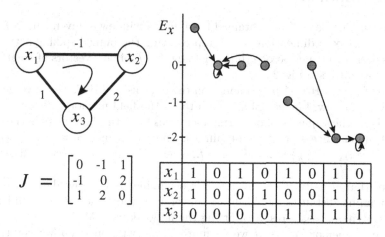

Fig. 1. Small Hopfield network. A 3-node Hopfield network with coupling matrix J and zero threshold vector θ. A state vector $\mathbf{x} = (x_1, x_2, x_3)$ has energy $E_\mathbf{x}$ as labeled on the y-axis of the diagram. Arrows represent one iteration of the network dynamics; i.e. x_1, x_2, and x_3 are updated by Eq. (3) in the order of the clockwise arrow. Resulting fixed-points **x*** are indicated by blue circles (Color figure online).

for memory denoising and retrieval since corrupted versions of patterns in $\mathcal{D}$ will converge through the dynamics to the originals.

In contrast to traditional rules used for this task such as the *outer-product learning rule* [11] (OPR) and the *perceptron learning rule* [17] (PER) that face a number of limitations such as low memory capacity, bad generalization properties and high computational cost, we here use *minimum probability flow* [19] (MPF) to estimate the parameters of a Hopfield network. Applied to estimating the parameters in an Ising model/Hopfield network, Eq. (1), the minimum probability flow objective function [8,19] is:

$$K_{\mathcal{D}}(J, \theta) = \sum_{\mathbf{x} \in \mathcal{D}} \sum_{\mathbf{x}' \in \mathcal{N}(\mathbf{x})} \exp\left(\frac{E_{\mathbf{x}} - E_{\mathbf{x}'}}{2}\right). \qquad (4)$$

Here, the *neighborhood* $\mathcal{N}(\mathbf{x})$ of $\mathbf{x}$ consists of those binary vectors which are Hamming distance 1 away from $\mathbf{x}$. The function in (4) is infinitely differentiable, jointly convex in the parameters, consists of only order $O(|\mathcal{D}|n)$ terms, and can be minimized using standard methods such as gradient descent. Notice also that when $K_{\mathcal{D}}$ is small, the energy differences $E_{\mathbf{x}} - E_{\mathbf{x}'}$ between points $\mathbf{x}$ in the dataset $\mathcal{D}$ and patterns $\mathbf{x}'$ in single-flip neighborhoods $\mathcal{N}(\mathbf{x})$ will be negative, making $\mathbf{x}$ a fixed-point of the Hopfield dynamics. Importantly to applications, much more is true: minimizing (4) given a storable set of patterns $\mathcal{D}$ will determine a Hopfield network storing those patterns as robust memories [8]. Moreover, the MPF objective function can naturally be turned into an online, neurologically plausible learning rule [9].

3   Our Method

The training data X are obtained by sliding a window of given length L over a binary matrix of dimension $N \times T$ representing the binned spiking activity of N cells over a time period of T bins, yielding $T - L$ binary vectors of length NL as training data, see Fig. 2.

After fitting a HN with NL nodes on the data using MPF, we converge each window of the raw, binned spiking data to its Hopfield memory.

We label the sequence of occurring memories by natural numbers in the order of their appearance so that we obtain a memory sequence $S = (s_1, \ldots, s_{T-L})$, with $s_i \in \{m_1, \ldots, m_k\} = M$, $k \leq T - L$, where M denotes the set of all distinct memories in S.

Note that usually $k \ll |S|$, as STP occurring in the raw data that have low Hamming distances are likely to converge to the same memory under the Hopfield dynamics as a result of fitting the network with MPF.

For each memory $m_i \in M$ we compute all pairwise one-step Markov transition probabilities to $m_j \in M$ ($1 \leq j \leq k$) using data from S and the entropy over this probability distribution for each m_i, which we call the entropy of the memory m_i and denote by $H(m_i)$.

The entropy of a memory is a measure for how predictable the following network state is, according to the observed data. Memories with a more restricted

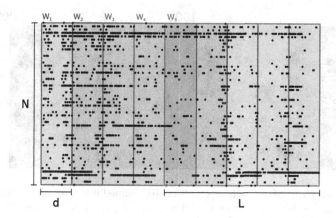

Fig. 2. Windowing of binned neural activity. To generate training data for the Hopfield network, spiking data of N cells are first binned and then training vectors are extracted using a sliding window. Windows of length L are shifted by d bins (here, we take d = 1) resulting in training vectors of dimension n = NL. The above illustration shows five overlapping windows.

set of following network states have lower entropy, ones with less predictable states have higher entropy. $H(m_i)$ can therefore be seen as a local measure (in time) for how deterministic the network dynamics evolve from that memory.

We then construct a directed graph with the elements of M as nodes. Two nodes m_i, m_j are connected by an edge (m_i, m_j) of weight w if their Markov transition probability $w = P(m_j|m_i)$ obtained from S is non-zero. We call this graph the *Markov graph* G_M of S. Paths and cycles (i.e. simple closed paths) in G_M along nodes with low entropy correspond to sequences of memory labels and thus sequences of STP of spiking activity that are prominently and reliably generated by the neuronal population.

4 Application to Data

We applied the proposed method to spiking data of recorded in the rat barrel cortex during repeated whisker stimulation [14] ($N = 16, T = 3.4 \cdot 10^4, L = 10$, 1 ms bins), see Fig. 3 for a raster plot of 50 trials of the experiment. For each trial, recorded spiking activity measured in 16 electrodes (multi unit activity, MUA) is shown. Whisker stimulation is performed at 1000 ms within each trial.

The number of different 160-dimensional patterns (corresponding to 10 ms of network activity) in the raw data is 161,171. After fitting a Hopfield network to the raw data and collecting the memories over the input data we obtain 577 distinct Hopfield memories, a 280-fold reduction in count, see also Fig. 4. The Markov transition probability matrix for the 577 memories is shown in Fig. 5, their probabilities and entropies in Fig. 6.

To ease data analysis, we further restrict the number of memories considered to the 50 memories of highest rank from this point on. The Markov Graph

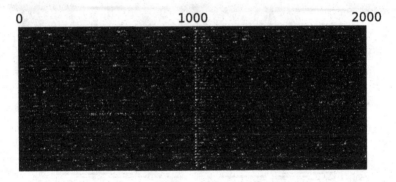

Fig. 3. Raster plots of 16 cells over 50 trials. Binned into 1 ms bins, stimulation of primary whisker at 1000 ms. White dots denote spiking activity. Horizontal axis shows time, vertical axis units/trials.

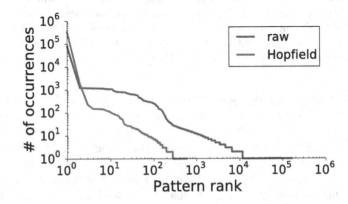

Fig. 4. Ranks of raw and Hopfield patterns of 10 ms length.

G_M is pruned accordingly, but node entropies are calculated on the full set of memories. To each Hopfield memory we associate memory triggered averages (MTAs, computed as the average of all raw patterns converging to the given Hopfield memory); these are shown in Fig. 7.

For this data set we find a 'central' node m_α (corresponding to memory label 1) in the Markov Graph G_M that has a high degree (sum of in- and out-degrees). This is characteristic for a situation in which the node is the termination (resp. starting) point of prominently occurring STP of network activity. Interestingly, the memory m_α occurs very frequently in the data ($p > 0.9$) and the node has low entropy. This we expect from a network's low-energy base state that it prominently rests in and repeatedly returns to. Using the information of the stimulus protocol, we indeed found that m_α corresponds to the resting state of the network (see top left MTA in Fig. 7).

We now look at cycles (i.e. closed, simple paths) in the Markov Graph G_M starting and terminating in some given node. We expect that cycles in G_M starting in m_α can give insight on how the network is driven out of its resting

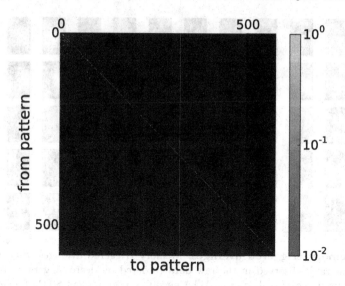

Fig. 5. Markov transition probabilities of all Hopfield memories (577) observed in the raw data.

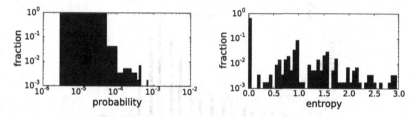

Fig. 6. Occurrence probabilities and entropies of Hopfield memories. Left: Occurrence probabilities of memories observed in raw data (cut at 10^{-2}). Right: Entropies of memories (calculated for each memory from its Markov transition probabilities) observed in raw data.

state by some stimulus and enters a transient sequence of excited states before falling back to the resting state. See Fig. 8 for the distribution of cycle lengths in the restricted Markov graph. Note that windows overlap by 9 ms in the present case, making the approximation of longer time-scale network dynamics via a first order Markov process (as paths in the Markov Graph) rather robust.

Tracing such cycles in G_M (and scoring them by their entropy, obtained as a weighted sum of the entropies of the cycle's nodes as a measure for how reliably that cycle is "visited" by the network dynamics), we find that the most STP associated with low entropy cycles indeed correspond closely to the average network response to whisker stimulation (that we computed from the raw data using knowledge of the simulation protocol), see Fig. 9. Note that our method was able to reconstruct the average network response without any knowledge of the stimulus protocol.

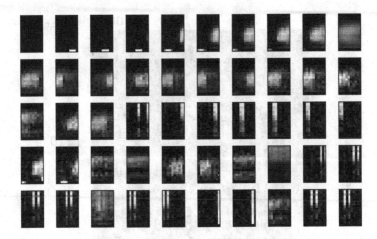

Fig. 7. Memory triggered averages. Memory triggered averages of 50 memories with highest rank observed in the raw data (ordered by decreasing rank, top left to bottom right). Each plot shows one MTA encoding a prominent STP of length 10 ms; a white pixel denotes high (1) spiking probability of a given neuron at a given time, a black pixel low spiking probability (0).

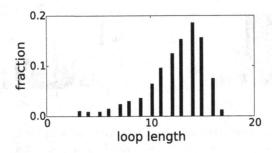

Fig. 8. Distribution of cycle lengths around base node 0 in reduced Markov graph.

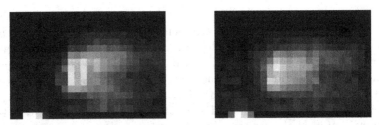

Fig. 9. Reconstruction of stable network response. Left: Stimulus triggered average obtained from raw data obtained using knowledge of stimulus protocol. Right: Likely network response reconstructed by our method, corresponding to a low entropy path in the Markov graph, not using any knowledge of the stimulus protocol.

5   Conclusion

We presented here a method for identifying and classifying recurring spatiotemporal patterns in parallel neural spike trains based on Hopfield networks. In contrast to previously proposed methods [5,6,15,16,18], it does not solely focus on (partial) synchrony detection or finding exactly recurring patterns, nor does it face combinatorial explosion in the number of neurons or time steps considered.

The trained Hopfield networks denoise the data, grouping similar patterns together in a way that respects the underlying statistics of the data. They are thus able to identify prominent patterns reoccurring in the dataset, possibly corrupted by noise, and eliminate the large number of spurious patterns occurring rarely. In its memories the network encodes different structural aspects of the spiking data such as prominent temporal firing sequences that usually are very difficult to identify in the raw data or using standard methods. Modeling the sequence of occurring memories as a Markov chain, we have shown that the method is able to extract salient features of parallel spike trains in a fully unsupervised way.

We thus propose the method as a novel tool in mining parallel spike trains for possibly low-dimensional underlying network dynamics. An open source software in form of a Python package [7] allowing for the wider application of the method is currently in beta test and to be released soon.

Acknowledgements. The authors would like to thank Yuri Campbell for helpful comments on an earlier version of this manuscript.

References

1. Abeles, M., Bergman, H.: Spatiotemporal firing patterns in the frontal cortex of behaving monkeys. J. Neurophysiol. **70**(4), 1629–1638 (1993)
2. Arieli, A., Shoham, D.: Coherent spatiotemporal patterns of ongoing activity revealed by real-time optical imaging coupled with single-unit recording in the cat visual cortex. J. Neurophysiol. **73**(5), 2072–2093 (1995)
3. Brown, E.N., Kass, R.E., Mitra, P.P.: Multiple neural spike train data analysis: state-of-the-art and future challenges. Nat. Neurosci. **7**(5), 456–461 (2004)
4. Cover, T., Thomas, J.: Elements of Information Theory, 2nd edn. Wiley, New Jersey (2006)
5. Gansel, K.S., Singer, W.: Detecting multineuronal temporal patterns in parallel spike trains. Front. Neuroinformatics **6**(May), 18 (2012)
6. Grün, S., Rotter, S.: Analysis of Parallel Spike Trains. Springer, Heidelberg (2010)
7. Hillar, C., Effenberger, F.: **hdnet** - hopfield denoising network. https://github.com/team-hdnet/hdnet (2015)
8. Hillar, C., Sohl-Dickstein, J., Koepsell, K.: Efficient and optimal little-hopfield auto-associative memory storage using minimum probability flow. In: NIPS Workshop on Discrete Optimization in Machine Learning (DISCML) (2012)
9. Hillar, C., Sohl-Dickstein, J., Koepsell, K.: Novel local learning rule for neural adaptation fits Hopfield memory networks efficiently and optimally. BMC Neurosci. **14**(Suppl 1), P215 (2013)

10. Hillar, C., Tran, N.: Robust exponential memory in Hopfield networks. arXiv e-prints (2014)
11. Hopfield, J.: Neural networks and physical systems with emergent collective computational abilities. Proc. Nat. Acad. Sci. **79**(8), 2554–2558 (1982)
12. Ising, E.: Beitrag zur Theorie des Ferromagnetismus. Zeitschrift fur Physik **31**, 253–258 (1925)
13. McCulloch, W., Pitts, W.: A logical calculus of the ideas immanent in nervous activity. Bull. Math. Biol. **5**(4), 115–133 (1943)
14. Minlebaev, M., Colonnese, M., Tsintsadze, T., Sirota, A., Khazipov, R.: Early gamma oscillations synchronize developing thalamus and cortex. Science **334**(6053), 226–229 (2011)
15. Picado-Muiño, D., Borgelt, C., Berger, D., Gerstein, G., Grün, S.: Finding neural assemblies with frequent item set mining. Front. Neuroinformatics **7**(May), 9 (2013)
16. Pipa, G., Wheeler, D.W., Singer, W., Nikolić, D.: NeuroXidence: reliable and efficient analysis of an excess or deficiency of joint-spike events. J. Comput. Neurosci. **25**(1), 64–88 (2008)
17. Rosenblatt, F.: The perceptron: a probabilistic model for information storage and organization in the brain. Psychol. Rev. **65**(6), 386 (1958)
18. Santos, L.V., Ribeiro, S., Tort, A.B.L.: Detecting cell assemblies in large neuronal populations. J. Neurosci. Methods **220**(2), 149–166 (2013)
19. Sohl-Dickstein, J., Battaglino, P., DeWeese, M.: New method for parameter estimation in probabilistic models: minimum probability flow. Phys. Rev. Lett. **107**(22), 220601 (2011)

Distance-Based Network Recovery
Under Feature Correlation

David Adametz[✉] and Volker Roth

Department of Mathematics and Computer Science,
University of Basel, Basel Switzerland
{david.adametz, volker.roth}@unibas.ch

1 Introduction

We introduce the *Translation-invariant Matrix-T* process (*TiMT*) for estimating Gaussian graphical models (GGMs) from pairwise distances. The setup is particularly interesting, as many applications only allow distances to be observed in the first place. Hence, our approach is capable of inferring a network of *probability distributions*, of *strings*, *graphs* or *chemical structures*. The basic building block of classical GGMs is the matrix $\widetilde{X} \in \mathbb{R}^{n \times d}$ which follows the Matrix-Normal distribution [1]

$$\widetilde{X} \sim \mathcal{N}(M, \Psi \otimes I_d). \tag{1}$$

The goal is to identify Ψ^{-1}, which encodes the desired dependence structure. More specifically, two objects (= rows) are conditionally independent given all others if and only if Ψ^{-1} has a corresponding zero element. Prabhakaran et al. [3] formulated the *Translation-invariant Wishart Network* (*TiWnet*), which treats $\widetilde{X}$ as a latent matrix and only requires their squared Euclidean distances $D_{ij} = d_E(\widetilde{x}_i, \widetilde{x}_j)^2$, where $\widetilde{x}_i \in \mathbb{R}^d$ is the ith row of $\widetilde{X}$. Also, $S_E = \widetilde{X}\widetilde{X}^\top$ refers to the $n \times n$ inner-product matrix, which is linked via $D_{ij} = S_{E,ii} + S_{E,jj} - 2S_{E,ij}$. Importantly, the transition to distances implies that means of the form $M = 1_n w^\top$ with $w \in \mathbb{R}$ are not identifiable anymore. In contrast to the above, we start off by assuming a matrix $X := \widetilde{X}\Sigma^{\frac{1}{2}} \sim \mathcal{N}(M, \Psi \otimes \Sigma)$, where the columns (= features) are correlated as defined by $\Sigma \in \mathbb{R}^{d \times d}$. Due to this change, the inner-product becomes $S_{MH} = XX^\top = \widetilde{X}\Sigma\widetilde{X}^\top$. In our setting only pairwise distances of squared *Mahalanobis* type are observed,

$$D_{ij} = d_{MH}(x_i, x_j)^2 = (\widetilde{x}_i - \widetilde{x}_j)^\top \Sigma (\widetilde{x}_i - \widetilde{x}_j). \tag{2}$$

The quantities d, X, $\widetilde{X}$, $S := S_{MH}$, Σ and $M = 1_n w^\top$ are treated as latent variables. The main difficulty comes from the inherent mixture effect of Ψ and Σ in the distances, which blurs or obscures what is relevant in GGMs. For example, if we naively enforce $\Sigma = I_d$, then all of the information is solely attributed to Ψ. However, in applications where the true $\Sigma \neq I_d$, we would consequently infer false structure, up to a degree where the result is completely mislead by feature correlation.

In a Bayesian fashion, we specify a prior belief for Σ. For a conjugate prior, this leads to the Matrix-T distribution. The resulting model generalizes *TiWnet* and is flexible enough to account for arbitrary feature correlation.

A. Feragen et al. (Eds.): SIMBAD 2015, LNCS 9370, pp. 209–210, 2015.
DOI: 10.1007/978-3-319-24261-3

2 Experiments

We apply TiMT it to the publicly available colon cancer dataset of Sheffer et al. [4], which is comprised of 13 437 genes measured across 182 patients. Using the latest gene sets from the KEGG database, we arrive at $n = 276$ distinct pathways. After learning the mean and variance of each pathway as the distribution of its gene expression values across patients, the Bhattacharyya distances [2] are computed as a 276×276 matrix D. The pathways are allowed to overlap via common genes, thus leading to similarities, however it is unclear how and to what degree the correlation of patients affects the inferred network. For this purpose, we run *TiMT* alongside *TiWnet* with identical parameters for 20 000 samples and report the annealed networks in Figure 1. Again, the difference in topology is only due to latent feature correlation.

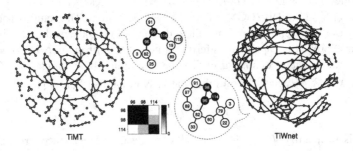

Fig. 1. A network of pathways in colon cancer patients, where each vertex represents one pathway. From both results, we extract a subgraph of 3 pathways including all neighbors in reach of 2 edges. The matrix on the bottom shows external information on pathway similarity based on their relative number of protein-protein interactions. Black/red edges refer to $+/-$ edge weight (Color figure online).

Without side information it is not possible to confirm either result, hence we resort to expert knowledge for protein-protein interactions from the BioGRID database and compute the strength of connection between pathways, leading to the conclusion that *TiWnet* overestimates the network and produces a highly-connected structure contradicting the evidence. This is a clear indicator for latent feature correlation.

References

1. Gupta, A.K., Nagar, D.K.: Matrix Variate Distributions. Addison-Wesley Longman, PMS Series (1999)
2. Jebara, T., Kondor, R.: Bhattacharyya and Expected Likelihood Kernels. In: Conference on Learning Theory (2003)
3. Prabhakaran, S., Adametz, D., Metzner, K.J., Böhm, A., Roth, V.: Recovering networks from distance data. JMLR **92**, 251–283 (2013)
4. Sheffer, M., Bacolod, M.D., Zuk, O., Giardina, S.F., Pincas, H., Barany, F., Paty, P.B., Gerald, W.L., Notterman, D.A., Domany, E.: Association of survival and disease progression with chromosomal instability: a genomic exploration of colorectal cancer. In: Proceedings of the National Academy of Sciences, pp. 7131–7136 (2009)

On Geodesic Exponential Kernels

Aasa Feragen[1(✉)], François Lauze[1], and Søren Hauberg[2]

[1] Department of Computer Science, University of Copenhagen,
Copenhagen Denmark
aasa@diku.dk
[2] DTU Compute, Copenhagen Denmark

This extended abstract summarizes work presented at CVPR 2015 [1].

Standard statistics and machine learning tools require input data residing in a Euclidean space. However, many types of data are more faithfully represented in general nonlinear metric spaces or Riemannian manifolds, e.g. shapes, symmetric positive definite matrices, human poses or graphs. The underlying metric space captures domain specific knowledge, e.g. non-linear constraints, which is available *a priori*. The intrinsic geodesic metric encodes this knowledge, often leading to improved statistical models.

A seemingly straightforward approach to statistics in metric spaces is to use kernel methods [3], designing exponential kernels:

$$k(x,y) = \exp(-\lambda(d(x,y))^q), \qquad \lambda, q > 0, \tag{1}$$

which only rely on geodesic distances $d(x, y)$ between observations. For $q = 2$ this gives a geodesic generalization of the *Gaussian kernel*, and $q = 1$ gives the geodesic *Laplacian kernel*. While this idea has an appealing similarity to familiar Euclidean kernel methods, we show that it is highly limited if the metric space is curved, see Table 1.

Theorem 1. *For a geodesic metric space (X, d), assume that $k(x,y) = \exp(-\lambda d^2(x,y))$ is positive definite (PD) for all $\lambda > 0$. Then (X, d) is flat in the sense of Alexandrov.*

This is a negative result, as most metric spaces of interest are not flat. As a consequence, we show that **geodesic Gaussian kernels on Riemannian manifolds are PD for all $\lambda > 0$ only if the Riemannian manifold is Euclidean.**

Theorem 2. *Let M be a complete, smooth Riemannian manifold with its associated geodesic distance metric d. Assume, moreover, that $k(x,y) = \exp(-\lambda d^2(x,y))$ is PD*

Table 1. Overview of results: For a geodesic metric, the geodesic exponential kernel (1) is only positive definite for all $\lambda > 0$ for

Kernel	Extends to general	
	Metric Spaces	Riemannian Manifolds
Gaussian ($q = 2$)	No (only if flat)	No (only if Euclidean)
Laplacian ($q = 1$)	Yes, iff metric is CND	Yes, iff metric is CND
Geodesic exp. ($q > 2$)	Not known	No

© Springer International Publishing Switzerland 2015
A. Feragen et al. (Eds.): SIMBAD 2015, LNCS 9370, pp. 211–213, 2015.
DOI: 10.1007/978-3-319-24261-3

Table 2. For a set of popular data spaces and metrics, we record whether the metric is a geodesic metric, whether it is a Euclidean metric, whether it is a CND metric, and whether its corresponding Gaussian and Laplacian kernels are PD.

Space	Distance metric	Geodesic metric?	Euclidean metric?	CND metric?	PD Gaussian kernel?	PD Laplacian kernel?
$\mathbb{R}^n$	Euclidean metric	✓	✓	✓	✓	✓
$\mathbb{R}^n, n > 2$	l_q-norm $\|\cdot\|_q, q > 2$	✓	÷	÷	÷	÷
Sphere $\mathbb{S}^n$	classical intrinsic	✓	÷	✓	÷	✓
Real projective space $\mathbb{P}^n(\mathbb{R})$	classical intrinsic	✓	÷	÷	÷	÷
Grassmannian	classical intrinsic	✓	÷	÷	÷	÷
Sym_d^+	Frobenius	✓	✓	✓	✓	✓
Sym_d^+	Log-Euclidean	✓	✓	✓	✓	✓
Sym_d^+	Affine invariant	✓	÷	÷	÷	÷
Sym_d^+	Fisher information metric	✓	÷	÷	÷	÷
Hyperbolic space $\mathbb{H}^n$	classical intrinsic	✓	÷	✓	÷	✓
1-dimensional normal distributions	Fisher information metric	✓	÷	✓	÷	✓
Metric trees	tree metric	✓	÷	✓	÷	✓
Geometric graphs (e.g. kNN)	shortest path distance	✓	÷	÷	÷	÷
Strings	string edit distance	✓	÷	÷	÷	÷
Trees, graphs	tree/graph edit distance	✓	÷	÷	÷	÷

for all $\lambda > 0$. Then the Riemannian manifold M is isometric to a Euclidean space.

Do these negative results depend on the choice $q = 2$ in (1)?

Theorem 3. *Let M be a Riemannian manifold with its associated geodesic distance metric d, and let $q > 2$. Then there is some $\lambda > 0$ so that the kernel (1) is not PD.*

The existence of a $\lambda > 0$ such that the kernel is not PD may seem innocent; however, as a consequence, the kernel bandwidth parameter cannot be learned. In contrast, the choice $q = 1$ in (1), giving a geodesic Laplacian kernel, leads to a more positive result:

Theorem 4. i) *The geodesic distance d in a geodesic metric space (X, d) is conditionally negative definite (CND) if and only if the corresponding geodesic Laplacian kernel is PD for all $\lambda > 0$.*

ii)   *In this case, the square root $d_{\sqrt{}}(x, y) = \sqrt{d(x,y)}$ is also a distance metric, and $(X, d_{\sqrt{}})$ can be isometrically embedded as a metric space into a Hilbert space H.*

iii)   *The square root metric $d_{\sqrt{}}$ is not a geodesic metric, and $d_{\sqrt{}}$ corresponds to the chordal metric in H, not the intrinsic metric on the image of X in H.*

The proofs rely on Schönberg's classical theorem [4], metric geometry and recent results on conditionally negative definite kernels [2]. Theoretical and empirical results on PD'ness of geodesic exponential kernels are summarized in Table 2.

References

1. Feragen, A., Lauze, F., Hauberg, S.: Geodesic exponential kernels: when curvature and linearity conflict. In: IEEE Conference on Computer Vision and Pattern Recognition, CVPR (2015)
2. Istas, J.: Manifold indexed fractional fields. ESAIM: Probab. Stat. **16**, 222–276 (2012)
3. Schölkopf, B., Smola, A.J.: Learning with kernels : support vector machines, regularization, optimization, and beyond. Adaptive computation and machine learning. MIT Press (2002)
4. Schönberg, I.J.: Metric spaces and completely monotone functions. Ann. Math. **39**(4), 811–841 (1938)

A Matrix Factorization Approach
to Graph Compression

Farshad Nourbakhsh[1], Samuel Rota Bulò[2, (✉)], and Marcello Pelillo[1]

[1] Ca' Foscari University, Venice Italy
[2] FBK-irst, Trento Italy

In the last few years, matrix factorization approaches have become an important tool in machine learning and found successful applications for tasks like, *e.g.* information retrieval, data mining and pattern recognition. Well-known techniques based on matrix factorization are, *e.g.* Singular Value Decomposition [1], Principal Component Analysis [2] and Nonnegative Matrix Factorization [3, 4].

A matrix undergoing a factorization in learning algorithms typically arises as a collection of feature vectors, each vector being a column of the matrix, or as a representation of the similarity/dissimilarity relations among data objects. In the latter case, we can easily interpret the matrix as the adjacency matrix of a weighted graph having the data objects as vertices. The application of matrix factorization for the analysis of graphs is mainly restricted to clustering [5, 6]. This paper aims at giving a novel viewpoint about the role of matrix factorization in the analysis of graphs and, in the specific, we show how matrix factorization can serve the purpose of compressing a graph.

Compressing data consists in changing its representation in a way to require fewer bits. Depending on the reversibility of this encoding process we might have a lossy or lossless compression. Information-theoretic works on compressing graphical structures have recently appeared [7]. However, they do not focus on preserving a graph structure as the compressed representation, which is instead what we aim at in our graph compression model. Our work is instead closer in spirit to [8], which proposes a summarization algorithm for unweighted graphs, and [9], which proposes a greedy procedure to determine a set of supernodes and superedges to approximate a weighted graph. Moreover, our work is related to the Szemerédi regularity lemma [10], a well-known result in extremal graph theory, which roughly states that a dense graph can be approximated by a bounded number of random bipartite graphs. An algorithmic version of this lemma has been used for speeding-up a pairwise clustering algorithm in [11].

A problem linked to graph compression that has focused the attention of researchers in the network and sociometric literature for the last few decades is *blockmodeling* [12, 13]. Blockmodels try to group the graph vertices into groups that preserve a *structural equivalence, i.e.* vertices falling in the same group should exhibit similar relations to the nodes in other groups (including self-similarity), and they differ by the way in which structural equivalence is defined.

© Springer International Publishing Switzerland 2015
A. Feragen et al. (Eds.): SIMBAD 2015, LNCS 9370, pp. 214–216, 2015.
DOI: 10.1007/978-3-319-24261-3

In this paper[1] we provide a novel viewpoint about the role of matrix factorization in the analysis of graphs and, in the specific, for the purpose of compressing a graph. The solution that we propose to compress a graph can be regarded as a blockmodel, where blocks and their relationships can be determined using a matrix factorization approach. The main contributions of the paper are the following: we link matrix factorization with graph compression by proposing a factorization that can be used to reduce the order of a graph, and we show that the same technique can be used to compress a kernel, by retaining a kernel as the reduced representation; we cast the discrete problem of finding the best factorization into a continuous optimization problem for which we formally prove the equivalence between the discrete and continuous formulations; we provide a novel algorithm to approximately find the proposed factorization, which resembles the NMF algorithm in [15] (under ℓ_2 divergence). Additionally, we formally prove convergence properties for our algorithm; finally, we establish a relation between clustering and our graph compression model and show that existing clustering approaches in the literature can be regarded as particular, *constrained* variants of our matrix factorization.

References

1. Horn, R.A., Johnson, C.R.: Matrix Analysis. Cambridge, University Press (1985)
2. Jolliffe, I.: Principal Component Analysis. Springer Verlag (1987)
3. Lee, D.D., Seung, H.S.: Learning the parts of objects by non-negative matrix factorization. Nature **401**, 788–791 (1999)
4. Paatero, P., Tapper, A.U.: Positive matrix factorization: a non-negative factor model with optimal utilization of error estimates of data values. Environmetrics **5**, 111–126 (1994)
5. Kuang, D., Park, H., Ding, C.: Symmetric nonnegative matrix factorization for graph clustering. In: SIAM International Conference on Data Mining, pp.106–117 (2012)
6. Rota Bulò, S., Pelillo, M.: Probabilistic clustering using the baum-eagon inequality. In: International Conference on Pattern Recognition, pp. 1429–1432 (2010)
7. Choi, Y., Szpankowski, W.: Compression of graphical structures: fundamental limits, algorithms, and experiments. IEEE Trans. Inf. Theory **58**(2), 620–638 (2012)
8. Navlakha, S., Rastogi, R., Shrivastava, N.: Graph summarization with bounded error. In: ACM SIGMOD International Conference on Management of Data, pp. 419–432 (2008)
9. Toivonen, H., Zhou, F., Hartikainen, A., Hinkka, A.: Compression of weighted graphs. In: International Conference on Knowledge Discovery and Data Mining, pp. 965–973 (2011)
10. Szemerédi, E.: Regular partitions of graphs. In: Problèmes combinatoires et thorie des graphes. CNRS, Paris, pp. 399–401 (1978)
11. Sperotto, A., Pelillo, M.: Szemerédis regularity lemma and its applications to pairwise clustering and segmentation. Energy Minimization Methods in Computer Vision and Pattern Recognition, pp. 13–27 (2007)
12. Holland, P.W., Laskey, K.B., Leinhardt, S.: Stochastic blockmodels: first steps. Soc. Netw. **5**(2), 109–137 (1983)

---

[1] F. Nourbakhsh, S. Rota Bulò, M. Pelillo. *A matrix factorization approach to graph compression with partial information*. International Journal of Machine Learning and Cybernetics, online 2015.

13. Lorrain, F., White, H.C.: Structural equivalence of individuals in social networks. J. Math. Sociol. **1**, 49–80 (1971)
14. Nourbakhsh, F., Rota Bulò, S., Pelillo, M.: A matrix factorization approach to graph compression with partial information. Int. J. Mach. Learn. Cybern. (2015, in press)
15. Lee, D.D., Seung, H.S.: Algorithms for non-negative matrix factorization. In: Adv. Neural Inform. Process. Syst. 556–562 (2000)

A Geometrical Approach to Find Corresponding Patches in 3D Medical Surfaces

Neda Sepasian[1, (✉)], Kundan Kumar[2], and Marcel Breeuwer[1]

[1] Department of Biomedical Engineering,
Eindhoven University of Technology, 5600 MB Eindhoven The Netherlands
[2] Department of Mathematics, University of Bergen,
Allegaten 41, Realfagbygget, N, 5007 Bergen Norway

The ability to identify similarities between shapes is important for applications such as medical diagnosis, registration and alignment of objects or images, and shape retrieval. Recently the usefulness of patch based registration for two dimensional medical images has appeared in various works [4]. Based on our knowledge this has not been explored for three dimensional medical surfaces registration. With the help of advanced acquisition techniques, 3D surface models for automated shape analysis, registration and statistical atlases has become rather ubiquitous [2].

The problem of patch correspondence finds similar or corresponding patches in different three dimensional surfaces. A main challenge of 3D patch correspondence is to find a suitable shape signature that can discriminate between similar and dissimilar shapes and can be constructed and compared quickly. Several approaches have been employed in resolving this problem including approaches based on using global features, such as Fourier or spherical harmonics, histograms of the shape features or local features such as shape moments. Recently, diffusion based techniques have been introduced which use the intrinsic geometry of the surface to construct surface descriptors. Exploiting the implicit geometrical structure also makes it independent of the co-ordinate system being used. These techniques include Heat Kernel Signature (HKS) or Wave Kernel Signature (WKS) [1] and construct shape signatures using the fundamental solutions of heat equation or Schrodinger equation, respectively on the surface. The corresponding kernel construction uses the eigen values and eigen functions of Laplace Beltrami operator on a 3D surface. These geometric features are invariant with respect to the co-ordinate system and are inherent to the surface properties.

Our approach consists of three steps: 1. We use the fast marching procedure to patch a given 3D surface or point cloud [5]. 2. We construct a Wave Kernel Signature for each patch. We form a statistics for the Wave Kernel Signature and construct a probability distribution [1]. 3. We compute the distance between the two probability distributions for different patches which can be used for patch correspondence. By exploiting the distance between the probability distributions allows to find the corresponding patch surface in different bone surfaces. Summarizing, our approach combines a PDE based segmentation approach and the statistical approaches for using the distributions of WKS feature descriptors as signatures for a patch.

Using the geometric features, first we identify the feature points. These points are selected based on the sharp changes in the curvatures. Let k_1, k_2 be the principal

© Springer International Publishing Switzerland 2015
A. Feragen et al. (Eds.): SIMBAD 2015, LNCS 9370, pp. 217–219, 2015.
DOI: 10.1007/978-3-319-24261-3

curvatures at point p, then the selection of feature points are obtained by first mapping the curvatures to $[0, 1]$ using Shape index $S(p)$. Denoting k_1, k_2 as the principal curvatures, we define $S(p)$ by

$$S(p) = \frac{1}{2} - \frac{1}{\pi} \tan^{-1} \frac{k_1(p) + k_2(p)}{k_1(p) - k_2(p)}.$$

Since $\tan^{-1}$ maps the real axis to $[-\pi/2, \pi/2]$, S maps the principal curvatures to $[0, 1]$. A higher shape index indicates convex surfaces and the smaller value indicates concavity. Furthermore, we choose thresholds for both the minimal and the maximum that are used to choose the feature points to make sure that these points do not concentrate in a small region. Given the feature points as initial source points, the distance maps are computed using a curvature dependent speed. To compute distance maps on the surfaces fast marching procedure is performed. This algorithm solves the front propagation problem and distance map computation formulated as a boundary value partial differential equation. Next, we use the Voronoi diagram for the given 3D surface and its distance map to perform a local surface patch construction. The Voronoi diagram consists of convex geometry enclosed by a closed curve and forms a partition for a 3D surface in disjoint subsets.

As introduced in [1] the wave kernel signature is obtained by using the wave function solving Schrödinger equation on a 3D surface. Let $\psi(x, t)$ solve the Schrödinger equation $\partial_t \psi = i\Delta\psi$, on a 3D surface, and $\lambda_k, \phi_k, k = 1, 2, 3, \ldots$ be the eigen values and eigen vectors, respectively of Laplace-Beltrami operator for this surface. The solution ψ is obtained by $\psi = \sum_{k=1}^{\infty} \exp(i\lambda_k t)\phi_k(x)f(\lambda_k)$, where f is a probability distribution of λ_k. Then the wave kernel signature (WKS) is defined by the time average of square of ψ. This gives, $WKS = \sum_{k=1}^{\infty} |\phi_k(x)|^2 |f(\lambda_k)|^2$. We compute a probability distribution for the eigenvalues of the Laplace Beltrami operator and use the KL divergence distance to compare the two respective distributions from any two patches.

The primary advantage of this approach is that the shape recognition problem is reduced to sampling, normalization, and comparison of probability distributions for the patches, which are relatively simple tasks when compared to prior methods that required reconstructing a solid object or manifold surface from degenerate 3D data, registering pose transformations, finding feature correspondences, or fitting high-level models. Moreover, this approach works directly on the original polygons of a 3D model, making few assumptions about their organization, and thus it can be used for similarity queries in a wide variety of databases. In fact, this approach also reduces the problem of point correspondence as once the patches are identified, performing this correspondence becomes more tractable. This is because the problem size scales much faster than the size for point correspondence.

Our proposed model incorporates the statistical distribution of geometrical information as well as the spatial information per individual patches. In the presence of pathology the morphological variability and the shape connectivity may suffer due to the surface reconstruction numerical errors and surface resolution. This may influence the reliability of the point-wise local estimation of surface features such as curvature. Hence, the classical point-wise shape curvature descriptors are insufficient, while including a bit larger area around the main feature points can make the selection more robust to the point-wise or sufficiently small region changes. The main question remains to be explored is the sufficient scale and number of patches on a single surface required in order to recognise and retrieve the similar 3D object patches from different individual models. Our algorithm has no prior models of any objects and is automated. In this work, we further explore the development of this framework for medical surface recognition and registration purposes.

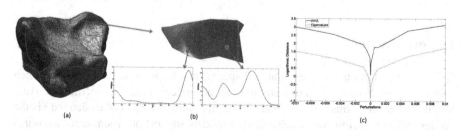

Fig. 2. (*a*) Segmentation of the distal part of a radius, red circles indicate the starting points (largest/smallest curvature). (*b*) A cut segment from the radius and WKS plots for two selected locations. (*c*) Logarithmic distance between one segment and corresponding perturbed segments with random noise.

References

1. Aubry, M., Schlickewei, U., Cremers, D.: The wave kernel signature: a quantum mechanical approach to shape analysis. In: 2011 IEEE International Conference on Computer Vision Workshops (ICCV Workshops). IEEE (2011)
2. Sepasian, N., Van de Giessen, M., Dobbe, I., Streekstra, G.: Bone reposition planning for corrective surgery using statistical shape model: assessment of differential geometrical features. In: Cardoso, M.J., Simpson, I., Arbel, T., Precup, D., Ribbens, A. (eds.) BAMBI 2014. LNCS, vol. 8677, pp. 49–60. Springer, Heidelberg (2014)
3. Barnes, C., Shechtman, E., Goldman, D.B., Finkelstein, A.: The generalized patchMatch correspondence algorithm. In: Daniilidis, K., Maragos, P., Paragios, N. (eds.) ECCV 2010, Part III. LNCS, vol. 6313, pp. 29–43. Springer, Heidelberg (2010)
4. Shi, W., et al.: Multi-atlas spectral patchMatch: application to cardiac image segmentation. In: Golland, P., Hata, N., Barillot, C., Hornegger, J., Howe, R. (eds.) MICCAI 2014, Part I. LNCS, vol. 8673, pp. 348–355. Springer, Heidelberg (2014)
5. Peyr, G., Cohen, L.D.: Geodesic methods for shape and surface processing. In: Advances in Computational Vision and Medical Image Processing: Methods and Applications, vol. 13, pp. 29–56. Springer (2008)

Similarities, SDEs, and Most Probable Paths

Anne Marie Svane[1] and Stefan Sommer[2,(✉)]

[1] Aarhus University, Aarhus Denmark
amsvane@math.au.dk
[2] University of Copenhagen, Copenhagen Denmark
sommer@di.ku.dk

1 Introduction

Differential manifolds, or even stratified spaces, can be used as data domains when vector space structure is too restrictive to accurately model properties of data. Similarity between objects on e.g. Riemannan manifolds are most often defined via the geodesic distance. However, stochastic data models suggest other similarity measures than geodesic distance when analyzing non-linear data. In this abstract, we will discuss a recent approach to statistics of manifold valued data where the data is considered as the results of random diffusions.

2 Diffusions and Anisotropic Distributions on Manifolds

The normal distribution is a standard choice for modelling data in Euclidean space. To treat manifold valued data, it is natural to seek for a generalization of the normal distribution to a distribution on manifolds. The isotropic normal distribution can be generalized to Riemannian manifolds via the heat diffusion, i.e. its density is a solution at time t_0 to the PDE

$$\frac{\partial}{\partial t} p(t, x) = \frac{1}{2} \Delta p(t, x), \quad \lim_{t \to 0} p(t, x) = \delta_{x,y}$$

where Δ is the Laplace-Beltrami operator on M. However, for normal distributions with anisotropic covariance Σ, holonomy prevents a globally defined analogue of Δ, so the construction does not transfer to this situation.

Another way of constructing the normal distribution is as the transition distribution of a Brownian motion. The Brownian motion can be generalized to manifolds by the Eells-Elworthy-Malliavian construction using stochastic development in the frame bundle. The corresponding transition distribution may be viewed as a generalization of the Euclidean normal distribution when Σ is anisotropic. This distribution can then be used for defining the mean or performing e.g. PCA, both in non-differentiable [1] and differentiable cases [2]. We shall describe the basic ideas in this abstract.

© Springer International Publishing Switzerland 2015
A. Feragen et al. (Eds.): SIMBAD 2015, LNCS 9370, pp. 220–222, 2015.
DOI: 10.1007/978-3-319-24261-3

3   The Frame Bundle and Stochastic Development

The frame bundle FM of a differentiable manifold M is the smooth vector bundle consisting of points $x \in M$ and corresponding frames (ordered bases) in the tangent spaces $T_x M$. A fundamental property of FM is the existence of $n = dim(M)$ globally defined *horizontal* vector fields $H_1, \ldots, H_n$. These correspond to infinitesimal displacements δx on M together with a parallel transport of the frame along δx.

Given a stochastic processes B_t in $\mathbb{R}^\times$ starting at 0, the *stochastic development* [3] of B_t is the stochastic process U_t on FM satisfying the Stratonovich stochastic differential equation $dU_t = H_i \circ dB_t^i$ with initial condition $U_0 = u_0$. If B_t is an anisotropic Brownian motion, the projection πU_t of U_t onto M may be considered as an anisotropic diffusion on M starting at πu_0.

4   Most Probable Paths

Among the stochastic paths of a stationary diffusion processes in $\mathbb{R}^\times$ that start at a point x and end at a point y, the straight line is the *most probable path*. On a manifold M, the most probable path for an isotropic diffusion process on M between $x, y \in M$ is defined to be the one that minimizes the Onsager-Machlup functional [4]. This functional involves the path length plus a curvature correction term, which means that the most probable paths are generally not geodesics. The Onsager-Machlup functional thus provides a different way of measuring similarity between points than the geodesic distance.

In [5], the most probable paths for anisotropic processes are formally described in terms of a sub-Riemannian metric on FM. The resulting paths are generally not geodesics. We are currently exploring in which sense this formal approach can be given a rigorous stochastic interpretation.

5   Outlook

For isotropic data, the Onsager-Machlup functional can be used to define similarities between points on manifolds. We are currently investigating the possibility to generalize this to the anisotropic situation. In particular, we would like to formalize the description of most probable paths of anisotropic diffusion processes in terms of the sub-Riemannian metric on FM considered in [5]. This would provide a foundation for estimating means and covariances on manifolds.

References

1. Nye, T.: Construction of Distributions on Tree-Space via Diffusion Processes, Mathematisches Forschungsinstitut Oberwolfach (2014)
2. Sommer, S.: Diffusion Processes and PCA on Manifolds, Mathematisches Forschungsinstitut Oberwolfach (2014)
3. Hsu, E.P.: Stochastic Analysis on Manifolds. American Mathematical Soc. (2002)
4. Fujita, T.: Kotani, S.i.: The Onsager-Machlup function for diffusion processes. J. Math. Kyoto Univ. **22**(1), 115–130 (1982)
5. Sommer, S.: Anisotropic distributions on manifolds: template estimation and most probable paths. In: Ourselin, S., Alexander, D.C., Westin, C.-F., Cardoso, M.J. (eds.) IPMI 2015. LNCS, vol. 9123, pp. 193–204. Springer, Heidelberg (2015)

Can the Optimum Similarity Matrix be Selected Before Clustering for Graph-Based Approaches?

Kadim Taşdemir[⊠] and Berna Yalçin

Department of Computer Engineering, Antalya International University,
Universite Cd. 2, 07190 Dosemealti, Antalya Turkey
kadim.tasdemir@antalya.edu.tr, h.k.berna@gmail.com

Keywords: Approximate spectral clustering · Similarity measures · Graph-based evaluation measures · Assortativity · Clustering coefficient

1 Extended Abstract

Spectral clustering, which is a relaxed graph-cut optimization approach based on eigen-decomposition of a Laplacian matrix derived from pairwise similarities, is able to extract clusters with various characteristics thanks to its independence from parametric models [1–3]. To address their high computational cost in large data analysis, they are applied via approximate spectral clustering (ASC). The ASC applies spectral clustering on a reduced set of data representatives either selected by a sampling approach or data quantization [4–7, 9]. [4] uses random sampling based on Nystrom method whereas [5] shows that selective sampling is the best sampling method with a similar success to k-means quantization. [6] uses k-means and random projection trees as quantization to conclude experimentally that the best sampling can be achieved by vector quantisation with minimum distortion. [7] compares neural networks with k-means and achieves superior ASC accuracies with neural gas quantisation. Alternatively, k-means++ [8], a successful variant of k-means with a novel probabilistic approach for initialisation, can be a good alternative for quantisation in ASC [9].

Besides making spectral methods feasible for large datasets, the ASC enables accurate similarity definitions harnessing different information types on the level of data representatives. For example, a reduced set of representatives partitions the data space into Voronoi polygons where each representative is the centroid of its corresponding data points distributed into these polygons. This not only provides a data density distribution which may determine separation among submanifolds, but also helps identify their topological relations with respect to the data manifold. [7, 9] exploit these information by defining various similarity criteria to utilize a local density

---

This study is funded by TUBITAK Career Grant No. 112E195. Taşdemir is also supported by FP7 Marie Curie Career Integration Grant IAM4MARS.

A. Feragen et al. (Eds.): SIMBAD 2015, LNCS 9370, pp. 223–225, 2015.
DOI: 10.1007/978-3-319-24261-3

distribution more detailed than the level of Voronoi polygons and an accurate manifold based neighborhood representation.

In addition to the variety of sampling or quantization methods for ASC, different representative sets are often obtained at each run even by the same method (due to random initialization and update in the implementation of these methods). Therefore, together with various similarity criteria, many partitionings can be obtained for a given dataset. The naive approach is to combine these partitionings into a consensus partitioning using an ensemble learning (such as maximum voting), which is shown outperforming the individual results [10]. However, ensemble approaches require to obtain all partitionings, which is time-consuming and computationally intense, especially for quantization based ASC.

An alternative solution can be to develop a novel selection criterion representing graph properties of the similarity matrices after getting the sets of data representatives so that one could decide whether a favored selection would exploit intrinsic data characteristics for the optimal clustering. Such a criterion (or different criteria) derived from similarity graphs can help: i) find the best representative set for a given sampling or quantization method, ii) find the best sampling or quantization method, or iii) select the optimum similarity matrix. Our preliminary experiments using traditional graph-based measures, such as assortativity, clustering coefficients and their local-global variants [11], are unfortunately unsuccessful in guiding the best representative set, sampling / quantization method or the best similarity criterion. Can the optimum similarity matrix be selected before clustering, for the graph-based ASC approaches? Is there such a criterion or is it possible to develop one?

References

1. Shi, J., Malik, J.: Normalized cuts and image segmentation. IEEE Trans. Pattern Anal. Mach. Intell. **22**(8), 888–905 (2000)
2. Ng, A., Jordan, M., Weiss, Y.: On spectral clustering: analysis and an algorithm. In: Dietterich, T., Becker, S., Ghahramani, Z. (Eds.) Advances in Neural Information Processing Systems, vol. 14. MIT Press (2002)
3. von Luxburg, U.: A tutorial on spectral clustering. J. Stat. Comput. **17**(4), 395–416 (2007)
4. Fowlkes, C., Belongie, S., Chung, F., Malik, J.: Spectral grouping using the Nyström method. IEEE Trans. Pattern Anal. Mach. Intel. **26**(2), 214–225 (2004)
5. Wang, L., Leckie, C., Ramamohanarao, K., Bezdek, J.: Approximate spectral clustering. In: Theeramunkong, T., Kijsirikul, B., Cercone, N., Ho, T.-B. (eds.) PAKDD 2009. LNCS (LNAI), vol. 5476, pp. 134–146. Springer, Heidelberg (2009)
6. Yan, D., Huang, L., Jordan, M.I.: Fast approximate spectral clustering. In: 15th ACM SIGKDD Knowledge Discovery and Data Mining (KDD), pp. 907–916 (2009)
7. Taşdemir, K.: Vector quantization based approximate spectral clustering of large datasets. Pattern Recognit. **45**(8), 3034–3044 (2012)
8. Arthur, D., Vassilvitskii, S.: k-means++: the advantages of careful seeding. In: 18th ACM-SIAM Symposium on Discrete Algorithms (SODA), pp. 1027–1035 (2007)
9. Taşdemir, K., Yalcin, B., Yildirim, I.: Approximate spectral clustering with utilized similarity information using geodesic based hybrid distance measures. Pattern Recognit. **48**(4), 1459–1471 (2015)

10. Moazzen, Y., Yalcin, B., Taşdemir, K.: Sampling based approximate spectral clustering ensemble for unsupervised land cover identification. In: 2015 IEEE International Geoscience and Remote Sensing Symposium (IGARSS), (2015, Accepted)
11. Opsahl, T., Panzarasa, P.: Clustering in weighted networks. Soc. Netw. 31(2), 155–163 (2009)

Approximate Spectral Clustering with Utilized Similarity Information Using Geodesic Based Hybrid Distance Measures

Kadim Taşdemir[✉], Berna Yalçin, and Isa Yildirim

Department of Computer Engineering, Antalya International University,
Universite Cd. 2, 07190 Dosemealti, Antalya Turkey
kadim.tasdemir@antalya.edu.tr, h.k.berna@gmail.com,
iyildirim@itu.edu.tr

Abstract. This is a summary of the paper published in [1] which proposes new hybrid similarity measures exploiting various information types such as density, distance and topology, to achieve high accuracies by approximate spectral clustering (an algorithm based on similarity based graph-cut optimization). The experiments in [1] on a wide variety of datasets show the outperformance of the proposed advanced similarities.

Keywords: Approximate spectral clustering · Geodesic distances · Hybrid similarity measures · Manifold learning

1 Extended Abstract

Spectral methods, recently popular approach in clustering, have a manifold learning algorithm based on eigenvalue decomposition of pairwise similarities of the data points. Due to its ability to extract irregularly shaped clusters, its independence from parametric cluster models, and its easy implementation, spectral clustering has been theoretically and empirically supported with successful applications in various areas such as information retrieval, computer vision, and image processing. However, its effective submanifold (cluster) extraction based on eigendecomposition has a drawback of high computational cost ($O(N^3)$, N: number of data points) due to the very same reason. This makes direct use of spectral clustering infeasible for clustering large datasets.

In order to address challenges in clustering large datasets with spectral methods, approximate spectral clustering (ASC) applies spectral clustering on a reduced set of data representatives either selected by a sampling approach or data quantization [2–4]. The ASC methods mainly focus on finding a suitable sampling or quantization method to find the data representatives, with a similarity criterion defined by (Euclidean) distance based Gaussian function. Both theoretical and empirical studies indicate that

This study is funded by TUBITAK Career Grant No. 112E195. Taşdemir is also supported by FP7 Marie Curie Career Integration Grant IAM4MARS.

A. Feragen et al. (Eds.): SIMBAD 2015, LNCS 9370, pp. 226–228, 2015.
DOI: 10.1007/978-3-319-24261-3

quantization based ASC generally achieves higher accuracies than sampling based ASC in expense of higher computational time. Additionally, [4] achieves superior ASC accuracies with neural gas quantization thanks to its relatively low quantization error.

Besides making spectral methods feasible for large datasets, the ASC approach enables accurate similarity definitions harnessing different information types on the level of data representatives. For example, the reduced set of representatives efficiently partitions the data space into Voronoi polygons (where each representative is the center), and the data points are distributed to these representatives. This not only provides a data density distribution which may determine separation among submanifolds, but also helps identify topological relations of these representatives with respect to the data manifold. [4] exploits these information to some extent by using CONN similarity defined in [5], to achieve high clustering accuracies than traditional distance based similarity definition. CONN is a weighted adjacency matrix where weights show local data distribution within the Voroni subpolygons with respect to neighbor representatives (producing a more detailed density distribution than the Voronoi polygons level). If the subpolygon of a pair of representatives is empty, then its connectivity weight becomes 0, indicating that those two representatives are not neighbors with respect to the data manifold (even though they are neighbors in the data space). This manifold based accurate definition of topological relations enables the use of geodesic distances for ASC without any user-set parameter.

Despite being an extensively used approach, geodesic distances are ignored in ASC, mainly due to the difficulty in determining the topological relations required for their truthful calculation with respect to the data manifold: the traditional approaches (k-nearest neighor, ϵ-neighborhood) require some parameters to be set optimally, yet, these emprically-set parameters may differ not only for each dataset, but also for representatives in the same data set.

In [1], we propose geodesic based similarities using topological information provided by CONN. We then fuse them with traditional (Euclidean) distance and local density information, to utilize all available information types provided by ASC. The proposed geodesic criteria outperform non-geodesic based similarities on a wide selection of datasets with respect to accuracy, adjusted Rand index and normalized mutual information. We refer to [1] for detailed discussion.

References

1. Taşdemir, K., Yalcin, B., Yildirim, I.: Approximate spectral clustering with utilized similarity information using geodesic based hybrid distance measures. Pattern Recognit. **48**(4), 1459–1471 (2015)
2. Fowlkes, C., Belongie, S., Chung, F., Malik, J.: Spectral grouping using the Nyström method. IEEE Trans. Pattern Anal. Mach. Intell. **26**(2), 214–225 (2004)
3. Wang, L., Leckie, C., Kotagiri, R., Bezdek, J.: Approximate pairwise clustering for large data sets via sampling plus extension. Pattern Recognit. **44**(2), 222–235 (2011)

4. Taşdemir, K.: Vector quantization based approximate spectral clustering of large datasets. Pattern Recognit. **45**(8), 3034–3044 (2012)
5. Taşdemir, K., Merényi, E.: Exploiting data topology in visualization and clustering of self-organizing maps. IEEE Transactions on Neural Networks **20**(4), 549–562 (2009)

Author Index

Printed in the United States
By Bookmasters